The Vulnerability Researcher's Handbook

A comprehensive guide to discovering, reporting, and publishing security vulnerabilities

Benjamin Strout

BIRMINGHAM—MUMBAI

The Vulnerability Researcher's Handbook

Group Product Manager: Mohd Riyan Khan

Publishing Product Manager: Khushboo Samkaria

Senior Editor: Runcil Rebello

Technical Editor: Nithik Cheruvakodan

Copy Editor: Safis Editing

Project Coordinator: Ashwin Kharwa

Proofreader: Safis Editing

Indexer: Manju Arasan

Production Designer: Alishon Mendonca

Senior Marketing Coordinator: Marylou De Mello

First published: February 2023

Production reference:1200123

Published by Packt Publishing Ltd.

Livery Place

35 Livery Street

Birmingham

B3 2PB, UK.

ISBN 978-1-80323-887-6

www.packtpub.com

To my dearest and oldest friend, Linda Mehlhorn. Thank you for your friendship and support over the years. It's meant the world to me.

– Benjamin Strout

Contributors

About the author

Benjamin Strout is a veteran of the technology industry and a passionate technology communicator. His experience in the healthcare, biotech, pharmaceutical, and fintech industries has led him to a role as a lead penetration tester at one of the largest healthcare conglomerates in the United States. The founder and point of contact of Maine's local DEF CON group (DC207), he has been featured as a guest speaker at various conferences. He has contributed to works as a technical reviewer and published 30+ CVEs for technologies in use worldwide. When not teaching others or tinkering with some technological curiosity, he's busy learning bluegrass licks on his banjo and playing with his cats, Dionysius and Louis Thanksgiving.

I could not have imagined writing this book without the support of my husband. Alex, thank you for reading my drafts, putting up with the late nights, and encouraging me to do this. In my career, I have immense gratitude for these awesome people for helping me on my path: David Freedman, Taylor Shain, Scott Allen, and the brilliant information security researcher Ryan Boutot. Many thanks to everyone at the DC207 group that keeps showing up monthly, keeping the hacking community alive in Maine. Finally, this book wouldn't be possible without the help of the ever-evolving SANS ICS HyperEncabulatation research.

About the reviewers

Avinash Sinha is a cybersecurity expert with 12+ years of experience and has worked with many global business unicorns, such as IBM, GE HealthCare, Schneider Electric, Airtel, Target, Aujas Networks, and UIDAI Aadhaar, securing them from next-generation threats.

He has managed and led teams for the successful execution of OT/IT/cloud security projects entailing security operations, enterprise security architecture, penetration testing, HIPAA, GDPR, threat intelligence, IR, red teaming, and cloud security assessment for O365, Azure, Citrix, and AWS.

He has a degree in computer technology, majoring in artificial intelligence and a postgraduate degree in international business from Symbiosis. He holds GICSP, GCFA, and SEC 541-Cloud Attacks and Monitoring certifications from SANS.

I'd like to thank my father, Rajendra Sinha, for constantly inspiring me, and my mother, for her love and blessings. Also, thanks to my lovely wife, Tanu, for taking care of me and keeping me healthy while my passion for cybersecurity extends beyond unusual times.

Every one of us has the responsibility to protect the world from constantly evolving threats. Special thanks to Jaykishan Nirmal, Vikram Dhar, and Anil Kumar PV for their guidance.

Vaibhav Kushwaha is a lead security engineer with a specialization in cybersecurity products architecture and R&D and has led teams for ASM, pentesting automation, network and web vulnerability scanners, and much more.

He started his career with pentesting but later gathered interest in security software R&D to innovate cybersecurity products and industry and also to automate boring and repetitive tasks.

Apart from this, Vaibhav also likes reverse engineering and working on cloud services and has worked on cloud connectors for multiple cloud services.

Disclaimer

The information within this book is intended to be used only in an ethical manner. Do not use any information from the book if you do not have written permission from the owner of the equipment. If you perform illegal actions, you are likely to be arrested and prosecuted to the full extent of the law. Packt Publishing does not take any responsibility if you misuse any of the information contained within the book. The information herein must only be used while testing environments with properly written authorizations from the appropriate persons responsible.

Table of Contents

3

Vulnerability Research – Getting Started with Successful Strategies   41

Part 2 – Vulnerability Disclosure, Publishing, and Reporting

4

Vulnerability Disclosure – Communicating Security Findings   85

5

Vulnerability Publishing –Getting Your Work Published in Databases   105

6

Vulnerability Mediation – When Things Go Wrong and Who Can Help   133

7

Independent Vulnerability Publishing   149

Part 3 – Case Studies, Researcher Resources, and Vendor Resources

8

Real-World Case Studies – Digging into Successful (and Unsuccessful) Research Reporting   165

9

Working with Security Researchers – A Vendor's Guide   181

10

Templates, Resources, and Final Guidance   203

Preface

Hello, intrepid explorer!

Vulnerability research is the practice of searching for security flaws in technical systems and then sharing that information with people who can fix these flaws. It's a fascinating process that helps improve the security and privacy of user data throughout the ever-growing technological world we find ourselves inhabiting. *The Vulnerability Researcher's Handbook* is a book that aims to explore, in depth, the process of what someone does with a new, never-before-observed information security vulnerability after it's discovered. For example, you might work in software development, operations, or information security roles. In such a case, you might wonder how vulnerabilities in publicly released software become known and ultimately addressed for the greater good of end users. The answer is that it takes coordinated effort, friction between parties, and grit from security researchers to overcome many of the challenges these scenarios introduce.

In this book, we'll introduce you to the world of vulnerability research for publicly released software by ensuring you understand the fundamentals around vulnerabilities and how they become dangerous. After that, we'll cover ways to begin selecting compelling research targets and then subject those targets to a methodology built on proven techniques that yield results. Finally, you'll be able to build plans to find security vulnerabilities.

We'll then cover the most complex step in this process: navigating the murky waters of working with vendors as you share your research and publish it to the world. We'll do this by learning about enthralling examples of vulnerability research and the many challenges security researchers like yourself need to overcome. Finally, as you work through the last chapters, you'll be armed with knowledge, various helpful templates to organize and standardize your research, and strategies to implement better vendor-research relations that you can begin to share or employ with software vendors.

I developed this book because it's the one I wish I had before I started working with vendors on disclosing vulnerabilities and persuading them to fix security problems in their products. Adopting technology systems and software to solve problems is (and has been) expanding into every niche that humans do. The entire software and hardware industry needs people more than ever who know how to share research in a way that benefits users and holds the right people accountable for fixing problems when they're found.

Ideally, I would expect you, the reader, to have strong technical skills that you can then apply to the soft skills you'll learn in this book. We don't teach you how to execute the latest in vulnerability research – several books, courses, and web content are released each year on this. We expect you'll be coming to the table or referring to these resources. Instead, this book aims to help you understand how publicly disclosed vulnerabilities are disclosed in the CVE system (or not) and how to find research targets and develop methods for organizing the arduous process of disclosing and publishing your findings in a responsible way that improves the world around us. Even if you don't possess highly technical skills, with this book, you'll find this entire process approachable, engaging, and very rewarding – so much so that you'll seek to grow that knowledge even more.

Who this book is for

This book is for security analysts, researchers, penetration testers, software developers, technology engineers, and anyone in leadership roles who wants to learn how vulnerabilities are found and then disclosed to the public. Before you start, we're expecting intermediate knowledge of operating systems, software, and interconnected systems. Prior experience with finding and disclosing vulnerabilities is optional. Nevertheless, some exposure to vulnerability scanners and other information security tools will help accelerate your journey to exploring research targets and finding and disclosing your first vulnerability.

What this book covers

Chapter 1, *An Introduction to Vulnerabilities*, includes a primer on what vulnerabilities are and how they're classified and organized. Then, you'll learn how security analysts find known vulnerabilities and what software they use.

Chapter 2, *Exploring Real-World Impacts of Zero-Days*, discusses the vulnerability life cycle and introduces zero-days, their exploitation, and their various dangers. Most importantly, you'll learn important terminology and how security research directly or indirectly creates these dangers, and the dilemmas of how to disclose such research.

Chapter 3, *Vulnerability Research – Getting Started with Successful Strategies*, defines security research, the strategies used, how to select targets and use test suites, and the tools that are commonly used for research.

Chapter 4, *Vulnerability Disclosure – Communicating Security Findings*, informs you of and defines the types of vulnerability disclosures you can use, and what strategies you can use to navigate the various challenges you'll face in making disclosures.

Chapter 5, *Vulnerability Publishing – Getting Your Work Published in Databases*, demystifies vulnerability publishing and the methods used to publish and provides practical examples and best practices that will help you confidently share your research with the world.

Chapter 6, *Vulnerability Mediation – When Things Go Wrong and Who Can Help*, defines what mediators are and how to find and utilize them best when things go wrong with vendor relationships.

Chapter 7, Independent Vulnerability Publishing, discusses what an independent disclosure is, the risks of using them, and how to avoid legal problems researchers commonly face from hostile vendors.

Chapter 8, Real-World Case Studies – Digging into Successful (and Unsuccessful) Research Reporting, uncovers real stories from vulnerability researchers, showing you how scenarios can unfold and how challenges were addressed by the researchers.

Chapter 9, Working with Security Researchers – A Vendor's Guide, turns the tables and speaks to vendors about the people reading this book, aiming to give researchers and technology leaders tools and information that they can use to foster good relationships in the unavoidable contact they'll have with researchers.

Chapter 10, Templates, Resources, and Final Guidance, shares test case templates and methods for using them, vendor communication templates, CVE disclosure templates, organizational templates, and finally, words of encouragement to those of you who use this information to improve the world of technology by researching and disclosing vulnerabilities.

To get the most out of this book

To get the most out of this book, we expect a beginner to intermediate knowledge of various techniques used, maintained, and developed by users and businesses. However, to apply the strategies and conduct research that will be reported, we expect advanced and possibly specialized knowledge on discovering security vulnerabilities using techniques defined in the frameworks covered in this book.

Download the color images

We also provide a PDF file that has color images of the screenshots and diagrams used in this book. You can download it here: `https://packt.link/1iZ9q`.

Conventions used

There are a number of text conventions used throughout this book.

`Code in text`: Indicates code words in text, database table names, folder names, filenames, file extensions, pathnames, dummy URLs, user input, and Twitter handles. Here is an example: "Mount the downloaded `WebStorm-10*.dmg` disk image file as another disk in your system."

Bold: Indicates a new term, an important word, or words that you see onscreen. For instance, words in menus or dialog boxes appear in **bold**. Here is an example: "Select **System info** from the **Administration** panel."

> **Tips or important notes**
> Appear like this.

Get in touch

Feedback from our readers is always welcome.

General feedback: If you have questions about any aspect of this book, email us at customercare@ packtpub.com and mention the book title in the subject of your message.

Errata: Although we have taken every care to ensure the accuracy of our content, mistakes do happen. If you have found a mistake in this book, we would be grateful if you would report this to us. Please visit www.packtpub.com/support/errata and fill in the form.

Piracy: If you come across any illegal copies of our works in any form on the internet, we would be grateful if you would provide us with the location address or website name. Please contact us at copyright@packt.com with a link to the material.

If you are interested in becoming an author: If there is a topic that you have expertise in and you are interested in either writing or contributing to a book, please visit authors.packtpub.com.

Share Your Thoughts

Once you've read *The Vulnerability Researcher's Handbook*, we'd love to hear your thoughts! Scan the QR code below to go straight to the Amazon review page for this book and share your feedback.

https://packt.link/r/1803238879

Your review is important to us and the tech community and will help us make sure we're delivering excellent quality content.

Download a free PDF copy of this book

Thanks for purchasing this book!

Do you like to read on the go but are unable to carry your print books everywhere?

Is your eBook purchase not compatible with the device of your choice?

Don't worry, now with every Packt book you get a DRM-free PDF version of that book at no cost.

Read anywhere, any place, on any device. Search, copy, and paste code from your favorite technical books directly into your application.

The perks don't stop there, you can get exclusive access to discounts, newsletters, and great free content in your inbox daily

Follow these simple steps to get the benefits:

1. Scan the QR code or visit the link below

https://packt.link/free-ebook/9781803238876

2. Submit your proof of purchase
3. That's it! We'll send your free PDF and other benefits to your email directly

Part 1 – Vulnerability Research Fundamentals

In this section, you will learn about the basics of vulnerabilities and vulnerability research. You will learn about different types of vulnerabilities and various exploits. You will also learn about the tools and techniques used by security researchers to find and analyze vulnerabilities. Armed with this knowledge, you will be well on your way to becoming a security researcher yourself.

This section comprises the following chapters:

- *Chapter 1, An Introduction to Vulnerabilities*
- *Chapter 2, Exploring Real-World Impacts of Zero-Days*
- *Chapter 3, Vulnerability Research – Getting Started with Successful Strategies*

1

An Introduction to Vulnerabilities

A **vulnerability** is a characteristic of something that makes that thing susceptible to hazards or damage. Technology is certainly not immune to vulnerabilities. For example, during the 1960s in the United States, AT&T observed one of the first widespread exploitations of vulnerabilities in technology. People found they could subvert telephone systems and avoid paying for services if they played certain tones into telephone receivers. These technology hackers learned that if they understood how the systems worked and what flaws might be present in these systems, they could take advantage of weaknesses in ways that could directly benefit them. Today, the same spirit and enterprising ways of challenging technology by using it in unintended ways are present and thriving.

Throughout our world, people are discovering and exploiting vulnerabilities found in software. Software drives the modern world in almost everything we do. Security researchers can find software and subsequent vulnerabilities in the simple applications you use on your phone, business applications that drive commerce, devices used in hospitals to save lives, and industrial controls that help ensure societal needs. These vulnerabilities can be used for cybercrime, to violate your privacy, disrupt infrastructure, and create national security risks. Unfortunately, the exploitation of these security vulnerabilities can be difficult to detect, especially in undisclosed vulnerabilities.

Despite the growing number of reported and unreported vulnerabilities, people continue to be victimized by these threats, which incur increasingly high financial and privacy costs.. So, what is being done about this? In this chapter, we'll explore how these threats are addressed by covering some fundamental concepts.

We'll go over the following:

- Software vulnerabilities and the CIA Triad
- How software vulnerabilities are classified and organized
- The vulnerability scanners that professionals often use to detect and fix flaws in software

- Some common security vulnerability types usually found in software
- The vulnerability life cycle and its impact on software

By the end of this chapter, you should understand what vulnerabilities are, how they get introduced to software, how vulnerabilities are organized and ranked, how to search for vulnerable software components, and the software vulnerability life cycle. Let's get started.

Introducing software vulnerabilities

Criminals want your data. One of the many ways they can obtain this data is by finding and exploiting vulnerabilities in software products that store your data. Since the adoption of the internet, there have been many such instances where criminals have exploited vulnerabilities, resulting in stolen banking information, health information, and corporate and state secrets.

Before we examine vulnerabilities, let's get a good idea of what software is. It's best to think about software as instructions that tell a computer what to do. Software can include any instructions or programs written for a device or machine. These instructions enable and empower users to do work such as word processing, sending emails, browsing the internet, and using social media sites such as Facebook and Twitter. Software isn't necessarily limited to just user-facing components in the form of applications. Software is built to power hardware components and microcontroller devices. Think about modern cars and consumer electronics – if you've bought anything with any semblance of computing technology in the 21st century, it's likely software has been written and is running these devices.

Software vulnerabilities, simply defined, are the defects and shortcomings of software. Think of vulnerabilities as logical errors or loopholes in the instructions we give to our computers. These errors or loopholes can impact three critical areas concerning vulnerabilities in software. In the information security industry, this is commonly referred to as the **CIA Triad**. CIA is an acronym for **confidentiality**, **integrity**, and **availability**, as illustrated in the following figure:

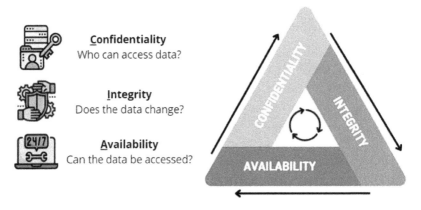

Figure 1.1 – The CIA Triad

Let's discuss these factors because they'll be essential to understanding how vulnerabilities are organized by severity.

The CIA Triad

Confidentiality is the extent to which data is kept private and hidden. Vulnerabilities that can impact this vector often manifest in ways that allow unauthorized users to view or export data they should not have access to. Exploits that impact this vector often disclose data that should not otherwise be disclosed.

Integrity refers to whether data is the same as when it was originally inserted into the software. Vulnerabilities that impact integrity often result in the changing of data. Consider the importance of information related to your banking or health information and how the integrity of those values is important. Exploits to this vector often include changing values from their original sets in a way that benefits the goals of an attacker.

Availability relates to whether the data can be accessed. Vulnerabilities in availability often result in downtime of the application or the disablement of certain features. Bad actors exploiting these vulnerabilities aim to disrupt the access or use of data and systems. Exploits here often result in legitimate users not being able to access data.

When thinking about vulnerabilities, it's important to know that they impact one or more of these factors in a way that is detrimental to the software. So, now that we understand what the three core concepts are in weighing and measuring vulnerabilities in software, how do they get organized and prioritized?

Organizing impacts

To help us organize and prioritize vulnerabilities, security researchers have developed methods and systems for scoring the impact of vulnerabilities. The most common scoring method you'll come across is the **Common Vulnerability Scoring System** (**CVSS**). The CVSS is an open source specification acting as an equalizing language that helps explore the severity of vulnerabilities and the impacts on the CIA Triad. In addition, the scoring system can be used as a sort of calculator that defines key base metrics about how bad vulnerabilities are. The calculation considers the following factors:

- Impact on confidentiality
- Impact on integrity
- Impact on availability
- How the vulnerability is exploited
- Complexity of the exploit
- Access needed to exploit the vulnerability
- Whether user interaction is required for exploitation

This set of data is calculated with a CVSS calculator (see *Figure 1.2*) and is usually attached to vulnerabilities in a vulnerability database:

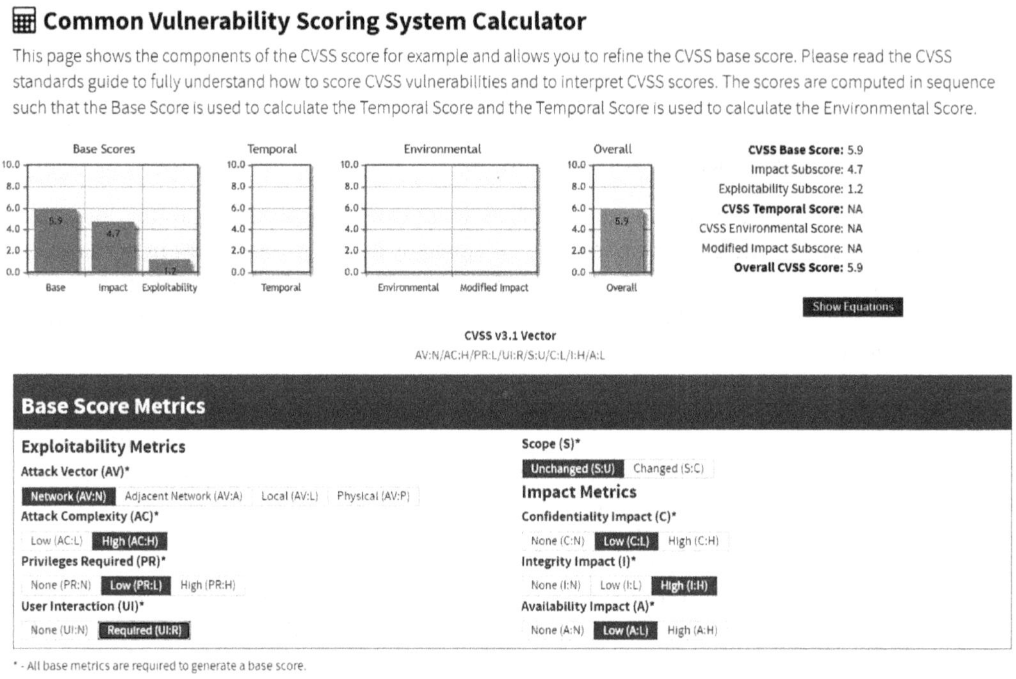

Figure 1.2 – An example of a CVSS score calculator

While we'll dig into different databases in future chapters, it's important to be aware of the most common vulnerability dataset, the MITRE **Common Vulnerabilities and Exposures (CVE)** list. Vulnerable software that has been publicly disclosed is assigned ID numbers through the CVE list. The CVE list feeds into large security vulnerability databases such as the US **National Vulnerability Database (NVD)** and many others. Each vulnerability in the list is simply called a CVE. Each vulnerability is assigned a CVE ID number, a CVSS score, and details relating to the vulnerability such as exploitation, research, a brief description of the vulnerability, and any other related information. A typical CVE record will look like this:

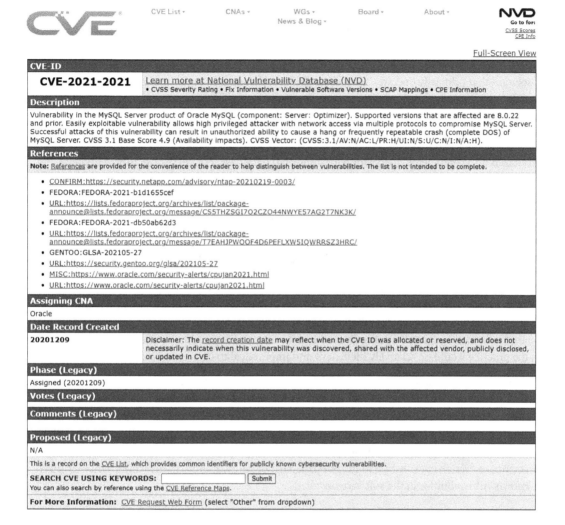

Figure 1.3 – An example of a CVE record, CVE-2021-2021

Every year, thousands of CVEs are added to the MITRE CVE list, then reported to the NVD. These vulnerabilities can impact various software, services, hardware, and more.

> **Note**
>
> The CVE list, CVE records, and subsequent datasets do not track vulnerabilities for **software as a service (SaaS)** products. For a vulnerability in this list and dataset, the software in question must be a customer-controlled product. So, for example, Google Docs is an office productivity solution that primarily operates as a web application that does not consist of installed elements under user control. Therefore, Google Docs is not eligible for CVE assignments and registration in vulnerability databases that house CVEs. Similarly, office productivity applications such as Microsoft Office now have similar cloud-based services – but they also provide thick-client installs of applications like Microsoft Word. In this example, the version of Microsoft Word that is installed on a computer is eligible for publishing on the CVE list, but not the cloud-based version.

Now we know how to find information on vulnerabilities and how that research is organized. So, how can security professionals leverage these resources?

Getting familiar with software vulnerability scanners

Many of the exploited vulnerabilities used today are known vulnerabilities registered in the CVE list and have an associated vulnerability score, CVE ID, and details about the vulnerabilities. As of writing this sentence, over 20 million vulnerabilities have been registered in this list. While it's entirely possible to gather information about the software used and then cross-reference it by searching through a CVE list, the practice would be relatively inefficient and impractical to do regularly.

To solve this problem, software developers have built solutions to detect these vulnerabilities. These kinds of applications are typically referred to as vulnerability scanners. Despite what you might be told by an enthusiastic vendor on the latest security features of their vulnerability scanner, these scanners are typically passive and do not discover otherwise unknown vulnerabilities. Instead, they only identify known flaws by running scripts that search for information about software. The scanners then compare versions of software to the published list of vulnerabilities to determine whether there are known vulnerabilities in the software installed.

Software development teams have been able to get these tools to work with detecting hardware, software versions, and even vulnerable networking equipment such as firewalls. In addition, vulnerability scanning systems let system administrators know what software needs security fixes to avoid the exploitation of vulnerable software. Modern systems usually do this in well-organized ways that prioritize the highest risk and provide reports and dashboards that various audiences can consume.

Vulnerability scanners allow cybersecurity professionals to identify, classify, and prioritize risks. There are many vulnerability scanning tools available to help identify these vulnerabilities. So, what are these common vulnerability scanning tools?

Common vulnerability scanning tools

This section introduces some of the common vulnerability scanning tools that are used by security practitioners. The list is not exhaustive, but it should give you a solid introduction to the basics of these tools and help with your understanding of the common tooling you'll likely find when you begin researching and using these tools.

Nmap

Nmap or **Network Mapper** is a free, open source network scanning tool created by the software developer Gordon Lyon. Take a look at the type of output Nmap typically generates when a user runs a scan:

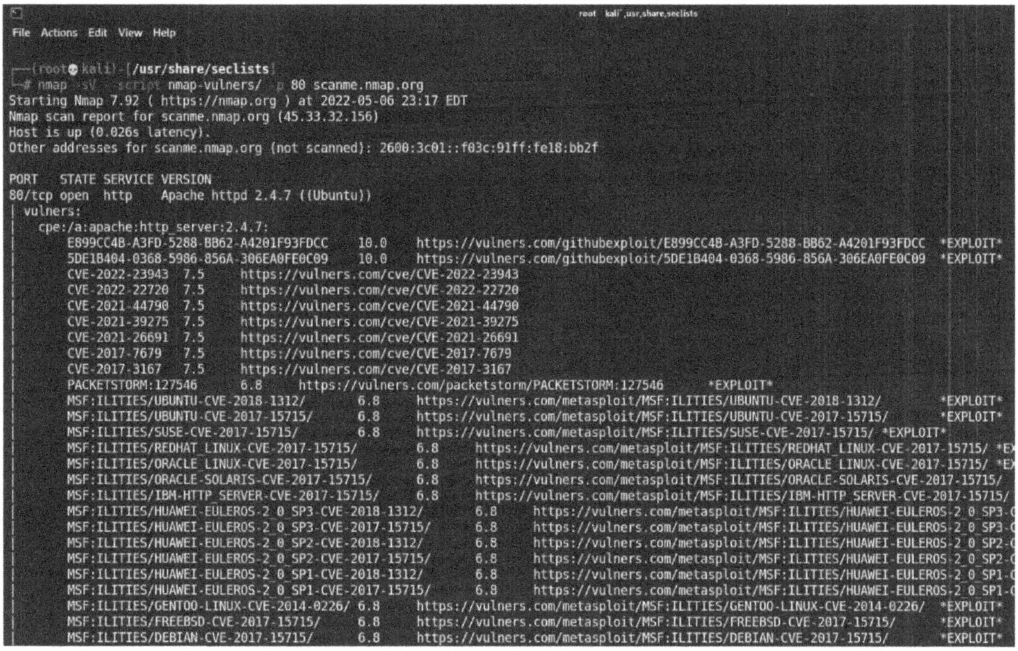

Figure 1.4 – A screenshot of Nmap output using the Nmap-vulners script

The tool can scan for a range of different services on a target host. It can be used to scan a single host or multiple hosts on a local area network or the internet. To say it's a vulnerability scanning tool is a bit reductive to the complexity of Nmap, but it's often used with scripts that specifically probe for vulnerabilities. Command-line inputs drive it, and scripts must be specifically requested to determine whether something is vulnerable.

OpenVAS

The **Open Vulnerability Assessment System**, more commonly known as **OpenVAS**, is a free, open source tool spun off the commercial product Nessus. OpenVAS's interface is pictured in the following figure with the Greenbone Security Assistant interface:

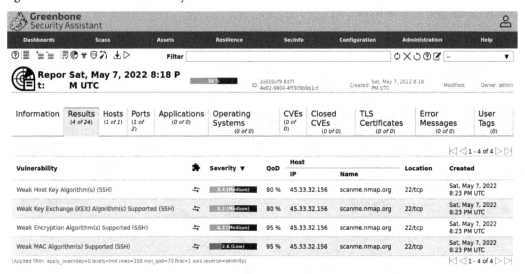

Figure 1.5 – The OpenVAS Greenbone Security Assistant dashboard

OpenVAS can help system administrators scan for well-known vulnerabilities against various operating systems and platforms. While it's open source, it's a well-supported tool. However, critics or detractors of OpenVAS often point out that the support for enterprises is poor, and extracting data out of the system can be difficult.

Nikto

Nikto is an open source command-line tool that can scan a webserver for vulnerabilities. Its usage is strictly limited to web servers and will require open web services to be of use. The output and interfaces are similar to Nmap, as seen in the following figure:

```
└─# nikto -h https://nmap.org
- Nikto v2.1.6
---------------------------------------------------------------------------
+ Target IP:          45.33.49.119
+ Target Hostname:    nmap.org
+ Target Port:        443
---------------------------------------------------------------------------
+ SSL Info:       Subject:  /CN=insecure.com
                  Ciphers:  ECDHE-RSA-AES128-GCM-SHA256
                  Issuer:   /C=US/O=Let's Encrypt/CN=R3
+ Start Time:        2022-05-06 23:09:57 (GMT-4)
---------------------------------------------------------------------------
+ Server: Apache/2.4.6 (CentOS)
+ The anti-clickjacking X-Frame-Options header is not present.
+ The X-XSS-Protection header is not defined. This header can hint to the user agent to protect against some forms of XSS
+ The site uses SSL and Expect-CT header is not present.
+ The X-Content-Type-Options header is not set. This could allow the user agent to render the content of the site in a differe
```

Figure 1.6 – A screenshot of Nikto output from the command line

Nevertheless, it's a great tool to use to check in on websites to get a better idea of what they might have for vulnerabilities. Much like Nmap, the output is limited, and detractors anecdotally point out that the rate of false positives is high.

Nessus

Nessus is one of the most deployed vulnerability assessment solutions across the information security industry. The easy-to-use interface and dashboard looks like this:

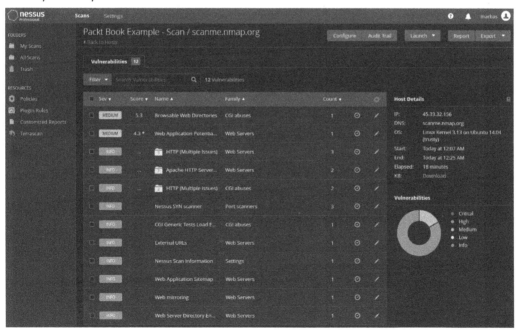

Figure 1.7 – Nessus scan example

Nessus works much like OpenVAS, allowing an operator to detect and audit the configuration and vulnerabilities on client computers, web servers, and more. This commercially available product also offers easy-to-export reports on the data it finds and various plugins that extend the scanning tools' functions.

Rapid7 Nexpose

Rapid7 Nexpose is a vulnerability scanner that can scan various targets for a wide range of vulnerabilities and misconfigurations. Take a look at the dashboard to compare and contrast it with Nessus in the following figure:

Figure 1.8 – Rapid7 Nexpose dashboard

It provides operators with a dashboard of results and tie-ins with other Rapid7 tooling used by penetration testers.

Qualys Vulnerability Management

Qualys Vulnerability Management is a commercial vulnerability scanner. Security analysts use this tool much like the other scanners previously mentioned. This aids in assessing the severity of the vulnerabilities so that they can be prioritized and corrected. It works much like OpenVAS, Nessus, and Nexpose.

> **Note**
> However powerful security vulnerability scanners are, they are strictly limited in their ability to search through their databases for known vulnerabilities. If there's not a scripted check for the vulnerability, it cannot be detected.

Now that we've talked about vulnerability scanners, let's get up to speed on the common kinds of software vulnerabilities you'll see in the wild.

Exploring common types of software vulnerabilities

While an exhaustive list of common software vulnerabilities is out of scope for this book, we should cover some of the most common software vulnerabilities that are being found and exploited. We'll split this up into two separate groups, web applications and client-server applications.

Web applications

Web applications are one of the most common entry points where organizations get breached. One of the most notable breaches of all time is the Equifax data breach in 2017. This breach occurred because Equifax had a vulnerable website that got exploited. This exploitation of vulnerable software was chained together with other vulnerabilities and exploits to ultimately result in the theft of confidential data. Organizations commonly have websites that feature tools and applications that help them conduct business with their customers and other organizations. These are just some of the common kinds of vulnerabilities found in these popular and widely adopted technologies.

Broken authentication and authorization

Broken authentication and authorization are one of the more common issues found in modern web applications. As a result of the vulnerability, attackers can access data they shouldn't be allowed to access through a valid account to the website or no account at all. A good example of broken authentication would be if an attacker could bypass the login page for the website to access and or manipulate data that doesn't belong to them. In contrast, broken authorization might result in an attacker logging in to that website with their own account, but when they access their account information, they could manipulate the application session to access the account information of another user.

Cross-site scripting

Cross-site scripting (**XSS**) is a technique used to inject malicious content into a website that can be used to run arbitrary JavaScript on a user's browser session. Attackers do this by finding poor input validation in code. This can be accomplished by finding places on websites that reflect information back to the users either through persistent storage or reflected values that can be present in a URL. There are three widely accepted variants of this vulnerability we'll briefly discuss:

- **Persistent XSS**: This vulnerability is exploited when users load websites that contain stored values with malicious JavaScript. To exploit this, attackers find places to submit data into the application in a way that saves those values as valid JavaScript, which is then, in turn, reflected back to a user.

- **Reflected XSS**: This variation of the XSS vulnerability allows attackers to exploit vulnerable inputs by giving victims URLs that contain malicious JavaScript. Typically, this kind of vulnerability is commonly present in search functions of websites.

- **DOM-based XSS**: This vulnerability exists when there is poor input handling in JavaScript, which exploits controls in something called the **Document Object Model (DOM)**. The DOM is a representation of windows and elements on a website and how data flows through these objects. To exploit these vulnerabilities, attackers need to insert malicious JavaScript, which can take advantage of how the objects are processed.

SQL and NoSQL injection

SQL/NoSQL injection is a type of vulnerability that exploits queries made to a connected database. Attackers exploit this kind of vulnerability by manipulating how data is queried in forms and/or requests to the server. When used, the vulnerability results in the disclosure of data such as passwords and personal information. In some cases, these vulnerabilities can be exploited in a way that allows an attacker to take over the underlying server that hosts the database. A variant of this vulnerability referred to as NoSQL injection is related to similar methods used to exploit non-tabular database systems that are connected to applications. The techniques have similar results but are executed in very different ways.

Command injection

Command injection is a type of vulnerability that is a lot like SQL injection. In command injection, though, attackers attempt to insert values into fields or processes in the web application that, if exploited, can run arbitrary commands on the server. This can give an attacker the ability to take complete control over the server and provide them with a foothold into networks they may otherwise not have access to.

Cross-site request forgery

Cross-site request forgery (CSRF) is a vulnerability that, when exploited, can cause users to perform actions for attackers. Standard exploitation techniques involve attackers sending users malicious links that serve requests if used by a user. One of the expected outcomes of distributing these malicious links to victims is actions that change the victim's password, email address, or other account information to initiate an account takeover.

Server-side request forgery

Server-side request forgery (SSRF) is a type of attack that exploits the trust that a server has in its client. It's very similar to the CSRF vulnerability type, but the specific focus of this vulnerability is the server and the trust it has with clients and other servers instead of the end user. Exploiting this type of vulnerability can result in the server making authenticated elevated privilege requests to itself or other internally accessible endpoints.

Business logic flaws

Business logic flaws are vulnerabilities introduced by failing to anticipate unexpected behavior or input in routine business processes. There's never a typical way to exploit these vulnerabilities. These vulnerabilities don't always follow similar patterns because the application developers always design the logic that dictates how an application ought to be used, and any attack patterns that emerge from the design must be considered on a case-by-case basis. Software developers often introduce these vulnerabilities by not handling the unexpected inputs and states that users may encounter.

> **Note**
>
> What's prevalent in web application security has changed significantly over the last decade. For the most up-to-date list of common security flaws found in web applications, please refer to the OWASP Top 10 list, which is updated frequently at the following link: `https://www.owasp.org/www-project-top-ten`.

Client-server applications

Unlike web applications, which seem to have incoming and outgoing trends in software flaws, traditional client-server applications, often known as thick clients or thick applications, change less frequently. These applications differ due to the fact that they are primarily used on an operating system, and the application typically needs to be installed or configured to run on that operating system. These applications often power web application components in server deployments, but they also help users accomplish tasks locally with the processing power of their workstations.

Information disclosure

This happens when applications require passwords, API keys, and personal information to be stored. Sometimes these details are stored in plain-text or encoded files, which can easily be accessed through decompiling applications or decoding the content.

Process hijacking

When applications are installed on operating systems, oftentimes, they are configured with incorrect or insecure permissions on their files, scheduled services, libraries, and more. Attackers can take advantage of these configuration problems by hijacking these components, often impersonating a legitimate application or user session.

Cleartext communications

This vulnerability refers explicitly to communications the application might be making over network protocols. Like our previous category of information disclosure, applications might be transmitting information that is unencrypted and contains sensitive values, which can be exploited if an attacker can intercept the network communication between the client and its network host.

Web application vulnerabilities

Sometimes, traditional applications install web applications that allow users to interact with components of the locally installed application. With these kinds of applications, even if the application is accessed locally, all the issues previously mentioned in the web application section can apply here.

Now that we have a good idea of what kind of vulnerabilities we might find out in the wild, let's examine the life cycle vulnerabilities typically have.

Inspecting the software vulnerability life cycle

The life cycle of vulnerabilities isn't always linear, but there are common themes that emerge, which we will explore through a discussion of the phases of this cycle. We'll talk about these in four stages that often overlap and or begin their execution simultaneously, as shown in the following figure:

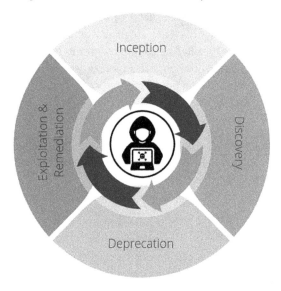

Figure 1.9 – The stages rarely follow a specific order, but they are consistent
through the inception and depreciation of vulnerabilities

Let's explore each stage in detail over the next few sections.

Inception

The first stage we'll cover is **inception**. In the life cycle, vulnerabilities get introduced through malicious or non-malicious activities during the inception stage. For example, developers might write insecure code, system administrators could deploy weak configurations, or malicious actors may purposefully embed vulnerabilities and back doors into the software. Understanding inception at times is difficult due to the various paths that vulnerabilities take when they're introduced.

For software and systems to be deployed securely, engineers need to know how to securely write code and deploy systems, or they should receive guidance from security practitioners. Security literacy, or rather the lack of it, may be why vulnerabilities get introduced, but it's not usually the only contributing factor. Developing software and maintaining operations is expensive, and organizations often seek to save money through various practices meant to accelerate product deployment. As a result, software developers and operation engineers are often stretched thin on projects, and products are rushed to get features and functionality embedded to acquire new customers or satisfy current customers. This pressure combined with poor security culture and/or education in the organization can often lead to outcomes where steps are skipped or security is placed on hold to ensure the product makes it to market. Remember, security always comes at a cost, and that cost often gets cut when businesses push to get applications or features to customers quickly.

Another factor to consider is the complexity of software systems and their deployed or supported infrastructure. If a system is complex, there are more opportunities for weaknesses to be introduced into the configuration and code.

Finally, malicious actors inserting vulnerabilities into code isn't as uncommon as one might think. It can take a few different forms. Attackers are often aided by an insider threat, such as a disgruntled employee who sells access to attackers. In other instances, sophisticated state-sponsored attacks often gain a foothold into the software of companies they seek to exploit. In 2020, such a campaign made worldwide headlines when attackers targeted the business software, SolarWinds Orion, resulting in CVE-2020-10148. This vulnerability identified highly sophisticated actors implementing a trojan in the Orion software, which was then deployed thousands of times to customers. While these types of attacks and their impact are difficult to quantify, many believe the full effects of this kind of vulnerability are often unseen and potentially have catastrophic outcomes when exploited by attackers.

Discovery

During the **discovery** phase, vulnerabilities are discovered through security research, where motivated actors seek to understand whether something is vulnerable. They do this by using various methods that test the software for the types of vulnerabilities mentioned in the common vulnerabilities section. The motivations for discovery can vary. Some people are simply looking to discover vulnerabilities to improve the security of software, while others seek to exploit software with other goals in mind.

Depending on the actor's motivations, the discovery stage presents the researchers with a choice to make. First, they need to decide how and whether they'll communicate their vulnerabilities to responsible parties. Once discovered, researchers would notify the software publisher directly in ideal circumstances. Once informed, the publisher can begin work on fixing the problems in the remediation stage. Unfortunately, disclosing and determining the next steps for vulnerabilities is rarely this simple or rewarding.

In many cases, the vulnerabilities are never communicated to software publishers. It's worth mentioning that disclosure decisions (if made at all) sometimes take an ethically questionable path. For example, there are some cases where security researchers decide to sell vulnerability research to security firms. Some of these firms specialize in the acquisition of vulnerabilities and operational exploits. These firms will buy exploits to incorporate into their security toolsets that they, in turn, sell to other software vendors, the original software vendor, or even nation-states that can incorporate these exploits in their cyber arsenals.

Exploitation and remediation

The **exploitation and remediation** stages can occur shortly after discovery. These two are linked in our life cycle and appear depending on how things unfold after discovering the vulnerability.

In some cases, a vulnerability is discovered, and then the researchers who found the vulnerability will inform vendors of their findings. Vendors will then create remediation plans or even software patches that they'll publish to customers that patch the security vulnerability.

Suppose information or software patches are released but they do not directly mention how the vulnerabilities work. In these cases, researchers sometimes try to reverse engineer the vulnerability based on the documentation or patches through careful observation to build functional exploits. This is quite common for security researchers working on or studying popular software products such as the operating system Windows. For example, with the disclosed vulnerability CVE-2019-0708, commonly known as BlueKeep, Microsoft released a patch in May 2019. Researchers reverse-engineered the patch to construct a working exploit in July, with the mainstream exploit kits receiving a working exploit later in the year during the month of September.

In other cases, some bug hunters can immediately release the exploitation information about their vulnerabilities to the public – sometimes for free and sometimes as something sold, as previously discussed in the discovery phase. Vulnerabilities that receive immediate releases can (and have) lead to widespread exploitation events.

Modern attack patterns typically show mass exploitation isn't far behind when vulnerabilities are discovered and information about them is released. Bad actors often begin scanning public resources on the internet for vulnerable software versions that match the vulnerability discovery. Provided exploitations are created and reliable, they're often added to hacker tools that can exploit the vulnerability.

Perhaps one of the most troubling attributes of this is how the public learns about these vulnerabilities. Even in the ideal circumstances of a researcher reaching out and sharing vulnerability information with companies, these actions, if not carried over public channels, can result in the vendor patching problems without any notice to the public or users about the impacted software and the risks associated with using outdated software. Unfortunately, this practice is insidiously common in the industry.

Deprecation

Much like in any life cycle, things end. Over time, software and vulnerable versions of that software will fall away from usage. Patches or remediations are provisionally added to newer versions. Eventually, legacy vulnerabilities will fall out of the purview of hackers, vulnerability scanners, or people looking for vulnerabilities.

Keep in mind that the process of eventual deprecation can take a lot of time, and older vulnerabilities should always be thought of and considered when reviewing technology. For example, the common bug Shellshock or CVE-2014-7169 is commonly found almost a decade after its public release. The vulnerability had been present in the software for over 30 years before being discovered, and the software is widely deployed throughout the worldwide technology ecosystem.

Another culprit for long deprecation cycles is unsupported but required services or systems. Consider for a moment the healthcare industry. Hospitals and healthcare organizations will often invest in blood chemistry analyzers, the hardware used for X-rays, and other imaging technology such as MRIs. These investments can amount to millions of dollars. Unfortunately, healthcare software publishers may not support the software on these devices for as long as a hospital intends to use the equipment it made investments in. These gaps can lead to issues where investments are not protected against exploitation, or exploitation is handled with other mitigating factors. Anecdotally, it's not uncommon to see software that is 15 to 20 years old on large equipment or major technology investments such as industrial control systems that power critical infrastructure deployments in the public sector.

Hopefully, this has helped you understand the life cycles of vulnerabilities and what you can expect when a vulnerability eventually appears in software.

Summary

In this chapter, you've learned about vulnerabilities, what they are, and how they relate to core concepts in the information security industry. First, we reviewed the standard tools industry professionals use to scan and find vulnerable components. We then discussed common vulnerabilities found in different types of applications. Finally, we discussed the usual life cycle of vulnerabilities.

Getting you familiar with these concepts lays a foundation that will be crucial if you're looking to research and report vulnerabilities yourself. Generally speaking, security practitioners need to understand vital foundational concepts around vulnerabilities, how they're ranked and organized, what tools to use to scan for them, and what course of action is taken when security researchers discover them. Now that you're armed with this foundational knowledge of vulnerabilities, you're prepared to learn more through research and how to approach your own vulnerabilities.

In the next chapter, we'll discuss the classification of vulnerabilities called **zero-days** and review case studies about their impacts on vulnerable software.

Further reading

- MITRE CVE list – `https://cve.mitre.org/cve/`
- Common Vulnerability Scoring System Calculator – `https://nvd.nist.gov/vuln-metrics/cvss/v3-calculator`

- Known Exploited Vulnerabilities Catalog – `https://www.cisa.gov/known-exploited-vulnerabilities-catalog`

- Nmap – `https://nmap.org/`

- Nikto – `https://cirt.net/Nikto2`

- Nessus – `https://www.tenable.com/products/nessus`

- Rapid7 Nexpose – `https://www.rapid7.com/products/nexpose/`

- Qualys Vulnerability Management – `https://www.qualys.com/`

- OWASP Top 10 Web Application Vulnerabilities – `https://owasp.org/www-project-top-ten/`

2
Exploring Real-World Impacts of Zero-Days

In the summer of 2016, the hacker group **The Shadow Brokers** (**TSB**) announced that they had exfiltrated and possessed cyber weapons used by the United States intelligence agencies over the social media platform Twitter. They intended to sell their findings at an auction on the dark web. However, after a few unsuccessful attempts to sell, they began leaking their stolen cyberweapons to the public. In April 2017, they revealed several zero-day exploits, one of which was the devastating CVE-2017-0144, often known as **EternalBlue**. By the end of April, the exploits for EternalBlue had infected computer systems throughout the world, with some researchers claiming over half a million assets were impacted.

By the time CVE-2017-0144 had been issued, Microsoft had released a security patch (MS17-010) just a couple of weeks prior. Companies with the ability to patch made the security fix a priority, but many did not or could not. In the previous chapter, we learned about the vulnerability lifecycle. Researchers frequently face a dilemma when researching security gaps aiming to exploit software. They could report the security flaw to the manufacturer so that it gets fixed, sell their research, or keep security flaws secret for eventual use and weapons development. In the case of the EternalBlue exploit, the United States government allegedly kept the vulnerability secret and developed sophisticated cyber weapons to use later in campaigns of technology espionage.

At one point in the lifecycle of the EternalBlue vulnerability, it was classified as a zero-day, and during that time, it was used and exploited without the knowledge of the manufacturer. Of course, all vulnerabilities are zero-days at one point, but when is a zero-day vulnerability classified as such, and what causes them to stop being zero-days? This chapter aims to clear up those ambiguities, discuss real-world vulnerabilities, and explore the ethics concerning zero-days. We'll dive into the following subjects in this chapter:

- We'll introduce zero-day vulnerabilities
- We'll learn key terminology that will help us understand how to talk about zero-days
- We'll review several real-world exploits of zero-days
- We'll discuss the ethics and dilemmas in terms of zero-day disclosure

These outcomes will be presented through the following main topics in this chapter:

- Zero-days – what are they?
- Exploring zero-day case studies
- Considering zero-day ethics

By the end of this chapter, you should understand zero-day vulnerabilities and their impact on modern business, as well as become aware of the ethical concerns regarding the handling of zero-days. By doing so, you'll be well on your way to finding, discussing, and disclosing your own zero-day vulnerabilities.

Zero-days – what are they?

Zero-day, sometimes styled as **0-day**, is a term used to talk about newly discovered vulnerabilities, exploiting vulnerabilities, and cyber-attacks. The word zero-day comes from a calculation used by security analysts to define the severity of a vulnerability. When the **window of vulnerability** equals zero, it represents the highest potential risk. It also aptly describes the exposure condition and the software manufacturer knowing about it, much less providing a security fix for such a discovery. As a result, zero-day vulnerabilities are very dangerous because there are no significant protections against them.

Generally speaking, zero-day terminology is often used incorrectly and interchangeably. So, let's get a good understanding of the terms you'll come across concerning zero-days and what they mean.

Zero-day vulnerability

A **zero-day vulnerability** is a type of vulnerability discovered by security researchers. This term usually refers to discovered vulnerabilities that have otherwise not been disclosed to a vendor or to the public. These vulnerabilities are typically known to an audience before the software publisher knows about the vulnerability. Zero-day vulnerabilities are generally found by security researchers and reported to the software vendor so that they can create a patch to fix the issue. In some cases, a researcher may choose to disclose the zero-day to the public so that users are aware of the problem and can take steps to protect themselves. Additionally, researchers may find it advantageous to step over these two standard options to keep the vulnerability secret or sell the zero-day to a vulnerability broker in other cases.

In the example of CVE-2017-0144/EternalBlue, which opened our chapter, the United States government allegedly discovered the zero-day vulnerability in the Windows operating system. They did this by purposefully exploring the security of the software, hoping to find zero-day vulnerabilities. Once discovered, they kept their findings secret.

Because a zero-day is usually undisclosed, there typically isn't a way to prevent the exploitation of the vulnerability, even in ideal circumstances. Zero-day vulnerabilities can be discovered before an attack that exploits the exposure, while an attack happens, or after an attack has occurred. A zero-day is what we'd classify as a newly discovered vulnerability in our vulnerability lifecycle.

Zero-day exploit

A **zero-day exploit** is when a malicious or non-malicious actor has developed a working exploit for a zero-day vulnerability. While not always the case, these are often refined into weaponized-like elements that can be delivered to vulnerable software. Therefore, this can also be referred to as the delivery mechanism used to exploit the vulnerability.

Again, in our opening vulnerability, CVE-2017-0144, the zero-day exploit was likely developed with the information discovered during the vulnerability research. In the case of TSB, they released the exploits, which consisted of EternalBlue, EternalRomance, and EternalSynergy. These zero-day exploits came bundled with tools and delivery mechanisms such as **DOUBLEPULSAR**. While DOUBLEPULSAR didn't specifically take advantage of CVE-2017-0144, it was used as a delivery and persistence mechanism that capitalized on the vulnerability.

When a zero-day is weaponized, it is often for a specific reason that is motivated by goals. These goals usually include the following:

- **Espionage**: Data exfiltration from a target organization to gain information that would otherwise be difficult or impossible to obtain

- **Sabotage**: Disrupting the operations of a target organization to gain an advantage over them or to cause them harm

- **Profit**: Using the zero-day to extort the organization or individual that is affected by it

While zero-day exploits can be used for many different purposes, they can also be used defensively. In some cases, security organizations will develop exploits or even purchase zero-days to test their own or client systems and see if they are vulnerable to attacks. The argument for companies to build in-house exploits for use in testing systems is that it provides a realistic understanding of risk, where highly motivated actors targeting specific industries will make similar investments.

In the case of the widely successful WannaCry ransomware attack following the release of EternalBlue, motivated attackers used the EternalBlue exploit in conjunction with other malware. These criminals did this to develop a weapon intended for profit by encrypting files, holding them hostage, and then demanding payouts from users; otherwise, their files would be encrypted forever.

Zero-day attack

A zero-day attack involves using a zero-day exploit. Attacks often consist of malware delivering an exploit to the target. In our EternalBlue example, there were uses of the exploit before it was leaked, but it could no longer be called a zero-day exploit or attack once the exploit was patched.

Security experts are concerned about zero-day attacks because they can be used to achieve exploitation goals on targets without any warning. In addition, once a new zero-day exploit has been used, it can be difficult for defenders to keep up with the ever-increasing pace of these attacks.

While zero-day attacks are challenging to protect from, in some cases, organizations have found significant benefits in a **defense-in-depth** strategy. Think of cyberattacks as a chain of events. Attackers rarely exploit one piece of software and move on with their lives. Instead, they chain attacks together to accomplish a goal (see *Figure 2.1*):

Figure 2.1 – Not having adequate controls within the chain can allow an attacker to be more successful

Defense in depth can help by breaking the chain of events by protecting other elements, which may help prevent the exploitation mechanism from being initiated or executed to allow an attacker to achieve a goal. Once again, exploring our EternalBlue example, in some cases, organizations used security controls that prevented the direct access of a specific port in Windows. These controls acted as a protection mechanism:

Figure 2.2 – Defense in depth can help break the chain of events that exploit zero-days

As a result, breaking the chain of attacks prevented the successful exploitation of a zero-day attack (see *Figure 2.2*).

An analogy of zero-day terminology

Zero-days are often weaponized and, much like weapons, they make a good analogy of how these terms can be used. Think about another weapon, such as a thermonuclear bomb. These weapons consist of dangerous raw materials such as uranium. While these are dangerous, they are not necessarily something that can negatively impact society widely unless designed explicitly to do so. Think of the raw materials that go into a bomb like this, our zero-day vulnerability. To weaponize raw materials (or vulnerabilities) to build a bomb, motivated actors need to refine them into something that can be used as a weapon, which is then packaged into a delivery mechanism, such as a nuclear missile. In our analogy, a zero-day exploit is just like our raw, weaponized materials, which now have an efficient means of delivery and exploitation. Much like conventional weapons, these are often tested before being used in attack campaigns. Finally, a zero-day attack involves using a weapon. Attacks often take place in ways that cause damage directly after an attack and sometimes later after use (see *Figure 2.3*):

Zero-day vulnerabilities are often just the raw elements of soft-ware, which can be refined.

Vulnerability

Zero-day exploits are refined vulnerabilities that have been turned into weapons.

Exploit

Zero-day attacks are deployed instances of the weapon that cause damage.

Attack

Figure 2.3 – Zero-days begin as vulnerabilities, are developed into exploits, and are used in attacks

Zero-day vulnerabilities often take time for the software developer to become aware of. Therefore, it might take months for a patch to be developed and deployed to users. Even when patches are developed, there's not always a guarantee that users will patch the software. Again, in our EternalBlue example, conservative estimates put over half a million devices hacked within the first 3 weeks of the exploit being available – even when a security patch was urgently communicated to customers about the grave risk.

Now, let's review some case studies of widely exploited vulnerabilities that entered and exited the zero-day nomenclature to better understand how scenarios like these unfold.

Exploring zero-day case studies

An excellent way to learn about zero-days is by reviewing instances of them being reported. Understanding how they were discovered, weaponized, and when patches were available can help us understand the process and give us questions to reflect on the potential problems zero-day disclosures can cause. So, let's review four cases of zero-day vulnerabilities found in the wild to understand how they're exploited. Since all of these vulnerabilities had disclosures, we'll call out the CVE ID, show the MITRE entry, present the description issued by the authorities, and discuss the vulnerability briefly.

Pulse – CVE-2019-11510

Kicking off our discussion of specific case studies, **CVE-2019-11510** relates to the Pulse VPN family of products. We will be discussing this because, during 2019 and 2020, it was one of the most serious unpatched vulnerabilities that attackers were actively exploiting. Let's take a look at the vulnerability's description.

Vulnerability description

In Pulse Secure **Pulse Connect Secure** (**PCS**) 8.2 before 8.2R12.1, 8.3 before 8.3R7.1, and 9.0 before 9.0R3.4, an unauthenticated, remote attacker could send a specially crafted URI to exploit an arbitrary file-reading vulnerability (see *Figure 2.4*):

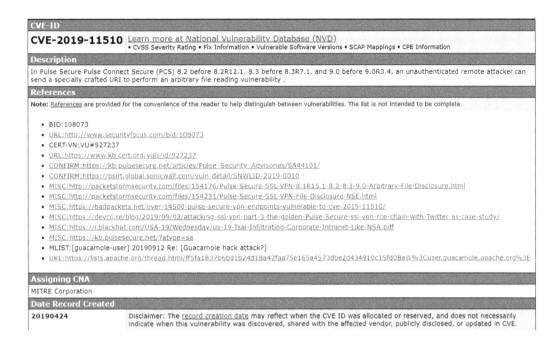

Figure 2.4 – MITRE CVE listing for CVE-2019-11510

Vulnerability discussion

CVE-2019-11510 is a critical vulnerability in PCS (formerly known as **Juniper SSL VPN**) that allowed for the arbitrary disclosure of files. Attackers could craft specialized requests to servers that hosted web applications that would allow passwords and usernames to be downloaded and extracted – all while remaining anonymous and not needing any sort of authentication. If successfully chained together with other exploits, victims could expect the vulnerability to result in a serious compromise, potentially allowing attackers into the network for unfettered internal network access. The vulnerability impacted many versions of the software and, according to the US-CERT and several post-exploitation reflections from companies who were impacted, the flaw could be exploited remotely without requiring any user interaction.

The problem Pulse Secure is meant to solve is securing remote access from users who want to log in to the enterprise network remotely from the internet. Weaknesses concerning access points for an enterprise network are always of great interest to security researchers, and this was no exception. This security bug came out of research that security researchers published directly to the vendor. Motivated researchers began looking at Pulse since it was used at Google and Twitter, among other large entities such as the United States government.

Thankfully, once the security researchers reported the vulnerability, the vendor quickly responded and fixed CVE-2019-11510 within a month of the initial report. Pulse issued a security patch to customers, and the original security researchers planned on not disclosing their findings until customers had enough time to patch the vulnerability. However, as discussed in the vulnerability lifecycle, the potential for security researchers to reverse-engineer patches became a reality soon after the vendor released their patch. Exploitation proof-of-concept code began popping up on the internet, and that code was refined into automated scanners, which could help automate the discovery and exploitation of Pulse software. So, revisiting our discussion on terminology about zero-days, the only real zero-day discovered here was the vulnerability. Later exploitations and attacks that occurred on systems due to this vulnerability were not technically zero days (see *Figure 2.5*):

Figure 2.5 – The only zero-day that manifested, in this case, was the vulnerability

Vulnerability takeaways

High-risk zero-day vulnerabilities and their inevitable weaponization rarely take a linear path. Interestingly, after the patch was released, other security researchers took a look at the patch and began reverse-engineering the patch to understand the potential exploit. It wasn't more than a few weeks until exploits were made public, and criminals began using the exploit code to attack companies.

It's also a good idea to examine customer response to the security advisory published by the vendor. Due to the widespread usage and the poor response in patching, security agencies over the next year monitored the exploitation. While the zero-day vulnerability was found and patched quickly, customers didn't apply the patch. Not applying the patch when it was issued opened the door to exploits that were widely used to attack large enterprises, government agencies, schools, and healthcare organizations.

One other interesting development in this particular case is that the original researchers who found the vulnerability and reported it to Pulse later began searching for companies with vulnerable systems, responsible disclosure policies, and bug bounties and exploited all vulnerable Pulse servers that met their criteria. Notably, their most interesting disclosed resources discuss finding the VPN in use at Twitter, then using this vulnerability in a chain of weaknesses to gain remote access to computer systems at Twitter. Twitter paid the researchers over $20,000 for disclosing this vulnerable asset.

Vulnerability reflection

It's important to remember that all involved parties believed they did the right thing. But reflecting on this vulnerability, ask yourself the following questions:

- Did the vendor correctly relay or inform customers that they were vulnerable? Many customers were still vulnerable after the patches were released.

- Were the security researchers who discovered the vulnerability right about not disclosing the vulnerability after the patch was released?

- Twitter paid out over $20,000 to security researchers who found a vulnerable VPN endpoint – there was a security patch available. Why do you suppose it wasn't patched, and could Twitter have saved itself a payout if security patches were applied?

- What would you have done differently through the disclosure process, if anything?

Confluence – CVE-2021-26084

Now, we will take a closer look at **CVE-2021-26084**, which was found in the immensely popular Atlassian **Confluence** software. This vulnerability was used throughout 2021 to help attackers achieve remote unauthenticated access to highly sensitive documents and OS-level access. Let's examine the vulnerability's description.

Vulnerability description

In affected versions of Confluence Server and Data Center, an OGNL injection vulnerability existed that would allow an unauthenticated attacker to execute arbitrary code on a Confluence Server or Data Center instance. The affected versions are before version 6.13.23, from version 6.14.0 before 7.4.11, from version 7.5.0 before 7.11.6, and from version 7.12.0 before 7.12.5 (see *Figure 2.6*):

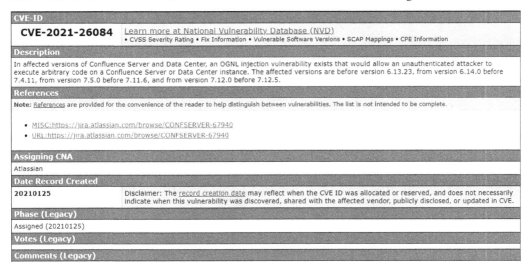

Figure 2.6 – MITRE CVE listing for CVE-2021-26084

Vulnerability discussion

Atlassian's software, Confluence, is probably one of the most used wiki-style documentation engines used in software development shops. The tie-ins with Jira, Bitbucket, and other Atlassian products make it an easy sell to customers invested in the ecosystem of products. If you've ever worked in a software development-focused organization or a startup, you've likely interacted, consumed, or directly worked on Atlassian software. **CVE-2021-26084** was a surprise to Atlassian, and researchers discovered it was being exploited in the wild. Attackers discovered exploiting the vulnerability involved sending Confluence Server simple crafted HTTP requests, which tampered with a parameter. Atlassian issued a patch and security advisory quickly.

This was not the first time that Confluence had been vulnerable to a critical security issue. In 2019, CVE-2019-3396 was exploited in the wild, resulting in remote code execution. Interestingly enough, security researchers found themselves keenly aware and interested in this vulnerability because Atlassian software was also being used in the US Department of Defense, NATO, and several other high-profile private and governmental organizations.

In contrast to the previous vulnerability in the Pulse VPN, this zero-day consists of the vulnerability, an exploit, and an attack:

CVE-2021-26084

Vulnerability	Exploit	Attack
✓	✓	✓

Figure 2.7 – Vulnerabilities, exploits, and attacks were all developed in this case

In some cases of zero-day discoveries, the vulnerability is discovered after it's been exploited, which is the case here (see *Figure 2.7*).

Vulnerability takeaways

The vulnerability was found, being exploited actively on the internet – and since Atlassian had previous experience with a similar issue, they had reflected and improved on previous responses. It could easily be said that Atlassian had an aggressive security response when the vulnerability was announced. For some users of the Confluence platform, Atlassian could send the customers notifications and alerts about the security of the software directly inside the platform. This functionality allowed site administrators to see this and know that urgent action was needed.

Anecdotally, users of the Confluence platform said they were also aggressively targeting product users with notifications via all possible channels by leveraging sales relationships. However, not everyone received this kind of support. In some cases, Atlassian chose not to support users who were not up to date on their licensing to get the security patches. As a result, some customers needed to pay expensive re-licensing fees to get their desperately needed security patches. Some might argue that this was unethical behavior from Atlassian, and some might attribute it to resolving delinquent customers. Regardless of either conclusion, Atlassian responded well in this case, given the terse notice and active exploitation in the wild.

Vulnerability reflection

Reflecting on how this vulnerability is different, let's take a moment to think about some questions we might ask ourselves in this particular case:

- The vulnerability was discovered after the attackers had deployed the zero-day exploit in an attack. What measures can you think of that might have helped slow down attackers?

- Could the attacks be prevented with controls? Why or why not?

- What are your thoughts on Atlassian's aggressive security response? Do you think it resulted in consumers patching the vulnerabilities at higher rates than the Pulse VPN?

- Should Atlassian have given users more information on detecting attacks that may have been executed against their Confluence Servers? How could this have been done?

- How do you feel about Atlassian not providing support for all customers of Confluence? For example, should they have withheld security fixes from customers who may not have had up-to-date licensing on their products and were not eligible for support?

Microsoft .NET CVE-2017-8759

In this example, we will be reviewing **CVE-2017-8759**, found in Microsoft's .NET platform. This case is intriguing because its discovery occurred after it had been exploited. For any threat-hunting researcher, this is a red flag that may indicate that they have uncovered an active exploitation campaign. Let's start by reviewing the description before diving into further discussion.

Vulnerability description

Microsoft .NET Framework 2.0, 3.5, 3.5.1, 4.5.2, 4.6, 4.6.1, 4.6.2, and 4.7 allow an attacker to execute code remotely via a malicious document or application, also known as the **.NET Framework Remote Code Execution Vulnerability** (see *Figure 2.8*):

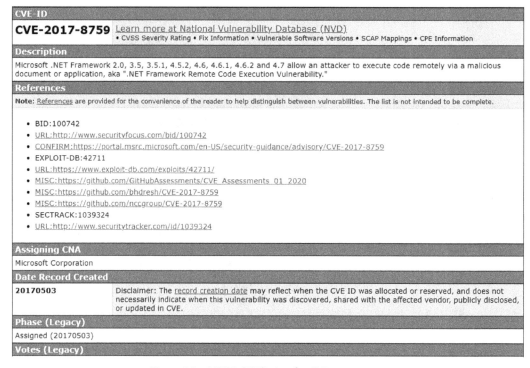

CVE-ID	
CVE-2017-8759	Learn more at National Vulnerability Database (NVD)
	• CVSS Severity Rating • Fix Information • Vulnerable Software Versions • SCAP Mappings • CPE Information
Description	
Microsoft .NET Framework 2.0, 3.5, 3.5.1, 4.5.2, 4.6, 4.6.1, 4.6.2 and 4.7 allow an attacker to execute code remotely via a malicious document or application, aka ".NET Framework Remote Code Execution Vulnerability."	
References	
Note: References are provided for the convenience of the reader to help distinguish between vulnerabilities. The list is not intended to be complete.	

- BID:100742
- URL:http://www.securityfocus.com/bid/100742
- CONFIRM:https://portal.msrc.microsoft.com/en-US/security-guidance/advisory/CVE-2017-8759
- EXPLOIT-DB:42711
- URL:https://www.exploit-db.com/exploits/42711/
- MISC:https://github.com/GitHubAssessments/CVE_Assessments_01_2020
- MISC:https://github.com/bhdresh/CVE-2017-8759
- MISC:https://github.com/nccgroup/CVE-2017-8759
- SECTRACK:1039324
- URL:http://www.securitytracker.com/id/1039324

Assigning CNA	
Microsoft Corporation	
Date Record Created	
20170503	Disclaimer: The record creation date may reflect when the CVE ID was allocated or reserved, and does not necessarily indicate when this vulnerability was discovered, shared with the affected vendor, publicly disclosed, or updated in CVE.
Phase (Legacy)	
Assigned (20170503)	
Votes (Legacy)	

Figure 2.8 – MITRE CVE listing for CVE-2017-8759

Vulnerability discussion

In 2017, Microsoft helped publish the **CVE-2017-8759** security disclosure. This disclosure was related to a previously unknown vulnerability in Microsoft .NET Framework. CVE-2017-8759 relied on social engineering to weaponize the vulnerability. This particular vulnerability manifested itself by delivering a malicious document. While samples vary, attackers relied on office productivity software (Microsoft Word and PowerPoint) to accomplish all the heavy lifting. Users would need to first be convinced to open a document; once the document was loaded, the malware was usually downloaded onto the victim's computer.

In the earliest observed instances of this active exploitation, attackers sent millions of documents. The consensus among security researchers is that the initial samples that were obtained (named *Project.doc* in the Russian language) pointed to a nation-state targeting Russian entities for geopolitical reasons. However, while this was the case, once the exploit was initially captured and released to the public, engineers began developing exploitation kits rapidly. Once an exploitation was available, criminal organizations began campaigns to steal banking information from users by sending millions of emails with malicious documents attached to them (see *Figure 2.9*):

Figure 2.9 – Vulnerabilities were discovered, refined into an exploit, and deployed as attacks

Vulnerability takeaways

This is a great vulnerability to study and review. First, the vulnerability was otherwise unknown – it was later discovered as a zero-day attack, where people were potentially being targeted by nation states. Security researchers then worked backward from the attack, understanding the exploit and the vulnerability. After that, the patch was released, but a lot of people lost money in online phishing scams, which saw opportunistic hackers seize the vulnerability for their purposes.

Vulnerability reflection

Microsoft patched things quickly once the vulnerability had been discovered and reported. But while reflecting on this vulnerability, ask yourself the following questions about this exploited zero-day vulnerability:

- How would you protect your organization from an attack like this? It required user interaction to be exploited.

- What would you have done if you found this attack within your environment?

- Could third-party vendors and products such as antivirus deter the download and execution of these malicious documents?

Citrix – CVE-2019-19781

In our final example, we'll take a look at **CVE-2019-19781**, which was found in the Citrix family of products. Citrix products are used to provide secure access to applications and, for that reason, can be enticing research targets. Let's take a look at the MITRE vulnerability description.

Vulnerability description

An issue was discovered in Citrix **Application Delivery Controller** (**ADC**) and Gateway 10.5, 11.1, 12.0, 12.1, and 13.0. They allow Directory Traversal (see *Figure 2.10*):

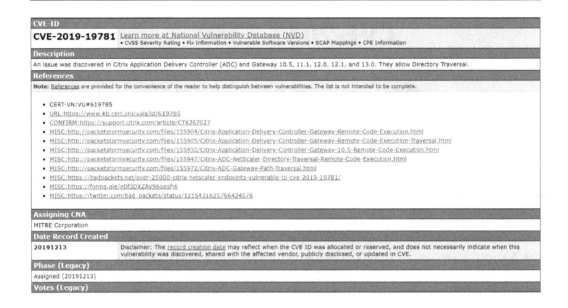

CVE-ID	
CVE-2019-19781	Learn more at National Vulnerability Database (NVD) • CVSS Severity Rating • Fix Information • Vulnerable Software Versions • SCAP Mappings • CPE Information
Description	
An issue was discovered in Citrix Application Delivery Controller (ADC) and Gateway 10.5, 11.1, 12.0, 12.1, and 13.0. They allow Directory Traversal.	
References	
Note: References are provided for the convenience of the reader to help distinguish between vulnerabilities. The list is not intended to be complete.	
• CERT-VN:VU#619785 • URL:https://www.kb.cert.org/vuls/id/619785 • CONFIRM:https://support.citrix.com/article/CTX267027 • MISC:http://packetstormsecurity.com/files/155904/Citrix-Application-Delivery-Controller-Gateway-Remote-Code-Execution.html • MISC:http://packetstormsecurity.com/files/155905/Citrix-Application-Delivery-Controller-Gateway-Remote-Code-Execution-Traversal.html • MISC:http://packetstormsecurity.com/files/155930/Citrix-Application-Delivery-Controller-Gateway-10.5-Remote-Code-Execution.html • MISC:http://packetstormsecurity.com/files/155947/Citrix-ADC-NetScaler-Directory-Traversal-Remote-Code-Execution.html • MISC:http://packetstormsecurity.com/files/155972/Citrix-ADC-Gateway-Path-Traversal.html • MISC:https://badpackets.net/over-25000-citrix-netscaler-endpoints-vulnerable-to-cve-2019-19781/ • MISC:https://forms.gle/eDf3DXZAv96oosfj6 • MISC:https://twitter.com/bad_packets/status/1215431625766424576	
Assigning CNA	
MITRE Corporation	
Date Record Created	
20191213	Disclaimer: The record creation date may reflect when the CVE ID was allocated or reserved, and does not necessarily indicate when this vulnerability was discovered, shared with the affected vendor, publicly disclosed, or updated in CVE.
Phase (Legacy)	
Assigned (20191213)	
Votes (Legacy)	

Figure 2.10 – MITRE CVE listing for CVE-2019-19781

Vulnerability discussion

Citrix **CVE-2019-19781** was one of the most commonly exploited vulnerabilities between 2019 and 2022. The CVE-2019-19781 flaw enabled threat actors to access and conduct unauthorized **remote code execution** (RCE) on a target system. This made it possible for attackers to execute malicious code and take control of an affected system.

Citrix ADC, formerly known as **NetScaler ADC**, and Citrix Gateway, formerly known as **NetScaler Gateway**, were affected by this vulnerability and colorfully codenamed as **Shitrix** by the greater infosec community. The vendor released a patch well over a month after the vulnerability was disclosed. Additionally, Citrix published mitigating suggestions, which should be deployed where possible (see *Figure 2.11*):

CVE-2019-19781

Vulnerability	Exploit	Attack
✓	✗	✗

Figure 2.11 – In this case, only the vulnerability was a zero-day; exploitation came after the disclosure

Arbitrary code execution (**ACE**) is a dangerous attack tactic that threat actors can use to gain elevated privileges and remote access to a target device. Once a flaw is discovered, ACE can be used to execute commands with malicious intent. Unfortunately, security patches were not immediately available, which prevented this vulnerability from being exploited; instead, to defend against this type of attack, Citrix published a series of steps that cybersecurity professionals could take to neutralize the threat.

Vulnerability takeaways

Citrix released guidance concerning the problem a few days before the security researchers disclosed their findings. Citrix published the CVE with the researchers and helped advise customers to perform mitigation steps in place of a patch. Patches were released over a month into the process of this vulnerability.

The detailed release from the security researchers helped other researchers quickly construct a working exploit. However, this exploit was later used en masse against Citrix servers that didn't have patches or mitigation techniques. Researchers stated that working with Citrix was collaborative, and they published mitigating steps quickly but not a patch.

When patched, some instances or installs of the ADC were corrupted so that even if they were patched, they were still vulnerable to exploitation. Almost a year after the initial publication, Citrix disclosed that further services were impacted by this vulnerability, advising customers to fix it but not directly. Critics often point to the security research company not providing enough time for Citrix to develop a patch. Still, the security researchers felt like disclosing a mitigating control was enough for them to publish their research a week or so after the CVE was published.

Vulnerability reflection

In this example, some praised Citrix's handling of the vulnerability, but they left customers unpatched for an unusual amount of time and didn't explicitly disclose vulnerable products. Consider how you might have handled this scenario by asking yourself these questions:

- Should Citrix have explicitly disclosed all impacted software to customers with a notice to patch?

- Were the mitigating controls that Citrix published enough to help curb risk?

- Did the security researcher disclose the vulnerability to allow the vendor time to patch it?

- Did the release of the security research help or hinder users because no patch was available?

With that, we have looked at four examples of CVEs that had zero-day exploitations in the wild. Each one has different characteristics, but they all share the commonality of being exploited before a patch was available. Understanding how these were exploited can help us better prepared in the future when we disclose our zero-day vulnerabilities. On that note, researchers should consider standard ethical practices when disclosing zero-days to ensure that users are protected from exploitation. Responsibilities associated with zero-days are a nuanced and complex topic, and in the next section, we'll examine the ethics and responsibilities of the involved parties.

Considering zero-day ethics

The ethics of zero-day disclosure is a topic that has been debated for years. However, the debate is not about disclosing the vulnerability but rather about when to do it and to whom to disclose it. There is no single answer to when and how to disclose a zero-day vulnerability. Each scenario involving multiple parties (typically, the researcher and the vendor) will need to be weighed. The most crucial factor to consider while disclosing is the users and the risk they'll incur if the zero-day is disclosed. Generally speaking, ethical concerns have been accepted regarding the responsibilities of these parties. Let's discuss these now.

Researcher responsibility

Some researchers believe that it is their responsibility to find and report vulnerabilities as soon as possible. This gives the vendor time to fix the issue before it becomes public and gives users time to update their systems. But what if the vendor doesn't see it that way? While major corporations with sophisticated security organizations might have internal policies and public posture when it comes to researchers reporting vulnerabilities in software, researchers need to realize that these companies make up only a small fraction of the software market of the software market.

At times, vendors will adopt hostile policies to security researchers, seeing the vulnerabilities reported as legal liabilities or operational overhead on a product that isn't making the vendor as much money as it once was. As a result, it's not uncommon for a security researcher to receive a cease-and-desist notice from lawyers representing the vendor's interest. In this case, is it ethical to sell the vulnerability to a security firm buying zero-days or putting public pressure on the vendor in other potentially hostile ways since the company itself is behaving in a hostile way?

There is no right or wrong answer here, and ultimately, it is up to the researcher to decide what they believe is the right thing to do. So, let's talk a little bit about a security researcher's responsibilities when it comes to disclosing vulnerabilities.

Responsibilities in vendor communications

The researcher should first define and discover ways of getting in touch with the vendor. This can take any form, but I advise finding and using an email address for the electronic records and evidence if that ever becomes something you need to produce. It may be advantageous to review whether there are any security disclosure policies ahead of time as well. Depending on their policy or lack thereof, disclosing research under a pseudonym might be better to avoid identification.

Consider the many pros and cons of contacting the vendor first and publishing the vulnerability via a public forum. Contacting the vendor first allows them to fix the issue before it becomes public knowledge, but it can take time for them to respond. On the other hand, publishing on a public forum makes the problem more visible and prompts the vendor to act more quickly. Still, it also means that more people are aware of the vulnerability before it is fixed, which can, in turn, lead to fast weaponization. So, first, it is highly recommended to reach out to the vendor, attempt to communicate with them, and agree on what is best for users. If this fails, explore other methods of getting this information to the public.

We'll talk about vendor communications at length in *Chapter 4*. Still, the key thing to remember is to make sure you're reasonably responsible in your research is that communication should happen. The responsible parties should be informed of the vulnerability and your explicit intent on publishing it.

Responsibilities to the public

Researching, finding, and knowing about security vulnerabilities is like having a superpower. As the saying goes, with great power comes great responsibility. It is the opinion of this author that security researchers should consider the impact on the public if the vulnerability were to be exploited. As researchers, our work should be used to strengthen the security of the user software experience, not weaken it. Therefore, sharing information about your research in the public space should only be done to take a harm-reduction course and follow actions that protect users from being victims.

In our previous section on vulnerability case studies, we saw multiple cases where researchers got their research to the public in a safer, more controlled way. This posturing led to security patches and allowed security-conscious organizations to fix flaws before they were weaponized. The net effect is generally positive, and it puts the public first. As researchers aiming to improve software security, we should aim for that positive impact.

Responsibilities to themselves

Researchers have a responsibility to themselves as well. They're unlikely to continue security research if they're incarcerated. It is essential to consider your research closely, ensuring that you're following applicable laws and researching systems you specifically own or have permission to test. Never test systems you have not received permission to test.

With that being said, ensure you're also protecting your livelihood. Strive to test systems by creating an isolated test environment for yourself to work in. This isolated environment should be separated from the assets you do any other work on and should not be tied back to, say, a day job or other conflicting interests. It's not uncommon for corporate entities to seek to punish you or your employer for research and disclosures.

We previously mentioned disclosing vulnerabilities under an alias or through a third party who will absorb the risk incurred with disclosing. This practice is commonplace for researchers who wish to avoid entanglement with corporate legal departments and avoid putting their jobs and reputations at stake.

Vendor responsibility

What is the responsibility of the vendor? Is it the vendor's responsibility to patch the zero-day as soon as possible? Or is it the vendor's responsibility to assess the risk and decide when to patch it? This, too, is rife with possibilities.

Modern, responsible, security-forward companies should adopt policies that allow security researchers to collaborate with them safely and constructively. For example, suppose a security researcher is reaching out to a vendor. In that case, they care about the greater good of users and likely want to collaborate, receive credit for their hard work, and add value to the vendor's software products in unconventional ways. It's almost like having a free (or low-cost, if compensation is awarded) security consultant. On the other hand, antiquated policies of first involving lawyers and defending the organization can ultimately create unnecessary weaknesses in your software by having the security researcher explore options outside of working with you.

Adopting and fairly offering safe harbor and responsible disclosure policies is how vendors modernize their security posture. We'll talk about this in *Chapter 9* with a deep dive into how vendors can best approach security researchers.

Vendor responsibilities to users

If the product is vendor-supported, users count on you to keep their data inside their products safe. Vendors have a responsibility to users to ensure that any weaknesses that can be exploited in detrimental ways that would impact users should be patched, or mitigation advice or assistance should be provided. Is the user on an older version of your software that isn't supported? Ensure they know of any vulnerabilities and offer incentives to loyal, long-time software users to upgrade to versions you're investing in with updates and security patches.

Ultimately, when user data is compromised due to the vendor's software product, they blame it on the vendor and may not observe nuances in the corporate or legal policy a vendor might have. This can result in a customer looking elsewhere for their next software purchase or, in the case of an enterprise licensing agreement, used as leverage to take deep discounts, cutting into potential profitability.

Vendor consumer responsibilities

Vendors often build their work and software on other software products. Vendors often develop their software with open source software libraries or even on top of consumer-grade operating systems. Vendors often argue that they're responsible for the software they designed explicitly for a platform, but not the security of the underlying platform. This bizarre take is often coupled with the onerous policy of placing on the customer responsibility for the underlying platforms, all while maintaining that the vendor will not support security changes made by the customer.

This kind of policy hurts users and disenfranchises them. Speaking once more about the EternalBlue vulnerability that kicked off the WannaCry ransomware attack, users lost their ability to provide essential business functions, because their unpatched and vendor-unsupported Windows XP devices were suddenly encrypted.

Let's speak plainly about this. Vendors who consume and then resell products are responsible for patching underlying software on top of whatever custom code they've developed. It's not enough to simply fix software and abandon customers afloat on a sea of dangersome risk. If a vendor sells their customer a package of hardware and software components, these components require support and periodic security patching.

Summary

You learned about zero-day vulnerabilities, exploits, and attacks in this chapter. First, we talked about each vector and how they relate to each other. Next, we reviewed four significant vulnerability disclosures in the past while discussing vulnerabilities, exploits, and attacks executed in some of those cases. Finally, we introduced ethics in zero-day culture, outlining an ideal mapping of who is responsible for what.

In the next chapter, we'll begin discussing how we can start doing research that will help you discover your zero-day vulnerabilities, how to pick targets, and what strategies you'll need to adopt to be successful.

Further reading

To learn more about the topics that we've discussed in this chapter, you can use the following resources for personal references:

- MITRE CVE List: `https://cve.mitre.org/cve/`

- EternalBlue Reference: `https://en.wikipedia.org/wiki/EternalBlue`

- Wired Magazine – Untold History of America's Zero Day Market: `https://www.wired.com/story/untold-history-americas-zero-day-market/`

- CVE-2019-11510: `https://cve.mitre.org/cgi-bin/cvename.cgi?name=CVE-2019-11510`

- CVE-2021-26084: `https://cve.mitre.org/cgi-bin/cvename.cgi?name=CVE-2021-26084`

- CVE-2017-8759: `https://cve.mitre.org/cgi-bin/cvename.cgi?name=CVE-2017-8759`

- CVE-2019-19781: `https://cve.mitre.org/cgi-bin/cvename.cgi?name=CVE-2019-19781`

3

Vulnerability Research – Getting Started with Successful Strategies

You're probably familiar with the old saying, *"If you fail to plan, you are planning to fail."* Having and executing a strategy plays an important role in most successes. Successful businesspeople, scientists, and even authors will tell you that accomplishing goals takes more than just hard work. It requires careful planning and execution of strategic steps. Without a clear plan of action, it is all too easy to get sidetracked or bogged down in the details. But with a well-thought-out strategy, you can stay focused on your goal and make efficient progress toward achieving it. In many cases, the difference between success and failure is simply a matter of having an effective strategy in place.

As we've explored in previous chapters, vulnerability research is the study of weaknesses and flaws in technology. This type of research can take many forms, from identifying new vulnerabilities to assessing the impact of known vulnerabilities. Vulnerability research is essential for keeping ahead of the ever-evolving threats posed by cyber criminals. By understanding how systems can be exploited, researchers can help to develop better security solutions and make technology safer for everyone.

When it comes to vulnerability research, strategies and planning must be considered. If you fail to plan on conducting and executing research, you're planning to fail. Some of the most successful strategies are those that are tailored to the specific needs of the researcher and the products they're evaluating. These strategies are something a novice might find difficulty in generating. With that said, there are some general principles that all vulnerability researchers should keep in mind when starting out, and these foundations can lead to advanced and specialized research.

In this chapter, we're going to teach you those very foundational things that can help you ramp up and begin researching vulnerabilities. We'll discuss vulnerability research, how to select great targets, and adopting a methodology for research, and dig into the techniques and tools that will make you successful in finding vulnerabilities.

Here's what we'll learn in this chapter:

- What vulnerability research is and how to conduct it
- Various types of strategies and resources available to us
- How to select the best targets for our research
- Test cases and test suites, defining how they're an important ingredient in successful vulnerability research
- Tools that will help us in our vulnerability research

Technical requirements

While not required for following along, having these materials and abilities ready would be helpful:

- A computer with internet access
- The ability to download and install software on the computer

By the end of this chapter, you should have a good understanding of what vulnerability research is, how to get started, how to select your first set of targets, and the common tools that researchers use to conduct and document research.

What is vulnerability research?

In *Chapter 1*, we introduced the idea of the vulnerability lifecycle. Early in this lifecycle, vulnerabilities get discovered through vulnerability research. Vulnerability research is a crucial part of keeping software safe and it's important to know what it is and how it works.

Vulnerability research is the process of identifying, analyzing, and reporting vulnerabilities in software or systems. It is an essential element of cybersecurity because it identifies previously unknown risks and can help ensure that attention is given to closing risks associated with insecure software. Vulnerability research can be done by anyone with an interest in keeping software safe, including security professionals, developers, and hobbyists. The consensus among the research community is that there's so much to research that, if given the opportunity to spend time, anyone can execute the necessary tasks that find vulnerabilities and contribute to research.

While the structure can vary in professional jobs that focus on vulnerability research, vulnerability researchers generally spend their days identifying security flaws in software and hardware systems. Their goal is to provide information that can be used by developers, hackers, or government agencies for the betterment of these technologies' cybersecurity measures.

There are many ways to conduct vulnerability research. Some researchers use automated tools to help them find vulnerabilities, while others use them to do manual analysis. Some focus on finding new vulnerabilities, some work exclusively on reverse engineering vulnerabilities from security advisories and patches, whereas others focus on improving existing methods for finding vulnerabilities or building elaborate exploits. Regardless of the focus, a great deal of vulnerability researchers share a common goal: to make software safer for everyone. So, how does a researcher – well, research?

Conducting research

To help simplify the key goal of understanding how research is executed, most researchers follow this typical path:

1. Identify a potential target to research.

2. Research the target to identify any possible weaknesses.

3. Try to exploit the identified weaknesses.

4. If successful, write a report detailing the findings of the research that details the vulnerability.

5. Submit the report to the relevant party (i.e., software developer, hardware manufacturer, etc.).

An analogy that is often used to explain vulnerability research is that of a lock picker. A lock picker's goal is to open a lock without the key. To do this, they must first identify a lock they wish to pick and perform any necessary research to gain an understanding of how the lock works. To do this, they will study the lock to identify any weaknesses through a practical visual inspection, technical inspection, a review of any manufacturer information, and potentially, information about other locks that have been picked that behave similarly. Once they have found a weakness, they will try different techniques to exploit it. If successful, they might document their success and use it to help make locks better.

Like our lock picker, a vulnerability researcher spends their time identifying the software they want to research. Once an appropriate target has been selected, researchers will then begin trying to understand how the target software works and if there are any signs of potential weaknesses. They do this by looking at the software practically through testing, reviewing the source code, reviewing manuals, and digging into other research to gain that vital level of understanding. Once weaknesses are identified, then techniques are used to exploit those weaknesses. In ideal circumstances, our researcher would report these vulnerabilities to a software manufacturer. But, much like our lock picker, they might not necessarily share this information or use it for other personally advantageous reasons.

It should be noted that not all researchers follow this path exactly. Some researchers may choose to only conduct research and not attempt to exploit any vulnerabilities that are found. Others may choose only to exploit vulnerabilities and not write any reports. The important thing to remember is that there isn't one correct way to do vulnerability research and any methods can be adopted and modified to meet a personal preference.

Getting started

If you're interested in getting started in vulnerability research, there are a few things you need to do. Revisiting the analogy of our lock picker, the lock picker had a baseline of knowledge about locks, the tools that are used to pick them, how to find more information about locks, and sometimes relevant experience to guide their actions. Like our lockpicker, we need to understand the basics of how systems work, how they can be vulnerable, what tools of the trade are commonly used, and how to use those tools to exploit weaknesses in software.

A verbose guide to vulnerability research and tool execution you'll need under your belt to successfully test for vulnerabilities is a little out of scope, and something we couldn't cover at length in a single chapter, or even a single book. We expect you're arriving at this chapter with some of the fundamental skills that a researcher might need to possess. Our aim here is to provide you with a foundational methodology that you can adopt. This methodology can help systemize and organize your work in a way that will help in the effective planning and execution of research projects. Although, even if some key concepts are missing, the practice of research and discussion of methodology should help inform your learning areas and grow your understanding regardless of skill level. Let's take a few moments to quickly discuss some of the best ways to learn these subjects, regardless of skill level.

How previously disclosed vulnerabilities can help

A key source of information that will help any aspiring researcher are reports on previously disclosed vulnerabilities and related exploitation resources. You can learn from these by reviewing a vast set of information found online. If you're looking to understand the key techniques that some researchers are discovering, a search engine can take you far in discovering a blog or articles that are specific to your research cases. A common constant in the information security community is that people like to share their findings to help inform future research. Another excellent way to learn is by learning more about vulnerabilities and previous disclosures. In our previous chapter, we dug into several zero-day vulnerability disclosures. In each case, there was a fascinating weakness or flaw that helped the vulnerability manifest.

Studying previously discovered vulnerabilities can give you an idea of what to look for when searching for vulnerabilities. However, piecing these resources together is a little difficult at first, so let's summarize the key resources that are a must-have when you begin to research previously disclosed vulnerabilities:

- The **National Vulnerability Database** (**NVD**): The NVD is a repository of information on known security vulnerabilities. It's a great resource for understanding the types of vulnerabilities that exist, as well as their severity (`https://nvd.nist.gov/`).

- The **Common Vulnerabilities and Exposures** (**CVE**) database: The CVE database is like the NVD, but often includes more research and resources for researchers. This can clarify not only what vulnerabilities exist but also how they might be exploited and reported (`https://www.cve.org/`).

- **Exploit-DB**: A database of exploits that are submitted by security researchers. This is an excellent resource for reviewing how vulnerabilities have been exploited in previous scenarios. The researchers typically base them on CVEs, but that isn't always the case. The code contained in Exploit-DB is usually unvetted; therefore, be cautious about what you download and understand it well before running it (`https://www.exploit-db.com/`).

- **Full Disclosure**: A mailing list that is dedicated to the disclosure of security vulnerabilities. By subscribing to this list, you will receive notifications whenever new vulnerabilities are disclosed (`https://seclists.org/fulldisclosure/`).

- Past **DEFCON** talks: DEFCON is the longest-running hacker conference in the world. It takes place every year in Las Vegas, Nevada. While not everyone can make it out to the conference, most of the past talks from DEFCON have been put online for people to review. Research at DEFCON is usually raw. It is presented by real researchers and doesn't come with commercial sales pitches. Some talks are so foundationally forming for specific areas of research they're still being referenced almost a decade after being published (`https://www.youtube.com/user/DEFCONConference`).

As you grow into your skills and begin to specialize, it can be helpful to begin searching for resources specific to what specialization you're interested in. For example, if you're looking for Windows vulnerabilities, a good resource to search for is the **Microsoft Security Bulletin.** If you're looking for Linux vulnerabilities, a good resource is the **Ubuntu Security Notice** feed. If you're looking for general web application vulnerabilities, a good resource is the **Open Web Application Security Project** (**OWASP**). If it isn't already, your favorite search engine should be your best friend in exploring potential vulnerabilities. The resources you need to further your knowledge are likely already out there waiting for you.

Additional resources you might explore are published materials on the subject. Let's say you're interested in understanding why your newest kitchen appliance needs a Wi-Fi connection to work. Specific books on security about your device may not exist, but there might be several publications on embedded device development that would help you learn how these devices are created by developers. Learning how devices are built and coded the way they are is a significant piece of understanding that is needed to know how weaknesses could be introduced. Don't stop there though, dig more into the challenges others might have faced with similar devices. Look at CVE disclosures for similar devices, find maintenance manuals that reveal hidden functionality of the device, or even take an online class in software development or hardware hacking to understand how the devices were constructed and how they operate. Whichever resources you choose, make sure that you take the time to understand the technology, even just a little bit, before you dive straight into looking for vulnerabilities.

Finally, remember that practice makes perfect – so don't be afraid to get your hands dirty and try things out for yourself! With this basic primer on how to find the information, you'll need to grow your research foundations. Let's talk about how we want to select research targets.

Selecting research targets

Beginning the initial process of picking a research target is exciting. There's so much software on the marketplace to choose from. Will you focus on desktop applications? Web applications? How about plugins developed for applications? Maybe the smart device that you bought and hooked up in your home? Before you begin rattling off or researching random software, you should remember that if we fail to plan, we're planning to fail. To be successful, we need a strategy for picking research targets. Let's go over some excellent ways to focus and strategize on what we'll select for research:

- **Keep it interesting** – With any research, you should choose a target that you're interested in. This will help you stay motivated during the research process.

- **Pick likely vulnerable targets** – You should choose a target that is likely to have vulnerabilities. This can be based on factors such as the complexity of the target, the age of the code base, and the number of users.

- **Pick something within your means** – Try to ensure that your target has something you can test readily without expending resources you do not have. For example, you might be really interested in researching security vulnerabilities in a Tesla. However, if you do not have the means to acquire a Tesla, or much less the ability to lose money because the research might damage the thing you're researching – it's not a good target.

- **Pick something you have permission to test** – While it might be interesting to focus on testing popular web applications hosted in some cloud environment, you may not have permission to test these, or you may have extremely limited options because the vendor operates authorized testing through a bug bounty program. You should avoid these, especially if you're looking to hunt for CVEs. Instead, focus on software that you can run on devices you own or are authorized to test.

- **Pick targets with high-value data and assets** – You should choose a target that is likely to be exploited. This can be based on factors such as the sensitivity of the data processed by the target and the potential impact of an exploit. For example, a piece of freeware that helps a user create greeting cards might be of less interest to a hacker than a lightweight customer relations management tool, which may take information such as credit cards, banking information, and valuable personal data.

- **Align research with your strengths** – You should consider your own skills and experience when selecting a research target. Choose a target that is within your skill set or something you're motivated to grow into so that you can be successful in your research. Otherwise, you might grow frustrated.

- **Ensure you have isolation environments** – Finally, we need to ensure whatever we pick is something we can isolate for testing. You might be very interested in testing mainframe software developed using COBOL in the 1980s. You might have a copy of the software readily available, but if you don't have a spare mainframe or the ability to emulate one then it's not a good pick.

While these high-level guidance points are helpful, it's better to have practical examples. Let's review an example of taking this guidance and applying it.

Finding targets that interest you

Since software drives our modern world, in most cases people have built software for a variety of purposes. Since we'll be trying to stay focused and engaged, let's pick a category of software that is of interest. For the sake of this exercise, let's say you're *really* interested in horses. If you take a quick look on Google, you'll find that owning and maintaining a horse costs around $10,000 every year in the United States. Owners spend a great deal of time, energy, and monetary resources to ensure their horses are well cared for. Because there's a lot to consider in relation to horse ownership (breeding, showing, riding, barn management, and medical needs), there might be software written for it to help. You could just begin searching for software with your favorite search engine, but one of the better ways to find niche software for research is by using **SourceForge** (`https://sourceforge.net/`).

After heading over to SourceForge and typing in `Horse Software` into the search bar, around 75 options appear for us to look over (see *Figure 3.1*):

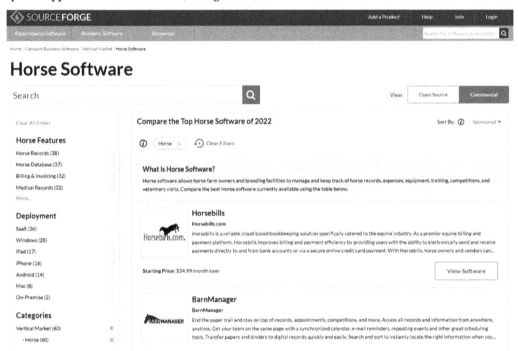

Figure 3.1 – Using SourceForge to find software you're interested in testing through the search feature

We've managed to find software that interests us personally (hypothetically), and we have a ton of options to pick from. Now, let's move into our next couple of categories, finding likely vulnerable targets with limited resources.

Likely vulnerable and downloadable software

The next thing we need to do is find software that is likely vulnerable and can be researched with minimal personal investment. Now, "likely vulnerable" software can fall under the umbrella of quite a lot of possibilities, but as a rule of thumb I might offer this suggestion: the older the software is, the more likely it's to be vulnerable. Another point of reference should be how the software is utilized. While SaaS solutions are often vulnerable, we might not always have permission to test them. SaaS solutions are always hosted on vendor-owned equipment. As such, they might be a little more locked down than if we were allowed to install the application on our devices such as computers or phones. Generally, the best place to do low-effort maximum-reward research is on applications that you have a lot of control over.

One additional consideration to make is the relationship to technology the software has. While not always the rule, software that non-technical industries use is often scrutinized less by security professionals. Our example where we selected horse-related software is a great target that has mostly a non-technical audience. It's unlikely there is a large enterprise market with high-security requirements or security conscious population as the primary consumers.

With these things under consideration, let's focus on an older application that can be installed on the Windows operating system. Over the years, SourceForge has been a great place to narrow down and filter the characteristics of software. This will allow us to focus on Windows-based applications, as seen in *Figure 3.2*:

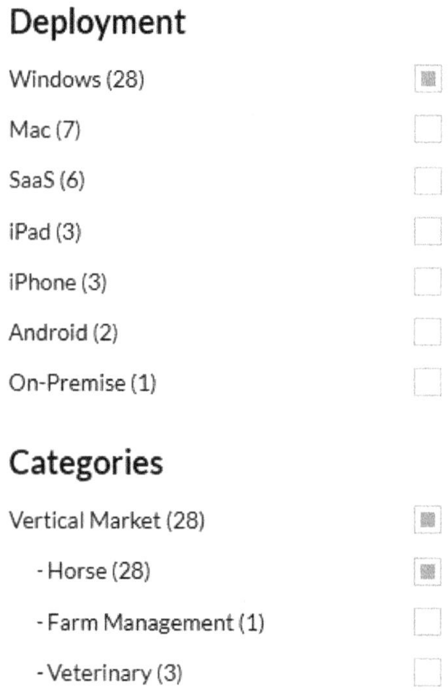

Deployment

Windows (28)	▦
Mac (7)	☐
SaaS (6)	☐
iPad (3)	☐
iPhone (3)	☐
Android (2)	☐
On-Premise (1)	☐

Categories

Vertical Market (28)	▦
- Horse (28)	▦
- Farm Management (1)	☐
- Veterinary (3)	☐

Figure 3.2 – SourceForge has filters that are useful in narrowing down our selection to specific targets

With our search criteria narrowed down, there are a few other attributes a researcher might be looking for. In our case, we're looking for software that we can download and try as soon as possible, and we're looking to do that without an exchange of funds, or personal investment. After looking at our options, as shown in *Figure 3.3*, a researcher might choose an option that has a free demo advertised and is available for us to download and install:

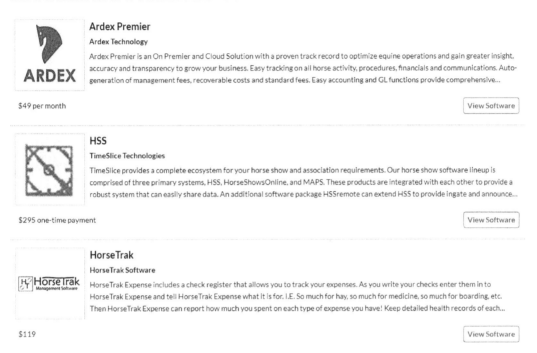

Figure 3.3 – Out of several options, the ones with available demos might be one of interest

Take a moment to review any marketing materials you might find, technical resources that you can download, and any other bits of information. As a researcher, you need to understand specifically in what context this software might be used so you can understand why someone might target this software. As shown in *Figure 3.4*, one of the things we're looking for in example materials is the ability to download software to test:

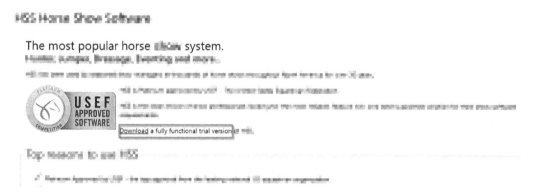

Figure 3.4 – Website materials can help uncover details that may make the target more enticing to research

Following what we've learned from the materials on the website, we have come to an understanding that the software we're investigating is being used for records management, personally identifiable information storage, credit card entry, and several other attributes. Additionally, the software looks like it was built several years ago – with the screenshots in our review of the marketing materials showing the date of 2018 (see *Figure 3.5*). Even just a few years of idle development cycles can grow the risk of security vulnerabilities significantly:

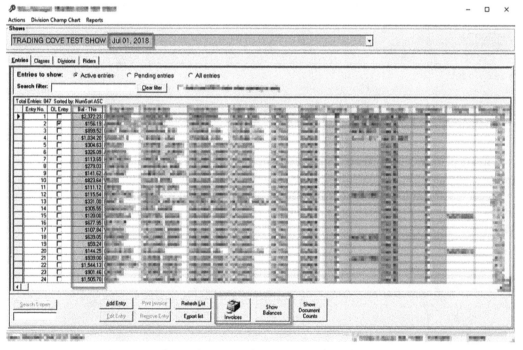

Figure 3.5 – Screenshots in marketing materials can help uncover
functionality before testing, like this ability to process invoices

So, to recap we've found software we're interested in. This software, which may have security vulnerabilities, is available to us to download and test and contains billing information and personal details. In matching our abilities, let's assume we're new to research. Thankfully, Windows software is an easy target, and a lot of vulnerabilities are easy for even a novice to test for (as we'll discover in our first test case). We now need to prepare our isolated environment for testing.

If you have a Windows PC, you can likely create isolated virtual machines hosting copies of the Windows operating system without much hassle. Microsoft offers this as an embedded feature in most operating systems as a tool called Hyper-V. There are also other favorite commercial and non-commercial options you can rely on for creating isolated Windows installs. We'll want to zero in on events that are happening on the computer where you're doing your testing. Therefore, it's best to install the software you're testing in an isolated environment to ensure there is no potential for cross-contamination with other applications. If you're unfamiliar with hypervisors or virtual machines, we have some suggestions in the *Tools* section of this chapter where we explore options available to build and run these isolated environments.

So, finally, we've got ourselves a great target, the ability, and the resources to do the testing. All our boxes have been checked. Let's now discuss how we'll test the software for vulnerabilities using test cases.

Exploring vulnerabilities with test cases

Once you have a great target (or targets), it's time to begin the research, Much like in our previous sections, planning and strategy should take a front seat to our approach. One way to do this is to create and/or use test cases. A test case is a set of instructions that can be used to discover potential weaknesses in software. Most security researchers choose to do a lot of this initial research and testing manually; however, as you become more familiar with potential abuses of systems, automation might be advantageous to explore. Now, we'll spend this next section defining what a test case is and how to effectively write them.

Test cases – a primer

In the world of software engineering, test cases are one of the primary tools quality assurance engineers employ to ensure that software doesn't have bugs in it. Similarly, professional bug-bounty hunters and vulnerability researchers alike have found significant benefits when adopting test cases. Simply put, a test case is a set of conditions or variables that will determine whether features are working as they should. Great test cases contain three elements:

1. **Summary and goals** – Here we'll want to summarize the reason for our test and the goals we have in mind while testing for a related weakness. In this section, we'll outline where and when this test will apply, and concisely define an objective.

2. **Testing instructions** – A good test case will have specific examples and instructions on how to execute testing against the specific weakness. This will include references to tools and techniques that might be used. Testing instructions should also contain additional references where applicable.

3. **Remediations** – As you discover vulnerabilities, it's helpful to have ready-made notes that explain the vulnerability and the remediations that are often used to mitigate the risk. When we begin to communicate our vulnerabilities to people who built the software, the number one thing they want to know is how to fix the problem.

While the purpose of a test case in software engineering is to verify the functionality of features, our use case will be different. We'll be focusing on determining if a software component is vulnerable to common types of vulnerabilities. A well-written test case should be clear, concise, and easy to understand; it should also be repeatable so that it can be used to verify that the feature continues to work as intended even after future changes to the code.

Creating effective test cases can be a challenging task. It is important to remember that the goal is to find bugs and/or find information that will lead to finding bugs, not to prove that the system works as intended. A test case should, therefore, be designed in such a way that it has a high chance of uncovering an issue, while at the same time being concise and easy to understand. In some cases, a test case may also include additional information, such as screenshots or log files, which can help to further understand the issue at hand.

So, where do we start in creating test cases? Well, the good news is that in most cases it's best to copy and use readily available resources.

Avoid reinventing the wheel

Writing and building effective test cases can be very difficult, especially for newer security researchers. How could you possibly invent a test case for a weakness when you do not know how to detect it in the first place? Thankfully, a lot of the hard work related to the creation of test cases is already done for security researchers. Let's talk about those resources now.

The OWASP is one of the best, if not the best, resources to reach for when you want to start exploring well-defined test cases. OWASP specifically focuses on web applications, but the organized and concise way testing resources are published is an example worth studying for everyone interested in the subject. Case in point for web applications, they have an excellent testing guide that includes comprehensive testing examples for web applications. The **Web Security Testing Guide** (**WSTG**) is in version 4.2, as of publishing this material, and consists of 400 pages of well-formatted, referenced testing materials that lay out a clear test case objective, demonstrations of how to test for the vulnerability, and notes on potential remediation (see *Figure 3.6*):

Web Security Testing Guide v4.2

- Union Operator: can be used when the SQL injection flaw happens in a SELECT statement, making it possible to combine two queries into a single result or result set.
- Boolean: use Boolean condition(s) to verify whether certain conditions are true or false.
- Error based: this technique forces the database to generate an error, giving the attacker or tester information upon which to refine their injection.
- Out-of-band: technique used to retrieve data using a different channel (e.g., make a HTTP connection to send the results to a web server).
- Time delay: use database commands (e.g. sleep) to delay answers in conditional queries. It is useful when attacker doesn't have some kind of answer (result, output, or error) from the application.

Test Objectives

- Identify SQL injection points.
- Assess the severity of the injection and the level of access that can be achieved through it.

How to Test

Detection Techniques

The first step in this test is to understand when the application interacts with a DB Server in order to access some data. Typical examples of cases when an application needs to talk to a DB include:

Figure 3.6 – Examples of test cases in the OWASP WSTG

In addition to the excellent WSTG, there are many more resources from OWASP that researchers rely on. The OWASP team posts resources related to APIs and mobile application testing, both of which are rapidly seeing exciting developments that incorporate structures much like the WSTG.

For test cases related to installable software, such as for Windows systems, UNIX-based systems, mobile testing, and embedded device testing, there's less of a unified front of resources. It's sometimes just up to the researcher to build effective sets of test cases, luckily this is something we'll learn more about a bit later in this chapter.

Test cases are exceptional for beginning your research and can help provide a template for budding researchers who do not have a great deal of experience in looking for bugs. A word of caution though, don't allow test cases to rule the exploration and testing of the application to a fault. Think of test suites like a cookbook. When you have a recipe, all the ingredients are listed right there for you. If you follow the steps, you can make a pretty good meal. However, sometimes you want to put your own spin on things because you're curious about how new flavors might work together. Maybe you don't have all the ingredients the recipe calls for, or the recipe in the book has a stain on it and you can't read the whole thing, so maybe you'll need to improvise. The same goes for test suites and test cases. Follow the recipe, but don't be afraid to get creative when you want to explore or if your test subjects don't meet the exact specification in your test cases.

With a good idea of the resources available to us, let's talk about what test suites are and how they should be used in an effective research strategy.

Building effective test suites

A test suite is a compilation of test cases that can be consumed by a tester. Think about the WSTG we discussed earlier as a test suite. When researching specific sets of software, it may be tempting to test everything under the sun, but sometimes that strategy is not the best for the outcome you're looking for. If, for example, you've decided that you want to focus on one specific kind of software and in that software, you've decided you wanted to focus on a type of vulnerability – you'll have a shorter path from point A to point B with a well-defined set of cases you want to test for. This can allow you to test software quickly and efficiently, focusing on your specific interests. If you leave the research undefined and take a 'test everything' approach where you execute every test case under the sun, you might eventually find something. However, a better-organized researcher in the same space of time will have executed testing against many targets, likely finding more vulnerabilities over time.

As we've established, test cases are great but where things come together is your testing suite. Test suites are a little odd in that they are both a high-level and low-level view of your testing. On the one hand, it's a way of categorizing and sorting test cases. But on the other hand, suites are also a compilation of everything you need to complete those test cases.

Test suites can be very helpful in scenarios where you need to organize key test cases together to target a specific technology you are researching. By having a test suite that focuses on a certain area, you can decrease the amount of time you spend researching and increase the amount of time you spend testing.

The best way to build a test suite is to use existing resources, which can inform how you should bundle test cases. There are many great security testing resources available online. Often, these can be adapted to your specific needs. We've discussed OWASP as a great place to start when looking for general security testing resources. Other resources, such as the NVD and MITRE, can help inform testing with a retrospective on previously discovered vulnerabilities. Another excellent resource that could help you construct an effective test suite is the **MITRE ATT&CK** framework. ATT&CK defines the types of attacks hackers will use, and it's used by defenders to map out patterns of defense. This can be most helpful as a reference for types of intrusions and attacks that are common. Taking common attack patterns and drafting them into bundled suites for testing is a great place to start in customizing your research. Each of these attack vectors in the ATT&CK framework is meticulously documented and well worth the investment of time to review.

Finally, it is important to remember that test suites are living documents and, as such, they should be updated on a regular basis. As new vulnerabilities are discovered, or as new versions of software are released, your test suite should be updated to reflect these changes. Keeping your test suite up to date will help ensure that it remains relevant and useful.

Writing your own test cases

Writing your own test cases is a way to become better versed in understanding vulnerabilities. In every researcher's life, they'll need to test applications that have very little in the way of compiled information about how to test for specific types of vulnerabilities. What we'll be doing now is walking through the creation of our own test case, which will focus on testing for a common weakness and vulnerability in Windows software; this is often called **DLL injection**.

Our first step in creating effective documentation is to utilize something that can help us organize our documentation. We'll be using one of the most popular open source, cross-platform tools penetration testers use: **CherryTree**. To follow along in this section, you can download and install CherryTree for Windows, macOS, or Linux operating systems at the CherryTree website (`https://www.giuspen.net/cherrytree/`). Once downloaded, install, and run the software. Once running, you should see something that looks like a text editor (see *Figure 3.7*):

Figure 3.7 – Opening CherryTree to get started

The best thing about CherryTree is that it has great organizational functionality, so let's take a moment to organize the structure of our test cases. CherryTree uses the naming convention of *nodes* to describe the hierarchical relationship we can create between documents. Since the kind of testing that we're doing is focused on Windows, let's create our first node, which organizes our testing into a test suite (see *Figure 3.8*):

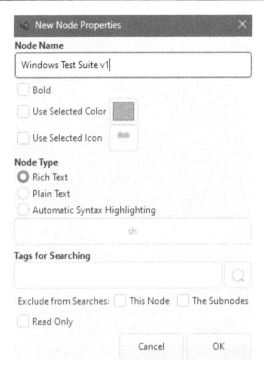

Figure 3.8 – Creating our first CherryTree node

We'll continue this process, and while it's ultimately up to you – here's the nesting relationship of notes that we'll create for this example. Our first node should describe the test case we'd like to review. In this case, we'll be creating a test case for **DLL Hijacking**. As we continue building our organized case structure, we should have a **TESTING NOTES** child node where we can keep our research notes, then another with **TEST CASE** to keep our test case notes (see *Figure 3.9*):

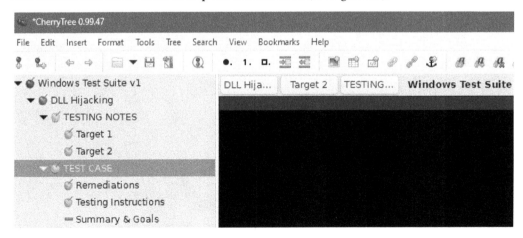

Figure 3.9 – Configuring relationships in nodes in CherryTree can help organize the content

This structure offers us the opportunity to create testing notes on things we're targeting, creating documentation for the summary of the test, testing instructions, and remediation. Let's dive right into building our test cases based on our initial criteria. Let's go through the process of filling out **Summary & Goals** for the test case.

Summary & Goals

To fill this section of our test case out, we'll need to make sure we understand what we're testing, the summary of the vulnerability, and what our goals are in testing it. First and foremost, if you don't know much about this vulnerability, let's do some initial research. You can use your favorite search engine to do most of the initial searching, but we suggest when initially researching to stick to resources we've previously mentioned, such as MITRE. For example, if we initially spend some time on MITRE's website, you might find their ATT&CK page, which is a comprehensive data structure that describes most vulnerabilities in the context of how they're used with examples. For our example of DLL injection, this is no exception and would serve as a great resource (see *Figure 3.10*):

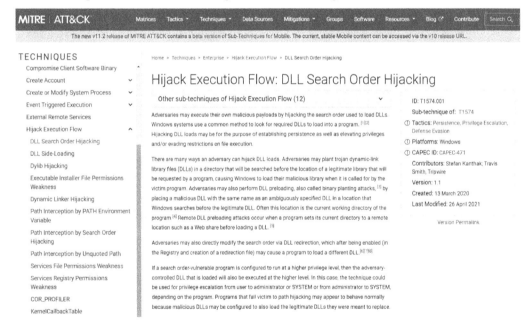

Figure 3.10 – MITRE ATT&CK is an invaluable research resource for researching hacking techniques

We now have CVE examples of DLL hijacking and information about hijacking techniques. If this is your first time exploring this kind of vulnerability, spend plenty of time learning about it. Once you understand it, begin building out your template summary. While you could just copy and paste, it might be of some value to spend the time to generate your own description, based on how you understand the vulnerability. Based on what we found, we might come up with the following summary based on our resources:

DLL hijacking is a type of vulnerability that leverages the way Windows loads DLLs to execute malicious code. This can be done either by placing a malicious DLL in a directory that is part of the system's search path or by modifying the registry to point to a malicious DLL. When an application attempts to load a DLL, Windows will search for the DLL in a predefined order. If the DLL is not found in any of the directories, Windows will search for the DLL in the current directory. This can be exploited by an attacker who places a malicious DLL in the same directory as a legitimate application that loads dynamic libraries. The legitimate application will load and execute the code from the malicious DLL, and the attacker can use this to gain control of the application or system.

DLL hijacking is a serious security vulnerability because it can be used to execute arbitrary code with the privileges of the application or process that loads the DLL. This can lead to privilege escalation and can allow an attacker to take complete control of the system. DLL hijacking is often used in conjunction with other attacks, such as social engineering or distributing malware.

Based on this information, we might summarize our goals as the following:

The goal of this test is to find weaknesses in the way Windows loads DLLs through poorly configured paths in software or permissions, which might be misconfigured in a way that would allow for privilege escalation and arbitrary code execution.

Our filled-out notes in the **Summary & Goals** section should look something like this when we're finished building our description (see *Figure 3.11*):

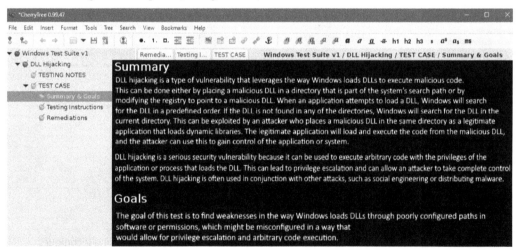

Figure 3.11 – Our summary and goals section should be filled out with the research as we understand it

Now that we have our initial template that defines our summary and goals, let's move on to how we'll find the best way to construct a test case for testing for this weakness.

Testing instructions

Testing instructions will most certainly vary from case to case, but in most cases, there is a wealth of information already available to us. There are a few different ways that you can test for DLL hijacking vulnerabilities. If you don't know this though, testing instructions might elude you. If this is new to you, start researching by using your favorite search engine. `How to test for DLL hijacking` or `DLL hijacking Tutorial` might be great starting points. While executing that search, one of the things we found was a comprehensive guide from the **hacktricks** website (`https://book.hacktricks.xyz/`), where six different approaches to testing were defined. These are good and again, with the idea of not reinventing the wheel, in this case, we'll just copy the types and test summaries to our test case. Make sure you reference your source materials in your notes (see *Figure 3.12*). While we might not be organically developing our own testing notes here, we can add and subtract elements as we see fit as we grow into developing our own methodology:

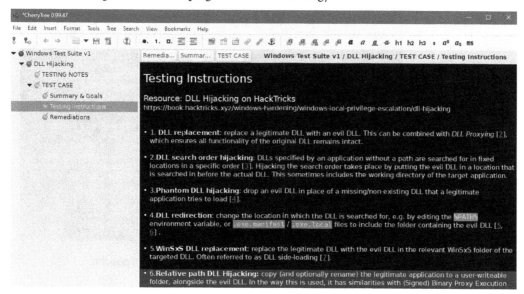

Figure 3.12– Avoid reinventing the wheel, build your testing notes
off already well-researched resources where possible

Let's continue with our next and final section on remediations, which will finish our first test case.

Remediations

Much like in previous sections, we'll lean again on the available resources. In our summary, we were able to observe some great resources related to remediation. However, one of the best resources that can give official guidance on these kinds of things is manufacturer instructions or developer resources. In the case of our example, we learned earlier that DLL hijacking is a type of weakness that impacts Windows systems only. With that in mind, spend time reviewing Microsoft's guidance on preventing these kinds of software problems. A quick search for resources related to this defines the vulnerability and provides the best instructions on how to mitigate the risks related to the problem. We'll add these to our test case just in case we need to notify a vendor that we found a vulnerability (see *Figure 3.13*):

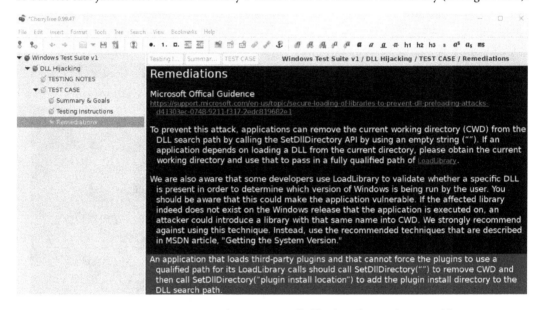

Figure 3.13 – Base your remediation notes off official guidance when possible

Great, so we now have our first test case. If you're just getting started in vulnerability research, this might the first and only test case you want to start with. While it's a great place to get started, we encourage you to continue finding vulnerabilities you're interested in that are related to the interest you have in this space. For our example, let's say we've added a few additional test cases related to testing Windows-based applications. Here's how three additional test cases might be structured in CherryTree (see *Figure 3.14*):

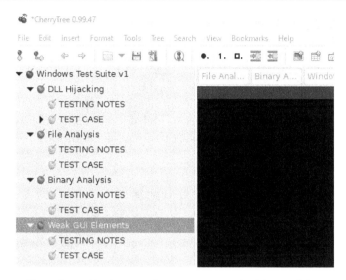

Figure 3.14 – Don't stop at just one test case, build several that
reflect the suite of tests you'd like to research

Once your test cases and suites are configured to your liking, what you might want to do now is save this as a template. CherryTree can let you use this as a template so when you begin a new research target, you can open a new copy and the **TESTING NOTES** section can be dedicated to the notes you take on the specific research target. To do this, click **File** and **Export to CherryTree Document** (see *Figure 3.15*):

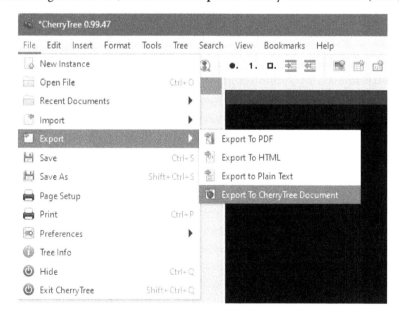

Figure 3.15 – Export your work as a template to save time in future research projects

Next time you open CherryTree and want to run new tests, you can import a CherryTree document as your template using the import function.

When creating your own test cases, it is important to consider what you want to accomplish with your testing. Are you looking for a specific type of vulnerability? Or are you just trying to get a general sense of the security of an application? By being clear about your goals, you can make sure that your test cases are focused and effective. Effective test cases are probably the best tool to have in your arsenal for discovering vulnerabilities. The next section will cover some of the other best research tools you'll need to learn to use to conduct certain research.

Introducing common research tools

Let's spend some time talking about some of the tools you'll need for vulnerability research. There are plenty of resources available online to help you get started, but we'll spend some time talking about the common tools that researchers lean on.

Note-taking, screenshot, and screen recording tools

As previously discussed, documentation is so important. As a result, a researcher needs to have good tools that they can use that will help categorize their research, sync it across multiple environments, annotate and record screenshots, and build video presentations of their research when necessary. Let's talk about very popular tools that are used to help aid in those needs.

Joplin

Joplin is a note-taking and to-do application with which you can sync your notes and tasks across all of your devices. It is available for Windows, macOS, Linux, Android, and iOS. You can use Joplin in your browser by going to the Web Clipper extension page and adding it to your browser.

With Joplin, you can create notes and to-dos, which can be organized into notebooks. You can also tag your notes for easy organization and search for them easily:

Figure 3.16 – An example of Joplin using Markdown notation

One key thing that researchers love about this is how well it synchronizes across devices, and how notes are formatted with a formatting language named **Markdown** (see *Figure 3.16*).

CherryTree

CherryTree is a hierarchical note-taking application that features rich text and syntax highlighting, storing data in a single .xml or .sqlite file. It can export to HTML, PDF and other formats. CherryTree is available for Windows, Linux, and macOS.

With CherryTree, you can create notes that are organized into nodes. You can also tag your notes and search for them easily. Your notes are stored in a single file, so they can be easily backed up or transferred to other devices:

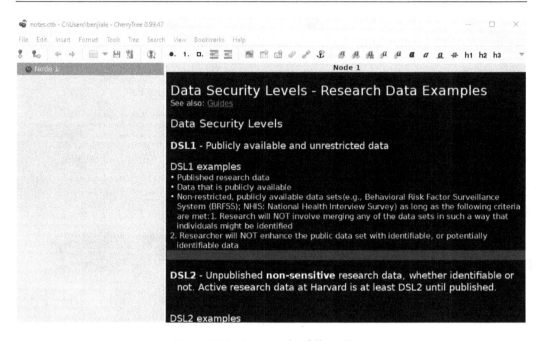

Figure 3.17 – An example of CherryTree

As also discovered in our previous example of writing test cases, it's a great tool that can be used to build templates that can be shared and used when needed to test specific software (see *Figure 3.17*).

Greenshot

You can use simple tools to create screenshot-based examples of your research, or you can supercharge your illustrative purposes with something such as **Greenshot**. Greenshot is a free and open source screenshot tool that supports Windows and macOS. It can capture screenshots of your entire screen, a selected region, or a specific window:

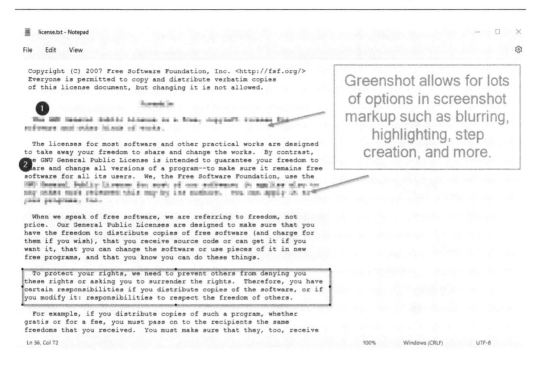

Figure 3.18 – Some of the many features of screenshot editing you can add with Greenshot

Best of all, Greenshot offers rich annotation and editing features that can allow you to write notes, and blur out and highlight elements in your screenshot (see *Figure 3.18*).

Open Broadcaster Software (OBS)

With **Open Broadcaster Software** (**OBS**), you can record your entire screen or a selected region. You can also Livestream your screen to popular streaming services such as Twitch and YouTube. OBS is a great choice for creating videos on your research to deliver to customers who might be consuming your research. Videos are a very effective way to communicate and share how vulnerabilities can be recreated (see *Figure 3.19*):

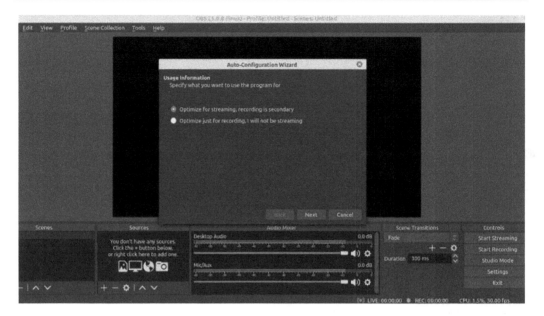

Figure 3.19 – An example of OBS being configured

Capturing media related to our testing is important. These should be good applications you'll find basic utility from, which will aid in clearly documenting your testing efforts. Let's now take a moment to talk about the technology we'll use to isolate our testing.

Hypervisors and virtual machines

A **hypervisor** is a type of software that allows you to create and run virtual machines on a physical computer. Hypervisors are used in both server and desktop virtualization.

Using a hypervisor will allow you to do vulnerability research on multiple virtual machines at the same time, without having to worry about impacting the stability of your physical machine. Additionally, some hypervisors come with features that make it easier to capture and analyze network traffic or perform other types of analysis.

Research-wise, the testing of software is best done in an isolated operating system or "sandbox" in order to minimize the risk of accidentally damaging your main system. This can be done using a **virtual machine** (**VM**) running on a hypervisor. Let's talk a bit about what hypervisors researchers commonly use.

VMware Workstation Pro

VMware Workstation Pro is a commercial virtualization software that supports Windows and Linux. It can create virtual machines on your computer, allowing you to run multiple operating systems at the same time. VMware Workstation Pro also offers many features for developers and testers, such as the ability to take snapshots of your virtual machine (see *Figure 3.20*):

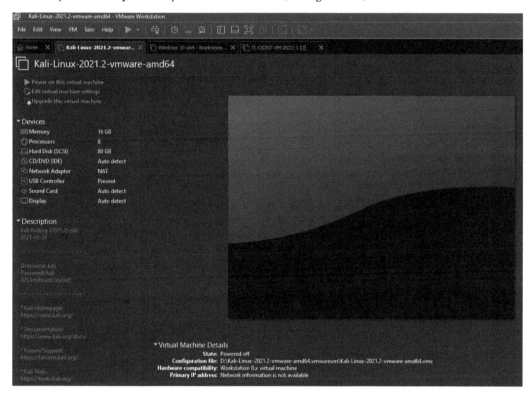

Figure 3.20 – An example of virtual machines used in VMware Workstation

Similar functionality is available to macOS users under the product name *VMware Fusion*.

VirtualBox

VirtualBox is a free and open source virtualization tool that supports Windows, macOS, Linux, and Solaris. It can run multiple operating systems simultaneously on a single computer. VirtualBox also offers many features such as snapshotting and cloning (see *Figure 3.21*):

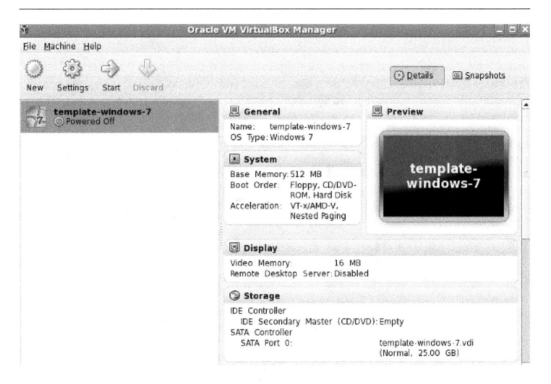

Figure 3.21 – An example of virtual machines in VirtualBox

It's very similar in a feature set with VMWare Workstation; however, it handles virtualization less efficiently and tends to be a little buggier than VMware Workstation.

Hyper-V

Hyper-V is a virtualization tool for Windows, which supports running multiple operating systems simultaneously. It can also be used to create virtual machines. Hyper-V also offers many features such as snapshotting and cloning:

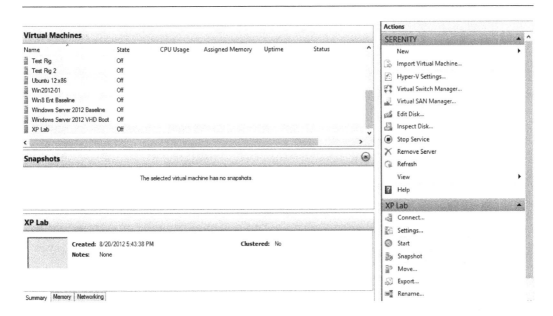

Figure 3.22 – An example of Hyper-V Manager in Windows

While the feature set related to Hyper-V is limited compared to our two other options, this has an advantage in that it's a feature in the Windows operating system and can be installed and configured in the Control Panel in most versions of Windows (see *Figure 3.22*).

Preconfigured virtual machines

Once you've acquired a hypervisor, you can build your own virtual machines from scratch, or you can acquire virtual machines that are preconfigured and load them into your hypervisor of choice. This is an awesome way to create isolated environments for testing, and save a lot of time in the process. Here are a few favorite resources for machines of various types.

Windows

Microsoft hosts and distributes many server versions and desktop software on pre-built virtual machines, which you can download and use for free at `https://developer.microsoft.com/en-us/windows/downloads/virtual-machines/`.

Linux

A good resource for many preconfigured Linux virtual machines is OSBoxes `https://www.osboxes.org/`.

Security-focused operating systems

A lot of researchers use specifically configured security virtual machines, which can help researchers get started with preconfigured tools. While not required, some of these can be helpful in saving you time in building out a common set of tools:

- Kali Linux (penetration testing and security research focused) `https://www.kali.org/get-kali/`

- Moblexer (mobile application security testing and research focused) `https://mobexler.com/`

- REMnux (malware analysis and reverse engineering focused) `https://remnux.org/`

- Trace Labs OSINT VM (intelligence research focused Kali Linux variant) `https://www.tracelabs.org/initiatives/osint-vm`

With a good hypervisor and virtual machines to conduct our research, let's spend some time talking about web application proxies.

Web application proxies

A web proxy is a piece of software that acts as an intermediary between your computer and the internet. When using a web proxy, all your internet traffic will go through the proxy server before it reaches its destination. This can be useful for many reasons, such as bypassing firewalls, filtering web content, and namely, discovering web application vulnerabilities.

For example, if you are testing a login page and want to see what data is being sent when you submit your credentials, you could use a web proxy to intercept that traffic. You could then examine the traffic to see if your credentials are being sent in plain text (which would indicate a serious security vulnerability). Let's look at a few examples of web application proxies now.

Burpsuite

Burpsuite is an interception proxy that supports Windows, macOS, and Linux. It can be used to intercept and modify traffic. Burpsuite also offers many features such as **fuzzing** and **bruteforcing**:

Figure 3.23 – An example of using Burpsuite to capture and view traffic on websites

Burpsuite is one of the most common Swiss-army knives that penetration testers have in their toolboxes when testing web applications. The educational resources and community supporting this tool are nothing short of excellent.

ZAP

ZAP is a free and open source web application security testing tool that supports Windows, macOS, and Linux. It can be used to intercept and modify traffic:

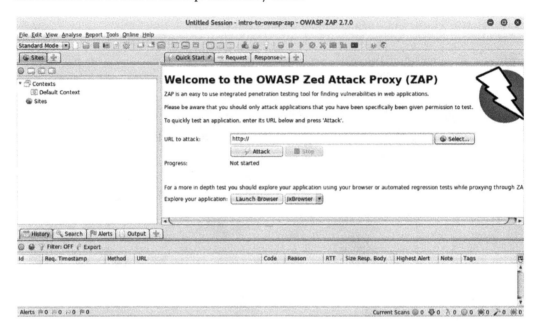

Figure 3.24 – An example of ZAP's default configuration

ZAP also offers many features such as fuzzing and bruteforcing, which can be useful for finding vulnerabilities in web applications (see *Figure 3.24*).

Fiddler Classic

Fiddler is a free web debugging proxy that supports Windows. It can be used to intercept and modify traffic:

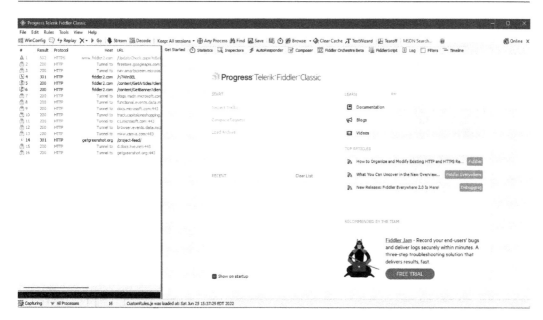

Figure 3.25 – Example using Fiddler to proxy and inspect web traffic

Fiddler also offers many features such as performance testing and HTTPS decryption (see *Figure 3.25*).

Debuggers and decompilers

A software debugger is a tool that helps you find errors in code. As such, it can be used to analyze the inner workings of a program. It does this by allowing you to step through your code line by line, so you can see what it is doing and where security vulnerabilities might be. This can be extremely helpful when you are trying to find and fix security vulnerabilities.

Debuggers are often found combined with decompilers, which allow you to reverse engineer compiled code. Essentially, it will allow you to take an executable file and convert it back into source code. This is useful for vulnerability research because it can help you understand how a program works and identify potential security vulnerabilities.

If you are new to debugging, there are plenty of resources available to help you get started. There are many different books and online tutorials that can teach you the basics. Once you understand the basics, you can start experimenting with different debuggers and find the one that works best for you. No matter what level of experience you have, a software debugger can be a valuable tool for security research. So, if you are not already using one, it is highly recommended that you start. Let's talk about a few of the more popular tools researchers are using today.

OllyDbg

OllyDbg is a free and open source debugger that supports Windows. It can be used to debug programs. This is useful for finding bugs and vulnerabilities in software through several avenues of testing:

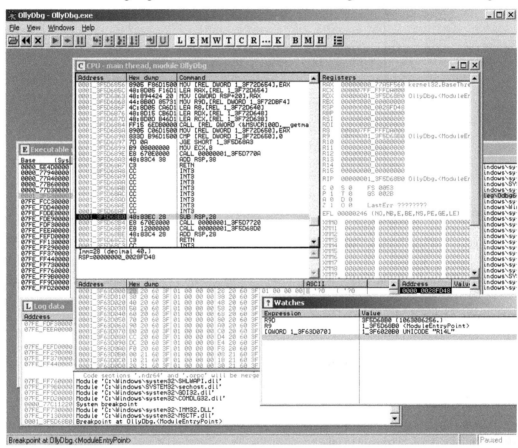

Figure 3.26 – An example of OllyDbg debugging a Windows application

OllyDbg also offers many features such as code analysis and disassembly, which can be useful for reverse engineering purposes (see *Figure 3.26*).

Immunity Debugger

Immunity Debugger is a free and open source debugger that supports Windows. It can be used to debug programs. Immunity Debugger also offers many features such as code analysis and disassembly, which makes it a similar choice to OllyDbg (see *Figure 3.27*):

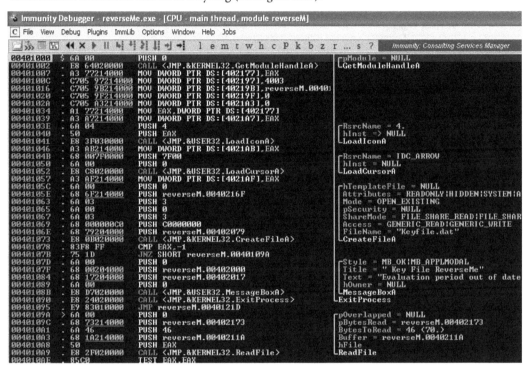

Figure 3.27 – An example of Immunity Debugger debugging a Windows application

Depending on the researcher, some prefer the colorized output in Immunity to OllyDbg due to the ability to differentiate text and focus on the most important elements.

Windbg

Windbg is a free debugger that is built by Microsoft to support software development in Windows. It can be used to debug programs:

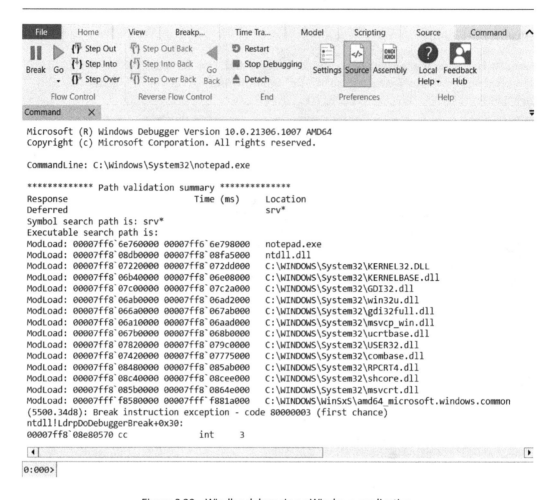

Figure 3.28 – Windbg debugging a Windows application

Windbg is probably the most up-to-date option on this list, but detractors may cite that Windbg has more use in development teams than security teams (see *Figure 3.28*).

Radare2

Radare2 is a free and open source reversing framework that supports Windows, macOS, and Linux. It can be used to reverse engineer programs. Radare2 also offers many features such as code analysis and disassembly:

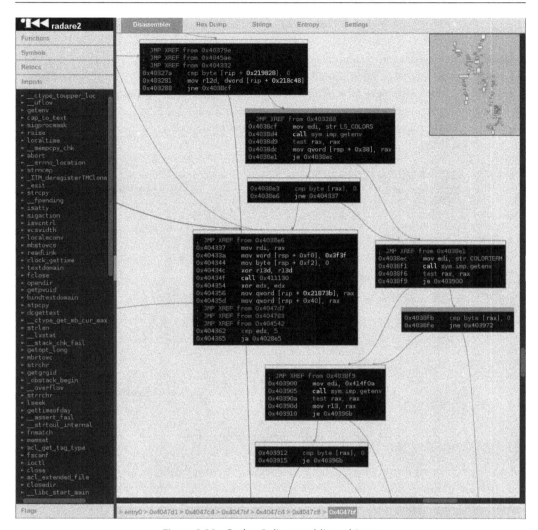

Figure 3.29 – Radare2 disassembling a binary

With Radare2, you can reverse engineer programs. This is useful for understanding how programs work and for finding vulnerabilities in them. Radare2 also offers many features such as code analysis and disassembly, which can be useful for creating patches or modifying programs (see *Figure 3.29*).

Ghidra

Ghidra is a free (and open source) software reverse engineering utility that supports Windows, macOS, and Linux. It was developed by the **National Security Agency** (**NSA**), an agency of the United States Government to help bridge a gap in tooling they felt existed. Ultimately this tool has been widely touted as an excellent resource that can help researchers reverse engineer binaries. With Ghidra, you can reverse engineer programs. This is useful for understanding how programs work and for finding vulnerabilities in them:

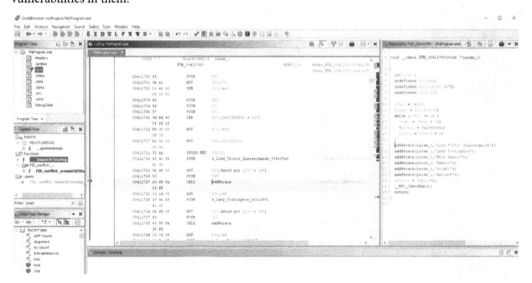

Figure 3.30 – Ghidra disassembling a binary

Ghidra also offers many features such as code analysis and **decompilation** (otherwise known as the inverse process of compilation), which can be useful for creating patches and exploits, and modifying programs (see *Figure 3.30*).

IDA Pro

IDA Pro is a commercial disassembler that supports Windows, macOS, and Linux. It can be used to reverse engineer binaries. With IDA Pro, you can reverse engineer binaries. This is useful for understanding how malware works and for finding vulnerabilities in software. IDA Pro also offers many features such as decompilation and debugging, which can be useful for reverse engineering software (see *Figure 3.31*):

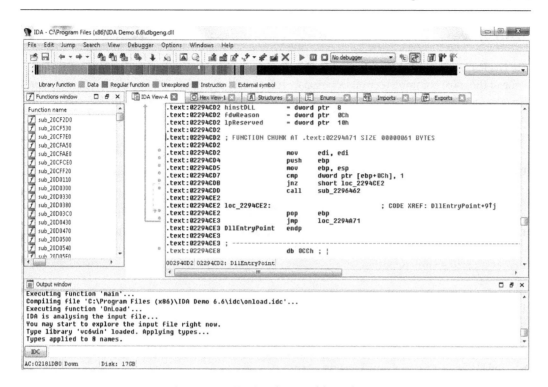

Figure 3.31 – IDA Pro disassembling a binary

IDA Pro is, without a doubt, the best tool available that can help disassemble software – but licensing fully featured copies (all decompilers) of the software to just one user, as of writing this material, can run to around $30,000.

Systernals Suite

We would be remiss to not include this phenomenal set of tools on our list. While technically not a decompiler or a debugger, it is an essential set of utilities and applications that can help and is extensively used in testing Windows applications. The suite contains over 70 free command-line tools, which will help in reviewing memory dumps, active directory configurations, running processes, thread-level process inspections, and so much more. If you're looking to research Windows applications, download these as soon as you possibly can, it's a goldmine.

As we close this chapter, all together, these tools represent an excellent arsenal of assets that you can use to build testing environments, take effective research notes and evidence, inspect network connections, debug, and disassemble applications. Undoubtedly, as you research and learn more about vulnerabilities, you'll add your own favorites to your arsenal.

Summary

In this chapter, we learned about what vulnerability research is and how to conduct it. We also looked at some of the most common techniques used in vulnerability research. We explored various types of strategies and resources that are utilized to discover new vulnerabilities. We also learned about some of the challenges faced by vulnerability researchers. We learned how to select the best targets for research. We dug into test cases and how they're an important method that can help you become more effective in finding vulnerabilities. We also learned which tools to become familiar with as we embark on our careers as vulnerability researchers.

All this information will be very useful as we conduct our own vulnerability research in the future and should have you setting out on your path of beginning your research. Though, when your research inevitably develops into the discovery of security vulnerabilities, what do you need to do next? In our next chapter, we'll talk about how researchers should conduct themselves and begin the communication process of reporting vulnerabilities.

Further reading

To learn more about the software and resources we've covered in this chapter, review these resources:

- The NVD – `https://nvd.nist.gov`
- The CVE database – `https://www.cve.org`
- Exploit-DB – `https://www.exploit-db.com`
- Full Disclosure – `https://seclists.org/fulldisclosure/`
- DEFCON Youtube channel – `https://www.youtube.com/user/DEFCONConference`
- SourceForge – `https://sourceforge.net/`
- CherryTree – `https://www.giuspen.net/cherrytree/`
- MITRE ATT&CK – `https://attack.mitre.org/`
- HackTricks – `https://book.hacktricks.xyz/`
- Joplin – `https://joplinapp.org/`
- Greenshot – `https://getGreenshot.org/`
- OBS – `https://obsproject.com/`
- VMWare Workstation Pro – `https://www.vmware.com/products/workstation-pro.html`
- VirtualBox – `https://www.virtualbox.org/`

- Hyper-V – `https://docs.microsoft.com/en-us/virtualization/hyper-v-on-windows/about/`

- Burpsuite – `https://portswigger.net/burp`

- ZAP – `https://owasp.org/www-project-zap/`

- Fiddler Classic – `https://www.telerik.com/download/fiddler`

- OllyDbg – `https://www.ollydbg.de/`

- Immunity Debugger – `https://www.immunityinc.com/products/debugger`

- WinDbg – `https://docs.microsoft.com/en-us/windows-hardware/drivers/debugger/debugger-download-tools`

- Radare2 – `https://rada.re/n/`

- Ghidra – `https://ghidra-sre.org/`

- IDA Pro – `https://hex-rays.com/ida-pro/`

- Systernals Suite – `https://docs.microsoft.com/en-us/sysinternals/downloads/`

Part 2 – Vulnerability Disclosure, Publishing, and Reporting

Disclosure, publishing, and reporting are critical phases in vulnerability research. In this section, you can expect to learn the right ways to disclose vulnerabilities to vendors and communicate your expectations to propagate remediation to their customers. Then, you'll learn how to publish your work to distributed security databases, which you can turn to when things go wrong during the disclosure process, and finally, how to share this information independently.

This section comprises the following chapters:

- *Chapter 4, Vulnerability Disclosure – Communicating Security Findings*
- *Chapter 5, Vulnerability Publishing – Getting Your Work Published in Databases*
- *Chapter 6, Vulnerability Mediation – When Things Go Wrong and Who Can Help*
- *Chapter 7, Independent Vulnerability Publishing*

4
Vulnerability Disclosure – Communicating Security Findings

In 2008, Dan Kaminsky discovered a severe vulnerability in the **Domain Name System** (**DNS**) protocol. This vulnerability was particularly dangerous because it could be used to redirect traffic from entire domains, such as *.com* or *.org*. This could allow for man-in-the-middle attacks, site redirection, and several other scenarios. It was a serious vulnerability with wide-reaching impacts.

Kaminsky understood the threat and immediately alerted Microsoft, who worked with him and many other vendors in secret to patch the issue. Once the patch was ready, Kaminsky held a press conference where he and the vendors announced patches that impacted the technology. At the press conference, few details were provided outside of the need to patch vulnerable systems. However, Kaminsky shared that all would be revealed in a talk at the BlackHat conference in Las Vegas, Nevada a few weeks after the press conference.

Vulnerability researchers took note and began speculating about Kaminski's vulnerability. Several researchers began sharing their thoughts on the bug on their blogs – some correct and incorrect details related to the exploitation were shared. Meanwhile, a researcher with some insider knowledge of the patching efforts accidentally released exploitation information in advance of Kaminsky's talk. Impacted customers had about 2 weeks to patch the vulnerability ahead of its accidental disclosure. Kaminsky shared with the press that while he had hoped vendors and the public had more time, they at least got a few weeks to patch before the vulnerability was exploited. While less than ideal, vendors received this short window of time to patch systems because Kaminsky communicated his security findings to the right people at the right time in a process called **vulnerability disclosure**.

When we inevitably find security risks, we need to communicate them collaboratively with software vendors. Unfortunately, sometimes, this involves us working in secret with vendors and only releasing information when all collaborators agree on the disclosure. While not all disclosures take this path, we can do a few things to ensure we have the best possible approach to communicating security findings. In this chapter, we'll dive into this topic by introducing the concepts around effective strategies for communicating security findings.

Here's what we'll learn in this chapter:

- We'll learn what vulnerability disclosure is and why it's important
- We'll discuss the different types of vulnerability disclosures and when to use them
- We'll introduce you to strategies you can pursue in disclosing vulnerabilities to impacted vendors
- We'll discover some common challenges you'll face and how to overcome them

These outcomes will be presented through the following main topics in this chapter:

- Vulnerability disclosure – what and why
- Different types of disclosures
- Initiating disclosures
- Approaching and overcoming challenges

By the end of this chapter, you should understand what vulnerability disclosures are and why they're important. You'll also have a good understanding of the different types of disclosures security researchers use. Finally, you'll know how to communicate with vendors and understand the common challenges associated with that initial disclosure.

Vulnerability disclosure – what and why

Let's begin this chapter by specifying what vulnerability disclosure is and why it's an important element of security research, software vulnerabilities, and the safety of software.

What is vulnerability disclosure?

Vulnerability disclosure is the process of revealing vulnerabilities to people. For example, vulnerability disclosures could be made to the public directly, to the vendor who built the software, to security consultancies, or a mixture of these parties. The idea is that if vulnerabilities are communicated to these parties, pressure to fix the vulnerabilities will build, and the vendor will need to take action to ensure their product and users are safe. In many cases, security researchers can make these disclosures to help make technology and its use safer.

We opened this chapter with a story about Dan Kaminski disclosing a vulnerability to Microsoft and other vendors about flaws found in DNS. The information security community has a variety of colorful thoughts on what should have happened or why this wasn't the best way for vulnerable software to be disclosed. Ultimately, it was up to the security researcher to determine the best course of action in disclosing the vulnerability, and in this case, vendors had an opportunity to develop a set of software patches, and the consumers of these products had an opportunity to patch the vulnerability before widespread exploitation took place. So, that's the best approach, right?

For every story about collaborative vulnerability disclosure, there's even more about disclosures that are much less collaborative. Case in point, when security researcher Leigh-Anne Galloway reached out to Myspace in 2017 about discovering a bug in Myspace that allowed unauthenticated access to user profiles, she didn't hear back from Myspace for months after repeatedly reaching out. In her mind, she thought the best thing to keep users safe was publishing her research on her blog (a link to the original disclosure can be found in the *Further reading* section of this chapter). Myspace fixed the issue within hours of her notifying them of publishing her blog. In this case, while contacting the vendor was something that happened, action was only taken by the vendor when the vulnerability was published publicly.

Our point is that vulnerability disclosures can look very different when the end goal is protecting users, and vulnerability researchers can approach disclosure differently to reach the end goal. Why does this matter, though?

Why is vulnerability disclosure important?

Depending on who you are and who you ask, you might get a few different answers on why vulnerability disclosures are important. From a researcher's perspective, vulnerability disclosures are important because they help identify risks to software users by ensuring public pressure is built against a vendor who might otherwise not want to fix the issue. This public pressure ultimately encourages vendors to create better products. Another value point to researchers is that it helps them achieve professional goals. Researchers who don't maybe do this for a full-time job want to break into the industry. Publishing research is a great way to help improve your resume and share your experience handling security concerns. From the vendors' perspective, disclosure about their products and security practices might be considered a liability.

In the United States, a governmental agency exists to protect food safety, named the **Food and Drug Administration** (**FDA**). The FDA was formed in 1906 after public outrage over the unhygienic conditions written about by Upton Sinclair in his novel The *Jungle*. Sinclair based the novel on his own experiences working undercover in the Chicago stockyards. Sinclair wrote of companies that would package and sell rotten meat, doctor spoiled products with chemicals, and even package severed appendages of employees into sausages. At the same time, workers with tuberculosis coughed and spat blood into the products being packed and sold to consumers. As a result, Sinclair and his fictionalized exposé were vilified in the meat packing industry. While in the United States, there is contention about governmental agencies and their efficacy, the practices found at the turn of the 19th century concerning food safety have vastly improved through regulatory compliance. Companies must meet specific requirements to package and sell food, and there is a consensus that products sold within the consumer market meet safety standards.

While not valid for every software manufacturer, a fair share of development shops mirror the conditions written in Chicago in 1906 about the meat packing industry. Modern software products are being packaged and sold under unsavory conditions, leading to unsafe products for consumers. It's safe to say that code quality hygiene is poor. Overworked, under-skilled workers build products, and software is rushed out the door without much consequence given to their security.

Even so, when companies are aware of vulnerabilities (or, in their view, liabilities) in their products, they can take steps to fix them. While this can be costly, vendors often take steps to prevent future cost expenditures by adopting a culture that focuses on implementing security early in the life cycle of the software development process.

Companies that are security-forward and think about the safety of their products may welcome a disclosure, but this will not always be the case. Sometimes, you'll find yourself talking to vendors who don't want to talk to you constructively about solving the problems found in their products, or much less publishing these findings. Simply put, vulnerability disclosure is a loaded topic for some vendors, but they need to learn that vulnerability disclosure is an essential element that can improve the quality of products at the end of the day.

We briefly discussed a couple of different scenarios involving different disclosures. Now, let's discuss these at greater length.

Different types of disclosures

Disclosures come in a few different forms. As a security researcher, you should expect that no disclosure will be the same. However, security researchers have reached a common consensus on different types of disclosures that achieve different goals. We'll explain each of these common types of disclosures and then discuss how to select the best one for your scenario and set goals.

Coordinated disclosure

Coordinated disclosure, often known as **responsible disclosure**, is when all information about a vulnerability is released, but only after the company has had a chance to patch it by working with a security researcher. In the scenario that opened our chapter on DNS, that's exactly what happened. This gives companies time to fix the issue before attackers can exploit it. Responsible disclosure requires all parties at the table to communicate about the risk and devise and execute a remediation plan.

The types of vendors who are prepared to operate security disclosures responsibly often publish a *responsible disclosure policy* on their websites. These policies may sometimes also fall under a *Safe Harbor* policy. An excellent example of such a policy has been published by the **Cyber Security and Infrastructure Security Agency** (**CISA**) through templates that companies can alter and adapt for their own disclosure needs:

What we would like to see from you

In order to help us triage and prioritize submissions, we recommend that your reports:

- Describe the location the vulnerability was discovered and the potential impact of exploitation.
- Offer a detailed description of the steps needed to reproduce the vulnerability (proof of concept scripts or screenshots are helpful).
- Be in English, if possible.

What you can expect from us

When you choose to share your contact information with us, we commit to coordinating with you as openly and as quickly as possible.

- Within 3 business days, we will acknowledge that your report has been received.
- To the best of our ability, we will confirm the existence of the vulnerability to you and be as transparent as possible about what steps we are taking during the remediation process, including on issues or challenges that may delay resolution.
- We will maintain an open dialogue to discuss issues.

Figure 4.1 – CISA's template shares expectations from both parties, so no party is left with uncertainty

For a link to this template, see the *Further reading* section of this chapter.

Good policies should clearly state what the vendors can do and what the researcher can do to work together. If a vendor has this type of policy, they're likely more security-forward, thinking about how to work with security researchers constructively. So, when does it make sense to use this disclosure method?

When should a security researcher use coordinated disclosure?

It is our advice, generally, that this is the first and foremost disclosure method that should be pursued by anyone who's looking for outcomes related to protecting users. We talked briefly about the Safe Harbor and responsible disclosure policies. Typically, companies with these policies have some method or process related to coordinated disclosure, which can help give you a good guide on what to expect when working with them.

Suppose a company does not have a coordinated disclosure process or policies. In that case, there's no reason why a researcher cannot attempt to collaboratively work with the vendor in the same fashion if they have no such policy. Of course, good vendors will want to work with you, but in these cases, you, as the security researcher, should plan on leading the way to ensure the best possible outcome. In the next section on communicating with companies, we'll discuss what that leadership entails.

While this might be the most common and preferred method of engaging with software vendors, several other methods can and have been used to achieve similar outcomes. We'll discuss private disclosures next.

Private disclosure

In a **private disclosure** model, researchers disclose the bug directly to the vendor, much like in a coordinated disclosure. The vendor then privately determines whether they publish or remediate this vulnerability at all. Typically, private disclosures are standard when an employed researcher finds software vulnerabilities in products that their company or products use that are owned or maintained by a third-party vendor. For example, this often happens in contracted penetration testing services when a paid expert tests products and only reports them internally to a paying client. Private disclosures can stop after the initial communication or report is issued. The receiving party of the disclosure likely will not publish details about the vulnerability and may or may not fix the vulnerability.

Why is this important? Well, to a company using a vendor's software, sometimes, the risk kept secret is an acceptable risk between parties. Sometimes, the risk is low or of medium importance to either party, or neither party has an interest in letting the public know about this risk.

When should a security researcher use private disclosure?

If you've been hired to work for a company through a contracted service directly, this required privacy in disclosure might be built into your contract. It is rare for contracts to have clauses for public or coordinated disclosure, so make sure you understand what you are legally bound to do in any contract. A curious development in private disclosure is that some companies become aware of the risk of any sort of public disclosure, and lawyers and security leadership of these vendors often put clauses or terms-of-use language into their products, which help insulate the company and provide legal avenues to seek damages if someone agrees to use the software and then pursues a course of action that aims to make any vulnerabilities public knowledge.

With that said, before any disclosure takes place, we advise that terms of use relating to the software are reviewed, and any contractual obligations are considered. Not every vendor is putative to security research, but enough are to the point where it can be troublesome in how you approach software vendors. Now, let's talk about the more disruptive disclosures: full disclosures.

Full disclosure

Full disclosure is when the researcher publicly releases all information about a vulnerability. This disclosure may include information about how to exploit the vulnerability and any potential mitigations. Some might argue users are immediately made aware of the issue and can take steps to protect themselves. That said, mitigation techniques are not always a guarantee of full disclosure. There are a lot of pros and cons to consider in full disclosure, and you should spend time considering them before putting the information about your research into public view.

Suppose attackers can exploit the vulnerability before it's patched. In that case, you may be embroiled in controversy related to any damages that may occur to customers who don't have security protections against your discovered vulnerabilities. Typically, though, the onus of consequence is on the software vendor for their inadequate response to security vulnerabilities when reported responsibly.

When should a security researcher use full disclosure?

Full disclosure should only be used as a last resort in most cases. This is usually when the vendor has not responded to coordinated disclosure, and the researcher believes that users are at risk of attack. For example, earlier in this chapter, we spoke of the Myspace disclosure. The security researcher, in this case, chose to do the full disclosure by writing about it on her blog after the vendor didn't respond to any messages for months. Only then did the vendor do something about it, patching the vulnerability in a few hours.

If you decide to pursue full disclosure, ensure that you have documented that you gave the company ample notice of the vulnerability with no response or uncooperative behavior. Remove any damaging or sensitive information in your disclosure and, depending on the size and impact, prepare for an influx of attention. The company may be inundated with media inquiries and pressure to fix the issue. In addition, you may see responses and colorful commentary from the information security community on why they did or didn't like how you handled it.

One alternative that is like full disclosure but carries less risk in disclosing vital exploitation information is partial disclosure. Let's take a quick look at this.

Partial disclosure

Partial disclosure is when select information about a vulnerability is publicly released directly by the researcher. Like full disclosure, this disclosure may include teasers and proof of the exploited vulnerability in an easy-to-consume media snippet. However, there usually is no specific information about how an exploit might be executed or specifics on the vulnerability itself. Usually, partial disclosures happen on social media platforms such as Twitter or personal blogs to help generate attention to an otherwise uncooperative or unresponsive vendor.

When should a security researcher use partial disclosure?

Much like full disclosure, partial disclosure needs to be examined closely before it's pursued. However, if the researcher's goal is to draw attention to the findings when other methods have failed, this is an excellent way to begin nudging the vendor in the right direction. Partial disclosures have often been used to build pressure, much like full disclosures, but with users in mind. Not disclosing all the details can help keep users safe from the immediate threat of exploitation. With that said, vulnerability disclosures can draw the attention of other researchers who want to reverse engineer or reexamine the software themselves, which can lead to full disclosure through a different party.

Now that we have a good idea about commonly used disclosures, let's take a quick detour to discuss coordinated disclosures through bug bounty programs. These are popular emerging ways for companies to offset disclosure to a third party.

Bug bounties and coordinated disclosure

We'd be remiss if we didn't take a moment to discuss **bug bounties** in this section. While bug bounties are not disclosure methods necessarily, they are programs that some security forward-looking companies use to help with coordinated disclosures. Essentially, bug bounty program providers work as middlemen who accept research from security researchers, validate it, and pass it along to a company that pays them. Typically, these providers hold deposits of money that they can and will disperse as an award if the company ultimately accepts the findings as valid. At the time of writing, the two most extensive bounty-hunting services that are open source and available to anyone are HackerOne and BugCrowd.

The big draw for security researchers is that by disclosing valid vulnerabilities, researchers are paid bounties for their disclosures. Vendors regularly publish bounty amounts from 10 US dollars to millions of US dollars. Usually, the programs predominantly focus on applications that are SaaS-based. In the previous chapter, we suggested against picking up and researching random SaaS-based solutions because it's illegal to test applications on servers you do not own without permission. Platforms like this help ease those legal burdens and help researchers test for security bugs in a way that helps define what is permissible to test and provides benefits to motivated researchers.

With that said, these companies usually define a narrow scope of what can be tested. Any vulnerabilities found may not be accepted for various reasons – some of which might lead to disgruntled researchers. Anecdotally, there have been many incidents where researchers failed to receive payments or have had their valid findings initially dismissed, but later fixed with no payments received for the disclosure.

> **Important note**
>
> Remember that these companies work as brokers and are not motivated financially to ensure researchers receive payouts, and they will usually side with the vendor when push comes to shove. Be aware of this.

Even with these concerns, we suggest checking out one of the several out there. Using HackerOne as an example, logging into the platform provides researchers with programs in which they're eligible to participate (see *Figure 4.2*):

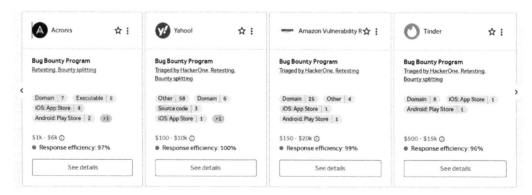

Figure 4.2 – HackerOne is a great resource for bug bounty research with thousands of active programs

Typically, each program comes with a robust scope and policy related to the program and how researchers can expect to interact with the program and receive awards for their research. *It's very important to remember to review all these rules and policies* (see *Figure 4.3*). Violating these may make you ineligible for awards and participation in other programs and may subject you to legal consequences, including criminal and civil actions against you:

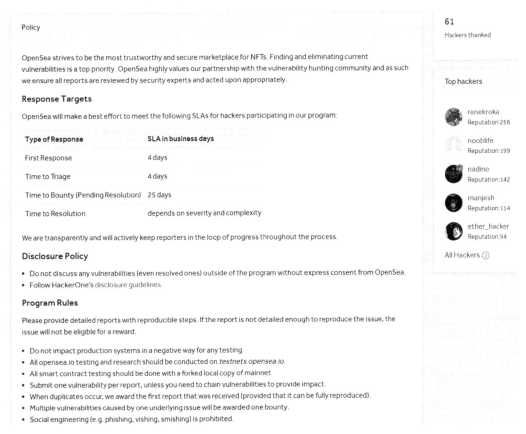

Policy

OpenSea strives to be the most trustworthy and secure marketplace for NFTs. Finding and eliminating current vulnerabilities is a top priority. OpenSea highly values our partnership with the vulnerability hunting community and as such we ensure all reports are reviewed by security experts and acted upon appropriately.

Response Targets

OpenSea will make a best effort to meet the following SLAs for hackers participating in our program:

Type of Response	SLA in business days
First Response	4 days
Time to Triage	4 days
Time to Bounty (Pending Resolution)	25 days
Time to Resolution	depends on severity and complexity

We are transparently and will actively keep reporters in the loop of progress throughout the process.

Disclosure Policy

- Do not discuss any vulnerabilities (even resolved ones) outside of the program without express consent from OpenSea.
- Follow HackerOne's disclosure guidelines.

Program Rules

Please provide detailed reports with reproducible steps. If the report is not detailed enough to reproduce the issue, the issue will not be eligible for a reward.

- Do not impact production systems in a negative way for any testing
- All opensea.io testing and research should be conducted on *testnets.opensea.io.*
- All smart contract testing should be done with a forked local copy of mainnet
- Submit one vulnerability per report, unless you need to chain vulnerabilities to provide impact.
- When duplicates occur, we award the first report that was received (provided that it can be fully reproduced).
- Multiple vulnerabilities caused by one underlying issue will be awarded one bounty.
- Social engineering (e.g. phishing, vishing, smishing) is prohibited.

61
Hackers thanked

Top hackers

renekroka
Reputation:256

nooblife
Reputation:199

nadino
Reputation:142

manjesh
Reputation:114

ether_hacker
Reputation:94

All Hackers ⊙

Figure 4.3 – Ensure you understand the policy found in each program before beginning your research

Bug bounties, for all their caveats, are worth exploring. As introduced in the previous chapter, you may enjoy this type of research over more unstructured research. One final thing that bounty hunters love is how communication is handled. Bounty programs help set up successful ways of communicating with software vendors and developers with minimal effort. These disclosures and even communication logs are often published on the platform. This can allow you to quickly understand what type of monies are being paid to researchers, how the researchers communicated with the bounty program, and, more importantly, how details on the vulnerability are published, which can help inform others of possible exploitation techniques (see *Figure 4.4*):

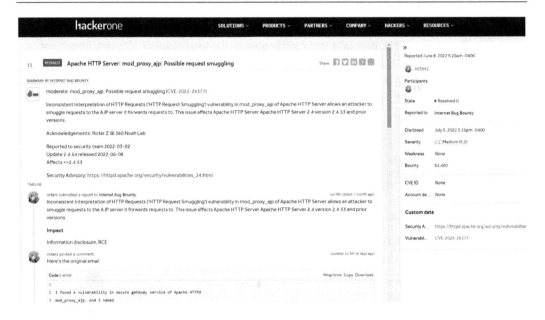

Figure 4.4 – Common disclosure log on vulnerabilities that shows payouts and communication logs

Bug bounty programs, for all their faults, have contributed to the improvement in disclosing vulnerabilities to vendors with concrete guidelines and mechanisms that provide tangible rewards for the researcher.

What if you're pursuing more unstructured research on programs that don't have bounties? Let's talk about how you should open conversations about vulnerabilities and some general best practices when initiating contact.

Initiating disclosure

Impressions count, and in the world of security disclosures, they can make or break a successful disclosure where you and the vendor are working together collaboratively. This section will help inform you and grant knowledge on how to best contact the responsible parties and make a great first impression. It will also provide helpful tips on what *not* to do.

Once you've found a vulnerability in a product, it's time to think about what to do next. It's the consensus that if you're hoping to protect users from software vulnerabilities, the best thing to do is initiate contact and attempt a coordinated disclosure.

Another item of note that will help your expectations is defining what you want out of the disclosure process. We can craft our communication strategy from this when we clearly understand what we want out of the process. Ask yourself the following questions to understand what you want:

- Do you want the vendor to simply know about the risk?
- Do you want the vendor to fix the vulnerability within a set period?

- Do you want to publish this research to the media or private blog?

- Do you want to submit your research to vulnerability databases so that other security professionals or the public know about this vulnerability and can act?

- Do you want to receive a reward for your research?

Understanding your intention in the disclosure process can help define how you act. Ideally, our general advice is to inform the vendor, share the research, publish any applicable information to blogs and vulnerability databases, and receive credit for your work. However, security disclosures can be a lot of effort, and you should prepare yourself to achieve the goals you're looking to achieve.

With your intentions set, you'll want to get started collecting preliminary information about the vendor and your research before you send an email to the company. Then, it would help if you gathered your intentions, **proof of concepts** (**POCs**), and evidence and brought it to the table to write a good disclosure. This is what you need to do to be expertly prepared:

- Gather all the relevant information about the issue, including any POC code or screenshots related to your research. Keep them organized and safe for future use if you need to produce further evidence or recall certain pieces of information.

- Discover if the software vendor has a security disclosure policy, a bug bounty program, or even a security and privacy policy. You need these to get in touch with the best possible person who can respond to your disclosure initiation.

- Check if the issue has already been disclosed to the vendor. For example, sometimes, if you're testing an older piece of software, a vulnerability may be an issue that has already been disclosed and published in their materials with published mitigation techniques.

- Build a compelling set of information that describes the vulnerability and creates clear instructions on how to recreate the conditions that demonstrate that a vulnerability is present. If possible, build a step-by-step guide with standard tools that could be downloaded and used by highly technical operators who may not have familiarity or access to specialty security research tools.

- If you want to contact the company, you need to decide if you'll do this anonymously, use a pseudonym, or your real name. If you're operating under the constraints of the law and even under the company security policy, you're usually safe to use your name. However, with that said, it should be noted that the company may investigate you, and the company may begin pointing its lawyers at you for cease-and-desist notices. Some researchers begin the communication anonymously or under an assumed name for the initial communication to determine if they're working with a cooperative company.

Once you have all the relevant information, you can start constructing the initial communication with the company. If you have found a security-related contact in your initial gathering or policy related to security disclosures, you'll want to initiate communication with those parties. Otherwise, a piece of general information on contacting the company or by using their customer service email will usually do the trick.

Your email should contain the following information:

- Explain that you're a security researcher with a security vulnerability you need to share with the company.

- If you're not officially contacting a security contact, ask to speak with one so that you may disclose details about the vulnerability.

- If speaking with a designated security contact, include all relevant information about the issue, including the step-by-step recreation instructions we built earlier.

- Share with them that you're available to collaborate and help fix the vulnerability.

- Let them know you plan on following up to see if they have any questions in the next 30 days if you don't hear anything back from them.

- Finally, let them know your intentions. Share with them if you plan on opening a **common vulnerabilities and exposure** (**CVE**) record, writing a blog, or would like to be credited with helping fix the security risk when the vulnerability is disclosed to customers. Again, it's important to preface this with an intent to disclose the vulnerability to set the stage for the expectation that the company will disclose it.

Your email should not, nor ever, include the following items:

- Threats about disclosing the vulnerability if they don't respond to your emails.

- Threats to exploit the vulnerability on customer systems or threats to release.

- Demands on receiving monetary rewards for your research.

- Ominous or cryptic language about vulnerabilities. These emails are usually scary for folks who've never received them in the past. Soften and specify the language so it seems like the email is from a friendly person, not a supervillain.

- Vague descriptions or recreation notes since they don't help explain the vulnerability well enough to communicate the risk.

- Insults, unprofessional language, or curt remarks about the vulnerability.

Remember, the first email should be one with a collaborative spirit. Try to approach the company as someone who wants to genuinely help and ensure that users benefit from this notice. So, once you've sent out your first email, what happens next? Let's talk about what you can expect.

What happens after disclosure?

This varies from case to case. First, the company will usually investigate the issue and determine if it's a valid finding. Then, they may contact you to talk about your initial communication or keep it internal to their teams. In most cases, it spurs conversations and work around patching the issue, which might happen without any notification.

In your initial email, you should have shared with the vendor that you would follow up in 30 days. If you haven't heard from them, try again. Ask how you can help and share a new plan to follow up with them in 30 days. The best practice is to give the company up to 90 days to respond to your request. If you still don't hear back from them, you have decisions to make. You now need to decide if you'll continue to contact them or if you plan to disclose the vulnerability using a full or partial disclosure. If you plan on opening a CVE, publishing that on a blog, or posting it in another vulnerability database, let them know. Avoid threatening language and state what your plan is moving forward.

Now, let's take a moment to examine a template you can use to build your initial communication with a vendor. This should take a lot of the confusion out of what your communication emails should look like if you want to create that great first impression.

Sample disclosure template

In this email template, we'll set up variables for your contact information, vulnerability information, and vendor information in curly brackets. You should aim to communicate in a friendly, collaborative way that includes your intentions and all relevant, helpful information about your research:

Hello {vendor name department},

My name is {researcher name}, and I'm an independent security researcher. I recently became interested in your software {software name} and spent some time reviewing the security of the platform.

This email is to inform you of the security vulnerabilities I discovered during my research. I'm sharing these with you because I'd like to help improve the security of your excellent software and reduce the chance of your customers being impacted by a security risk being exploited by a criminal.

There are {vulnerability count} in {software name}, specifically in the {version number} version. In the next section, I'll describe these vulnerabilities:

Vulnerability 1

{CWE mapping name and ID}

This vulnerability is found in the {where the vulnerability was found} section of the application. This weakness can result in {CWE impact description}, which may impact your customers in {scenario how this vulnerability would impact the user}.

To recreate this vulnerability, you can follow these steps for which I've provided screenshots to help illustrate a proof-of-concept.

{Recreation steps}

Vulnerability 2

{Additional vulnerabilities}

As part of my research, I plan on {releasing blog/publishing CVE} for which I'd like to receive any contributor credits when you fix and disclose this vulnerability to your customers. Additionally, I'd like to offer any assistance I can to help fix this problem impacting {software name}.

I hope to hear from you soon. I know this is a lot to process, so I'll follow back up in 30 days if I have not heard from your team on our next steps. If you need any assistance or help, please reach out to me via email {email address}.

Thanks,

{researcher name}

This is a great first start and will clearly state what you want, when you will follow back up, what vulnerabilities were found, and how to recreate a proof of concept. Additionally, we must cover the impact, define the software's name and version, and reiterate the researcher's email address in the message body if the reply-to address gets removed from forwarding and sharing this with other parties.

While this is a great start and will likely set you up for a positive experience, we'll discuss what challenges you might face and how to approach them in the best way possible.

Approaching common challenges

Vulnerability disclosure is rarely a linear or straightforward process. Even with an excellent introduction email and approaching the situation with a collaborative spirit, things can get off track quickly. So, let's spend some time talking about those challenges now.

Duplication of efforts

While this might be one of our more uncommon challenges, it's worth discussing. At times, vendors may (rightfully) claim that another security research has brought attention to the research you're sharing with them, and you need not worry. If you're invested in research, how do you proceed?

Deeper inquiry

Vendors might get frequent researchers contacting them, depending on the popularity of a product they offer to the market. The first thing you should offer to do is to share notes on the vulnerability proof of concept if you have not already. Researchers do not always arrive at the same conclusions, and sometimes, the vulnerability they're working on seems similar enough to some other vulnerability they're working on, and they make assumptions without verifications.

Discuss plans

If you've been able to verify that your vendor is indeed working on it or is aware of the vulnerability you've shared with them, ask them what their plans are. Vendors might know about something but confirm they have plans to fix it. If they don't have plans, it's time to encourage them to do just that. If the vulnerability is eligible for a CVE, ask if they've opened one yet. If they haven't, share with them that you'd like to help out by opening the vulnerability on their behalf.

Author anecdote

As the author, I can share one of my personal experiences working with a vendor to close a vulnerability. After approaching the vendor, they claimed to know of the vulnerability and said they were working on a fix for it. When we spoke about their plans to fix the problem, their *fix* was to upgrade customers and eventually deprecate the software. I reminded them that paid, in-service customers would not accept this as a fix and a patch should be issued due to the sensitivity of the data stored on the platform. At that point, I shared I'd be opening a CVE on their behalf. My impacted parties had a patch in their environment 8 months later. Sometimes, it's worth clarifying what the plans are to ensure there are plans to begin with.

Letting go

If the vendor is right and you've delivered a duplicate, and a good plan is in place, you might be out of options. Sometimes, letting go and checking back in when a patch is released is the right thing to do if there's already another invested researcher. If you're invested in seeing this vulnerability closed out, you can always offer to help test the patch when it comes out, or you can ask to be notified when the security fix is released.

While duplicate research might be one of those things you see only once in a while, a more common problem seen in the industry is unresponsive vendors. Let's discuss this now.

Unresponsive vendors

While we briefly discussed this in our communications planning, one common challenge is that companies may not be responsive to your reports. This can be frustrating and disheartening, but there are a few things you can do to increase your chances of getting a response.

Verify your contacts

Make sure you're contacting the right person or team – attempt creative ways of communicating with the team if you're having difficulty with your initial methods. For example, connecting with and contacting likely responsible parties/employees on LinkedIn (security officers, finical officers, security practitioners, and so on) is a great way to start a conversation. A quick message to the tune of *"Hey, I saw you worked at X company. Did you get the security vulnerability I sent to the company? I've been having a hard time reaching anyone and thought you might be able to help."* can go a very long way.

Be persistent

The old saying, *the squeaky wheel gets the grease*, applies here. Continue to prod for progress updates and offer to help politely. The more you're heard, the more likely this will be worked on if the vendor isn't otherwise responsive. As you continue to follow up, ensure your tone and approach are even and professional.

Be patient

Ensure you're giving them a reasonable amount of time to respond. Vendors have their fair share of financial difficulties, politics, and technical illiteracy, which may slow progress. Months can go by without contact – it doesn't necessarily mean that the vendor isn't working on a patch. They might be secretive about the development, do not trust you, or do not believe you need to be looped into information about their operations. That's fair and you should try to be patient in these circumstances.

Another common challenge is that vendors may have received your report but have decided not to fix it for a few different reasons. Let's discuss those now.

Uncooperative vendors

Vendors can either start or become uncooperative for several reasons. For example, vendors may believe that the security vulnerability isn't something that should be fixed due to perceived low risk or that it's a product they're not actively promoting or selling and, therefore, not worth the expenditure of resources to address. Another contributing element might be that the vendor simply does not have the staff to correctly process the information in your disclosure. Finally, vendors can sometimes take an approach where they distrust you right out of the gate. If you run into this issue, you can try the following techniques.

Paint a clear picture of the risk

Spend time constructing language on why the security vulnerability needs to be fixed. Attempt to construct this language in a way that appeals to their customers in plain language. Try to dig into the customer impacts and use them as motivators. However, try to be careful with your language to avoid sounding threatening. For example, while writing *"This is important, and I could hack this today and steal all of your customer data"* might be true, it sounds hostile. Tweaking this message to something more like *"This is important. As shown in my proof of concept, your customer data is at risk of criminals exploiting this vulnerability and causing a huge financial liability to you and your customers. How can I help in closing this risk?"* is much more effective.

Offer to help more actively

They might need more help in understanding and communicating this problem to their businesses. Or it might be that the right people are not looking at this problem. Clarify the issue you're running into and respond with an *"I'll help!"* response if you're invested in the resolution. Ask if they need help communicating the risk and impact to developers. Ask if they need help with mitigating controls. Ask if they need help in drawing up disclosure notes. If you take some workloads on to make disclosure easier, they might be more responsive to fixing the vulnerability. Additionally, it's not entirely unheard of for researchers to get offers to work for companies that assist in improving their products.

Remind them of your intentions

Restate your intentions firmly. Suppose you're looking to open a CVE, and the vendor doesn't want to work on the vulnerability and has clearly stated that; it might be prudent to ensure they understand the next steps. Remind them that, as a researcher, you plan to execute your plan for disclosure without them if necessary. Remind them that CVEs are an internationally shared database of security vulnerabilities, and the product and company will be tied to and associated with this disclosure. Share with them that you'd like to publish that information *with them, not without*.

One unusual challenge in the disclosure process is when a vendor is no longer in business. So, let's discuss our limited options there.

Failed vendors

Perhaps making insecure software was not profitable enough for the vendor to continue making money to operate as a business. This is possible and happens to software that may be published and used worldwide but no longer supported by the vendor because they no longer exist. If this is the case, you have just a couple of options here.

Reach out to the community

There may be a community of users who still use this software. Try researching user groups or websites that feature mentions of the product. Reaching out to these resources and letting them know of potential security vulnerabilities is usually welcome and can result in collaborative action.

Unofficial support

Suppose a developer or maybe a critical resource at the company has taken on supporting the legacy software as a consultant. Usually, this information might be published on resources such as LinkedIn or even directly on the vendor's website if it is still online. It's worth trying to at least take a cursory look for signs of this kind of thing.

Full disclosure ahead

Full disclosure is usually the best path for unsupported legacy products made by people who have moved on with their careers. However, since it's unsupported software, it likely won't receive a patch. Consider this in your disclosure. Perhaps don't provide a working exploit or public proof of concept if you cannot provide a mitigating control.

Finally, vendors may not take kindly to your contact and might respond to your disclosure with hostility. Let's discuss these possibilities.

Hostile vendors

In the event you begin encountering hostile vendors, you should prepare yourself for unpleasant interactions. The vendor may pursue legal action or social engineering attacks designed to discredit you. If you're not otherwise informed of tactics used by hostile vendors, it might seem corrupt and a little surreal.

For example, in 2019, a security researcher was assaulted by the COO of a company named Atrient. The company sells widely deployed kiosks to Las Vegas casinos that customers used to redeem winnings. The researcher attempted to contact the vendor to alert them of unencrypted personal information using the kiosks. The vendor ignored the disclosure. After several attempts to contact the vendor, the researcher partially disclosed it on Twitter. The tweet was noticed by Las Vegas casino security operators and subsequently by the **Federal Bureau of Investigation (FBI)**.

After getting the attention of casino security leaders, the FBI then helped proctor and facilitate a call between the vendor and the researcher, committed to fixing the bug in a few months, and Atrient told the researchers they'd receive a bounty if they signed a non-disclosure agreement. The researchers were never paid. The COO saw the researcher at a conference shortly after the company announced new products they were launching and violently grabbed the researcher, tearing away his conference badge. Atrient didn't stop there, though. They continued to run misinformation campaigns against the researcher, stating they were threatened with extortion and further hacking.

Thankfully, the researcher was on the right side of things. There was videotape evidence of the assault, and extensive communications were preserved and saved concerning researcher collaboration with the vendor and the FBI.

While this is a rare example of a disclosure gone wrong from the vendor side, we sincerely hope that you don't run into scenarios where executive officers feel they need to assault you physically. Let's talk about common tactics you might encounter and basic measures you can take to protect yourself.

Discrediting tactics

One common tactic used by hostile vendors is trying to discredit the researcher who found the vulnerability. This is done to invalidate their work and make it less likely that other people will take them seriously in the future.

There are a few different ways this can be accomplished. One standard method is to paint the researcher as someone who is not competent or trustworthy. This can be done by spreading false information about them or their work or hiring someone to pose as a researcher and make spurious claims about the original researcher's work.

Another tactic is to try to damage the researcher's reputation by making it appear as though they have acted unethically. This can be done by leaking private information about the researcher or planting false information that makes it appear as though the researcher has misbehaved.

The best thing you can do is retain copies of your research and communications – publishing your content or working with others to get your story out there. Cybersecurity media outlets and magazines might be interested to hear your side of the story.

Legal action

Some vendors may choose to take legal action against researchers who disclose vulnerabilities. This could include filing a lawsuit or initiating a criminal investigation. In some cases, these actions may be frivolous and intended solely to intimidate researchers into silence. In other cases, they may be legitimate attempts to punish researchers who have violated terms of service or other agreements.

Researchers should be aware of the possibility of legal action and consult with a lawyer before disclosing anything or contacting the hostile vendor regarding the vulnerability.

Closing this chapter on this subject, it's no surprise that security researchers sometimes choose to use assumed names when communicating with vendors. Nevertheless, it might be the best way to avoid unintentionally disturbing a vendor with an aggressive approach to security disclosures.

Summary

In this chapter, we learned about vulnerability disclosures. First, we discussed what they are and why they're essential. We then discovered the different types of disclosures and when to use them. Then, we outlined the basics of communicating security disclosures with some best practices. Finally, we discussed challenges related to disclosures and helpful suggestions for getting to your desired goals in communicating vulnerabilities. Now that we have a great understanding of disclosures, what happens next? We need to publish our vulnerability to a database such as the MITRE CVE or NVD in many cases if the software meets a certain criterion. In the next chapter, we'll cover everything you need to know to get your research published in those databases.

Further reading

To learn more about the software and resources we've covered in this chapter, review these resources:

- An Illustrated Guide to the Kaminsky DNS Vulnerability: `http://unixwiz.net/techtips/iguide-kaminsky-dns-vuln.html`

- It's not Yourspace, it's Myspace: `https://leigh-annegalloway.com/myspace/`

- Vulnerability disclosure policy template: `https://www.cisa.gov/vulnerability-disclosure-policy-template`

- HackerOne: `https://www.hackerone.com/`

- BugCrowd: `https://www.bugcrowd.com/`

- Casino Screwup Royale: A tale of "ethical hacking" gone awry: `https://arstechnica.com/information-technology/2019/03/50-shades-of-greyhat-a-study-in-how-not-to-handle-security-disclosures/`

Vulnerability Publishing – Getting Your Work Published in Databases

In September 2017, the security researchers working at Armis Labs published research on weaknesses in the Bluetooth protocol. They named these weaknesses and the associated vulnerabilities **BlueBorne**. BlueBorne vulnerabilities allow attackers to gain access to a device without the user's knowledge or interaction. The attacker can then take complete control of the victim's device. The researchers discovered that there were eight vulnerabilities in the Bluetooth protocol that could be exploited to carry out this kind of attack. These vulnerabilities affected all devices that use Bluetooth, including smartphones, laptops, and **Internet of Things (IoT)** devices. Their research was published in an extensive 41-page white paper, which gave background on the protocol running on approximately 8.2 billion devices worldwide. With this research paper, Armis helped lay the groundwork for modern-day Bluetooth research and helped the industry reconsider security in widely adopted technology. In each provided example of research in the BlueBorne whitepaper, the team detailed a vulnerability tied to a **Common Vulnerability and Exposure (CVE)**. Before releasing this whitepaper talking about these CVEs, they needed to be disclosed and published.

At this point in our journey, you should have a great grasp on vulnerabilities, zero-days, vulnerability research techniques, and disclosing your findings. As previously discussed in our initial two chapters, CVEs are unique identifiers assigned to vulnerabilities when they have been disclosed to an organization authorized to reserve and publish this data. But how do they get published in this database? Is this our only option for publishing vulnerabilities? Does it always make sense to publish to databases?

In this chapter, we'll explore those questions about getting your work published to the public so others can benefit. This is especially important for CVEs, which are commonly used to share and express data on vulnerabilities. Here's what we'll learn about in this chapter:

- What publishing is and the details related to getting vulnerabilities published

- Our options and what we can select for vulnerability publishing methods

- Examples of publishing vulnerabilities to **CVE Numbering Authorities** (**CNA**) and **CVE Numbering Authorities of Last Resort (CNA-LR)**

These outcomes will be presented through the following main topics in this chapter:

- Demystifying vulnerability publishing

- Selecting the right publishing methods

- Practical examples of vulnerability publishing

- Best practices for publishing vulnerabilities

By following the advice in this chapter, you will be well on your way to getting research published in vulnerability databases. Let's get started by demystifying the vulnerability publishing process.

Demystifying vulnerability publishing

Let's begin this chapter with what vulnerability publishing is, the importance of publishing in the vulnerability life cycle, and the overall impact publishing has on the information security community, users, and you.

Vulnerability publishing is the process of making information about a security vulnerability public to increase awareness and allow others to take steps to protect themselves. Typically, publishing can take varied forms. In our opening example of BlueBorne, there was the publishing of a monumental whitepaper, but should that be technically considered the publishing of the vulnerability? Well, in this case, the publishing of the vulnerabilities came before the disclosure in the form of requesting and publishing CVEs. The researchers first requested CVEs from the MITRE organization, a process we'll review later in this chapter in the *Practical vulnerability publishing examples* section. This typically happens right after the disclosure phase, as we discussed in our previous chapter, *Vulnerability Disclosure - Communicating Security Problems*. Once the vulnerability has been disclosed, the vulnerability can be patched, or mitigating controls can be published to the public. However, if the vulnerability disclosure is not met with a vendor response, publishing can still take place, provided a process is followed with or without the vendor's intervention.

A good example of a vendor not responding to a vulnerability disclosure would be that of the *MiCODUS MV720 GPS tracker* research published in July 2022. *MiCODUS* is a software and hardware manufacturer that builds GPS tracking devices that are used in fleet management. The **Cybersecurity and Infrastructure Security Agency of the United States** (**CISA**) issued the advisory number ICSA-

22-200-01, where they referenced five CVE disclosures related to the device. The security research referenced things such as insecure configurations and passwords, all relatively easy things to discover by a knowledgeable researcher. However, the impact was severe. These trackers allow for the remote configuration and control of vehicles in the form of remote kill switches, geofencing, disabling of alarms, and route information. The implications of these vulnerabilities were that loss of life could occur if they were exploited. The researchers initially tried to work with the vendor and began contacting them as early as September 2021. In their first communication with the vendor, they shared almost no specifics regarding the vulnerability. They received an email from the vendor's sales team stating that the vulnerabilities were being worked on. The vendor refused to talk to the researchers about the vulnerability and did not respond to any further questions about the issue. In January 2022, the researchers reached out to CISA in a request to help, a request CISA accepted. CISA began trying to work with the vendor; however, they ran into similar problems when communicating with the vendor and were unsuccessful in getting the vendor to cooperate or collaborate on improving the security of the GPS tracker. In July 2022, the research was jointly released by the researchers and CISA, with no mitigations or vulnerabilities fixed by the vendor at the time of the publication (`https://www.cisa.gov/uscert/ics/advisories/icsa-22-200-01`).

In relation to CVEs, when the details about the vulnerability have been published in a public medium such as a CISA disclosure, a mediated disclosure, vendor disclosure, or even independent disclosure, then the CVEs can be *published* by the security research or vendor. As fascinating as vulnerability research publications are, why would researchers even go through the trouble of getting this information to the public?

Why publish vulnerabilities?

When discussing the vulnerability life cycle, which was introduced in *Chapter 1, An Introduction to Vulnerabilities*, we mentioned how vulnerabilities do not always get published. Why might someone look to publish vulnerabilities, though? Well, there are many reasons why security researchers may choose to publish vulnerabilities. In some cases, they may want to increase awareness of the issue so that others can take steps to protect themselves. In the case of MiCODUS, the researchers published their findings to help inform the public of the risk of using these devices and the threat they posed to the national security of the United States. Not all researchers are driven by these motives, though; some might want to help improve the content of their resumes and firmly establish their work and experience to attain other jobs. In other cases, they may want to pressure the vendor into patching the issue more quickly. And in some cases, they may simply want to share their findings with the information security community so that others can learn from their work.

Whatever the reason, publishing is probably the easiest (albeit longest) of all the steps in the vulnerability life cycle, and this process arguably benefits the researchers and the public significantly. These certainly are important reasons to publish, but let's spend some time discussing a few additional angles now.

In the BlueBorne vulnerability introduced in this chapter, once the research was disclosed, it led to the discovery of new high and critical security vulnerabilities. In the wake of the 2017 whitepaper, many security practitioners were left wondering how many more Bluetooth vulnerabilities were under the surface of these initial findings. Some speculated that it was possible that many more would come into existence with additional research.

They were not wrong in their suspicion. Research attracts research, and a year after publishing this report, security researchers worldwide were publishing new Bluetooth vulnerabilities with increased severity than in the years prior and in greater quantities. Publishing is important because it helps to bring security research to the information security community, which in turn helps scrutinize technology through diverse skillsets and understanding. This process ultimately improves the quality of the technology by improving its security.

When you publish research, you draw attention to vulnerabilities and encourage more research. Vulnerability publishing can be a great way for security researchers to share their findings with the community so that others can learn from their work. Researchers are not built alike; what one person sees may differ from the next, and the increased attention ultimately leads to greater knowledge forcing technology to become more secure or risk obsolescence.

Another consideration as we think about the importance of publishing is that users of the technology usually benefit. When vulnerabilities are found and published, it increases awareness of the issue and allows others to take steps to protect themselves. Executives begin asking questions about risk in relation to the adoption of technology in their enterprises, users become more informed and educated in security, and in most cases, this overall concern generates pressure on the software manufacturer to improve their products. If you simply stop at the vulnerability disclosure phase, you might miss these key benefits in publishing, and if pressure is not generated, it can cause the software manufacturer to delay fixing flaws found in software or simply avoid fixing the problems to begin with.

Much like in our previous chapter, where we discussed the initial disclosure of the vulnerabilities, there are always risks in opening this information up to the public. Let us discuss a few of those now.

What are some of the risks involved in vulnerability publishing?

Like all things in life, there are risks with any action taken, and vulnerability publishing is no exception. At the time of publishing this text, there have been great improvements over the previous decade when it comes to vulnerability publishing. Large and/or modern software manufacturers have generally got better, making software more secure, and have adopted methods for accepting vulnerabilities and publishing them without much effort from the researcher.

The risks involved are usually very much like the risks involved with disclosure. Security researchers should be aware before publishing who they are working with and try to determine if publishing might result in hostile actions from the software manufacturer. If the vendor was hostile in the disclosure process, expect them to be as much or more so in the publishing process.

Finally, whenever you publish information about vulnerabilities, you should expect that information may likely be misused by attackers. In the whitepaper *Improving Vulnerability Remediation Through Better Exploit Prediction*, the researchers found that out of the published vulnerabilities between 2009 and 2018, roughly only 5% of them were ever exploited. Out of the 5% of these vulnerabilities, only half of these had published exploits. It would suggest that if you plan on releasing vulnerability details, not publishing a proof-of-concept exploit may reduce the chances of the vulnerability being exploited.

In the example we shared earlier about the software and hardware manufacturer MiCODUS, researchers likely heavily weighed whether they should release data on the vulnerability. In this example, the vulnerabilities were not fixed, but in consideration with a mediating party, CISA, the researchers and mediation team thought that not releasing the data would be more dangerous than releasing it. Ultimately, this publication led to some online retailers pulling the product from their stores, and this information helped users make more informed decisions on whether they should use a technology that is vulnerable and is serviced by a company that does not care about vulnerabilities enough to respond to researchers or agencies of governments. We will talk more about mediation groups such as CISA, who can help you make these decisions, in our next chapter, *Vulnerability Mediation – When Things Go Wrong and Who Can Help*.

In other cases, vulnerabilities may be patched more slowly if they are not made public. Sometimes, it is just enough to let the vendor know you're planning on publishing your findings and that you'll open a disclosure with a vulnerability database to inspire action. These risks should not deter security researchers from publishing vulnerabilities, but they should be aware of them and take steps to mitigate them. Now that we've completed this section demystifying the vulnerability publishing process, let's dive into the most popular options for publishing vulnerabilities.

Selecting the right vulnerability publishing method

When you first start researching vulnerability databases, you might find yourself easily overwhelmed by the various options which you have. Sometimes, the databases have redundant publishing components, or they may help further for-profit organizations, and there are often confusing rules to determining who should be told and when. To help simplify, let's talk about key publishers of research in relation to traditional applications and **software as a service** (**SaaS**) solutions, and then we'll talk about a couple of outliers you should be aware of that may fit your publishing goals.

CVE

One of the most common ways of publishing vulnerabilities is by using the CVE system. As previously discussed in earlier chapters, CVE is a publicly available database that is used by many different organizations, including vendors, security researchers, and bug bounty programs.

For a vulnerability to be added to the CVE List, the software needs to be independently maintained by the end user in some capacity, with the user having the ability to disable insecure components. This generally excludes SaaS products unless part of the SaaS solution is hardware owned by the user. To help drive this point home a bit further, let's go through a few examples to identify whether the application is CVE-eligible or not:

- **A Windows application installed on your computer**

    - **CVE eligible**: Applications that are installed locally on a device are managed by the user and therefore are eligible for CVE publishing.

- **A Windows application installed on a server you can only access through remote connections**

    - **Not CVE eligible**: A common new method of offering SaaS is to provide limited remote access via web services to traditional Windows applications. Since these assets are entirely controlled by the vendor, they are typically ineligible for CVEs.

- **Open source software libraries**

    - **CVE eligible**: Open source software is one of the common components which routinely receive CVE disclosures and is generally eligible for CVEs.

- **Closed source software libraries**

    - **CVE eligible**: Even though some software libraries are closed source, if you have access to one and can directly interact with it by adding it to the software you're developing or can observe it in software you own, it's eligible for a CVE.

- **Applications that can be downloaded and installed on a computer, but the data is stored in the vendor's cloud**

    - **Partially CVE eligible**: Even though elements related to the software are SaaS-like, most of the computing power is likely stored locally, and therefore the software and any SaaS-related elements which interact with the software are eligible for CVE disclosures.

- **Software hosted entirely in the cloud but requires the download and use of Chrome browser extensions**

    - **Partially CVE eligible**: Depending on the scope and what the browser extension is used for, the components related to the browser extension are eligible.

- **An IoT device that talks exclusively to the cloud and must be configured on the vendor's SaaS platform**

  - **Partially CVE eligible**: In our example where we discussed the MiCODUS hardware, the vendor's cloud-based API was up for disclosure due to the fact that it directly impacted the local user devices. If there were independent components outside of what was user-controlled, such as a blog on the MiCODUS marketing website that had cross-site scripting, those would not be CVE-eligible because they are independent of the consumer elements.

- **Cloud-based SaaS application**

  - **Not CVE eligible**: Basic cloud-based SaaS applications are not eligible for CVEs because they do not consist of user-controlled elements.

Another element to discuss in relation to CVEs is the role of the CNAs. CNAs are organizations that have entered a relationship with MITRE and have agreed to participate in the CVE numbering program. (You can read more about them at https://www.cve.org/ProgramOrganization/CNAs.) CNAs have the authority to assign CVE IDs to vulnerabilities and publish vulnerabilities. CNAs typically consist of large corporations such as Microsoft, Alibaba, Google, and Meta. When requesting a CVE, (something we'll show later in this chapter, in the *Practical vulnerability publishing examples* section), you'll need to determine whether the software you've tested belongs to an already registered CNA. If it does, there are procedures you'll need to follow to request a CVE from that CNA. If the software you've tested does not belong to a CNA, you'll need to request a CVE from a CNA-LR. There are very few CNA-LRs; as of publishing this material, there are only two—one being MITRE and the other being CISA for industrial control systems. This relationship is shown in *Figure 5.1*:

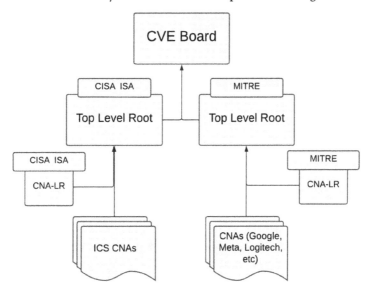

Figure 5.1 – Example of the CVE reporting hierarchy

In the organizational chart of the CVE disclosure, once a CNA or CNA-LR has received the request, the information goes through one of the *top level roots*, which has its own procedures for processing the vulnerability.

One additional piece of information vital to understanding the process for getting CVEs published is the three-part process vulnerabilities go through before being published. Let's talk about each one of these parts now:

1. **CVE request**: The first part of getting a CVE is the request process. Depending on whether you'll be using a CNA or a CNA-LR, this process might look different. In both cases, though, the request must happen with the information required, which usually involves the researcher submitting information about the vulnerability to the authority. To move to the next step, the information must be complete and meet the specifications of the CNA or CNA-LR. If the initial request doesn't meet the specifications, the request will be returned for more qualifying information.

2. **CVE assignment**: Once the CVE request has been approved by the authority processing the request, a CVE ID is assigned to the vulnerability. This CVE ID is set to **RESERVED** and is published in the database pending the final step, publishing. Typically, an assignment happens right after a researcher discloses the vulnerability and the intent to publish a CVE:

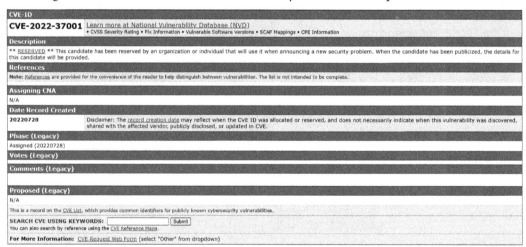

Figure 5.2 – Example of a CVE in a RESERVED status

3. **CVE Publishing**: Once the vulnerability details have been made public by the software manufacturer, security researcher, or both, the CVE can then be published. To do this, the researcher or the software manufacturer will submit publishing details and the official notification. Once the details have been submitted and approved, then the CVE will be made active, and the **RESERVED** status will be lifted, unmasking the original request.

Now that you have a good idea of how basic CVEs work, let's now talk about CVE CNA intermediates for publishing vulnerabilities in traditional application components.

CVE CNA intermediates

Publishing is hard work, and some companies and organizations have made it easier to publish vulnerability details via their services. However nice, these are usually for-profit companies that use your research to sell their products. Let's talk about a few of these now.

VulnDB

VulnDB is a product owned and operated by pyxyp. Its goal is to index a global database of vulnerabilities and then assign risk to them:

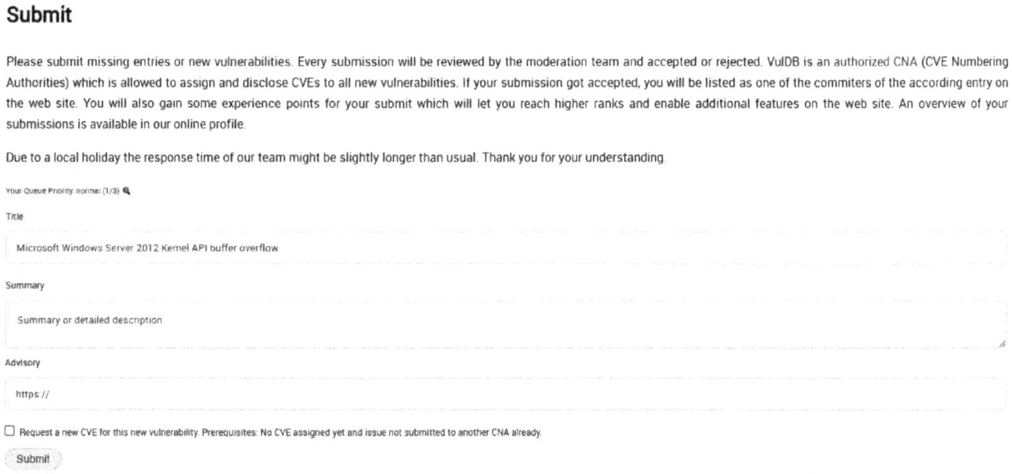

Submit

Please submit missing entries or new vulnerabilities. Every submission will be reviewed by the moderation team and accepted or rejected. VulDB is an authorized CNA (CVE Numbering Authorities) which is allowed to assign and disclose CVEs to all new vulnerabilities. If your submission got accepted, you will be listed as one of the commiters of the according entry on the web site. You will also gain some experience points for your submit which will let you reach higher ranks and enable additional features on the web site. An overview of your submissions is available in our online profile.

Due to a local holiday the response time of our team might be slightly longer than usual. Thank you for your understanding.

Your Queue Priority: normal (1/3) 🔍

Title

Microsoft Windows Server 2012 Kernel API buffer overflow

Summary

Summary or detailed description

Advisory

https://

☐ Request a new CVE for this new vulnerability. Prerequisites: No CVE assigned yet and issue not submitted to another CNA already.

Submit

Figure 5.3 – VulnDB vulnerability submission form

This product is something that is offered as a free service with additional paid offerings. They operate as a CNA, where if you submit vulnerabilities to them, they can open CVEs on your behalf and then credit you for the research in addition to unlocking more features depending on how often you submit to the VulnDB platform.

Snyk

Snyk is a for-profit organization specializing in the discovery, indexing, and disclosure of vulnerable **open source software** (**OSS**) libraries. Most of the technology used in SaaS products is built with a high number of open source libraries. The infamous Equifax breach was caused by unpatched OSS libraries. As such, companies have invested in technology that will inspect OSS for vulnerable components:

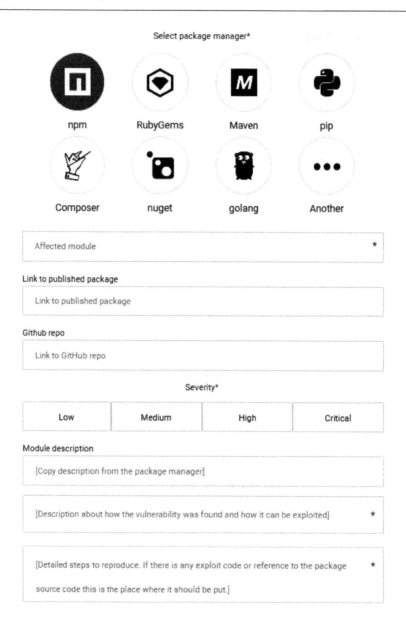

Figure 5.4 – Snyk vulnerability submission form

To set itself apart from the competition, Snyk closely works with researchers to get vulnerability information to customers as fast as possible by providing a method of verifying and indexing vulnerabilities submitted by researchers. If you're a security researcher looking at open source components, Snyk is an easy way to get your vulnerability details published. Snyk is a CVE CNA, so they can verify and publish vulnerabilities to the CVE database on your behalf.

huntr.dev

huntr.dev is a team of hackers who have collectively pooled resources to build a program that pays researchers and maintainers of OSS built on GitHub:

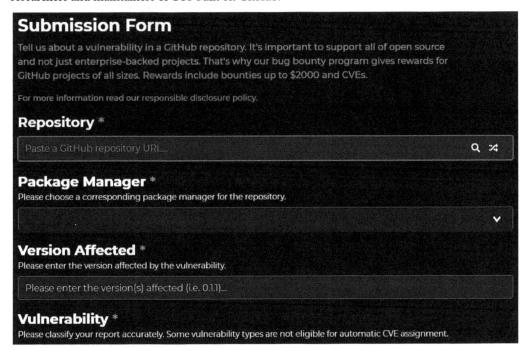

Figure 5.5 – huntr.dev vulnerability submission form

On this platform, researchers disclose vulnerabilities, the platform begins a disclosure process to the maintainer, and the issue is tracked until it is fixed. It's an open platform for both security researchers and maintainers of projects on GitHub only. Much like Snyk, the huntr.dev team is a CNA and will automatically open CVEs and publish them provided that the findings are accepted on the platform.

Zero Day Initiative

Much like Snyk and huntr.dev, the **Zero Day Initiative** (**ZDI**) can open CVEs on your behalf but only does so, provided that the researcher's findings are validated, accepted, and rewarded. ZDI initiates this process only after the researcher submits the vulnerability and ZDI offers to purchase the vulnerability. Acceptance and offer criteria are based entirely on whether the product in the research is widely used and how the flaw is exploited. Details are murky, though, and this qualifying criterion is not published anywhere. Rewards are offered in the form of payments of US dollars and tokens called *ZDI rewards points*.

This is what a ZDI vulnerability submission form looks like:

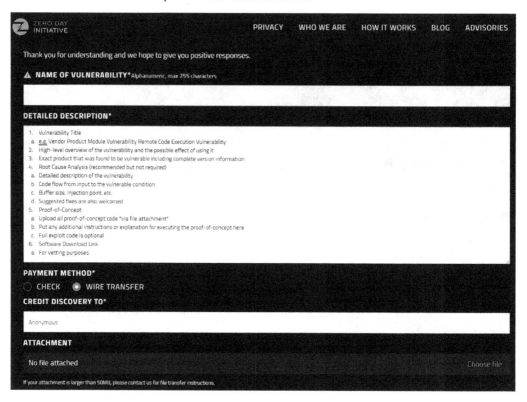

Figure 5.6 – ZDI vulnerability submission form

While all these options cover the publishing of CVEs, let's talk about ineligible applications for a moment, as they encompass many application services in use by users today.

Ineligible application publication options

In most cases, there are no databases or publishing guidelines around the disclosure of vulnerabilities or weaknesses found in SaaS-based applications that do not fit into the criteria of a CVE. In this scenario, a disclosure to the software vendor would be the recommended option and place where the researcher's work might end. As discussed in *Chapter 3, Vulnerability Research – Getting Started with Successful Strategies*, in most cases, when SaaS providers are informed of the vulnerabilities, there's usually no additional publishing that happens outside of what the vendor or researcher chooses to disclose.

That said, some companies do publish release notes in relation to customer-facing changes in their software products, and with more security-forward companies, sometimes those notes do include a thank you and notice to researchers.

In some bug bounty programs, the programs can publish the findings and share them with the community. If your bug details are made public, you can refer to them or even write about them in a blog. Before doing any of these things, though, ensure you refer to any disclosure policy or guidance provided by the bug bounty provider to avoid violating terms of service.

Overall, though, there is no unified database where you can publish vulnerabilities in SaaS applications. In *Chapter 7*, we'll talk a little bit more about self-publishing options if you do want to talk about vulnerabilities, but public knowledge of SaaS applications is something that is sorely lacking.

Vulnerability publishing isn't right for everyone; sometimes, researchers are motivated to publish exploits to further their research. Let's talk about those motives and where you can submit exploitation details if that might be something you'd want to focus on in the future.

Exploitation databases

One of the curious ways that vulnerable software gets *published* but perhaps not published in vulnerability databases is through exploit databases. These are websites where people can upload and share exploits for vulnerabilities.

It's important to know that not every CVE has an exploit, and conversely, every exploit does not have a CVE. Some exploitation databases don't usually discriminate or split hairs on who owns what. Where CVE rules might say that SaaS applications are out of scope, those rules might not exist in the realm of an exploitation database.

There are a few reasons why someone might want to publish their exploit in an exploit database rather than submitting it to a vulnerability database. First, they may not be interested in getting the software patched and instead just want to be able to use the exploit themselves or sell it to someone else. Second, they may not think that the vulnerability is significant enough to warrant a patch. And finally, they may not want to go through the hassle of submitting it to a formal database.

Depending on the database you use, you could feasibly speed up the vulnerability patching process. For example, 0day.today will publish vulnerabilities for you as CVEs, notify vendors, and, most importantly, leave you as an anonymous resource. Let's talk about a few of these exploitation databases now.

A word of caution

Exploit databases are very interesting places to find code and exploits in software. That said, if you're interested in downloading or executing any of the code, please be aware that downloading and running code without careful review can be dangerous. Take caution and try to understand any code before running it, and if you do run it, please do so in an isolated environment. You never know what might be lurking in pieces of shellcode published by a malicious security researcher.

0day.today

0day.today is one of the more fascinating exploit databases around. Think of it like a marketplace of exploits, of which some are free, and some are paid. They cater to the research community by providing anonymous, validated zero-day exploits and, more importantly, a place to publicly share vulnerabilities, which is an important step to gaining a CVE in some circumstances:

Figure 5.7 – 0day.today exploit database homepage listing free and paid exploits

Validated researchers who contribute (or even sell) exploits to gain access to even more data about exploits and specialized access to events allowing you to connect with other researchers to talk about vulnerabilities. 0day.today hosts around 37,000 exploits as of writing this content.

ExploitDB

ExploitDB is probably the most popular exploit database. It was created in 1998 by HD Moore (the creator of the Metasploit framework) and is now maintained by Offensive Security:

Figure 5.8 – ExploitDB's homepage listing available exploits

The website contains a searchable database of exploits, as well as a collection of useful tools and resources for security professionals. If you find an exploit that you want to use, you can either download the raw exploit code or sometimes install it directly within the Metasploit framework.

Packet Storm

A common place where security researchers might submit code is the long-running site Packet Storm. Packet Storm acts as an archive of security research and tools. As such, they collect and archive tooling, exploit code, and security advisories. It is an excellent place to look for historical security research data. Researchers can publish exploit code and reference tools they've made through their easy, non-discriminatory submission process. This is what Packet Storm's exploit files look like:

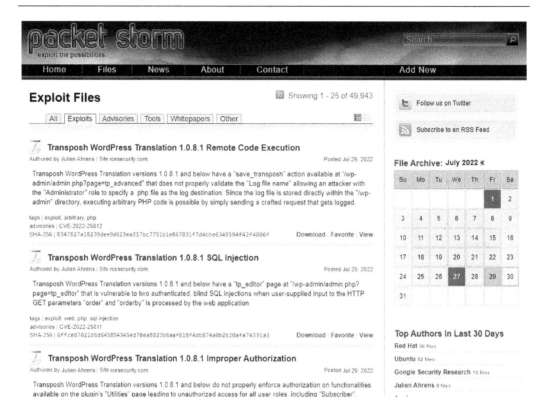

Figure 5.9 – Packet Storm's exploit files indexes thousands of historic vulnerabilities

Much like the CNA providers who open CVEs, each exploitation database has its own rules and guidelines on submissions. Before submitting anything to an exploit database, you should review those rules to avoid unnecessary confusion or resubmissions.

You should now have a good understanding of vulnerabilities that can be published to databases, who you can potentially work with to get your findings into databases, and finally, what exploit databases are and why they might be a good fit for your goals. With this understanding, let's now spend some time reviewing CVE publishing under a few examples of disclosure.

Practical vulnerability publishing examples

In the next section, we'll be doing a step-by-step review of the publishing process of two different types of CVE disclosures, one of which will focus on CVE disclosures with a CNA and another on a CNA-LR. For this example, we'll come up with a sample vulnerability. Let's say we're reporting a cross-site scripting vulnerability in software related to a small business e-commerce platform—we'll call it *Ecom-o-matic* for the sake of these examples. Let's get started with a CNA-sponsored CVE disclosure.

Note

Disclosure always *precedes* publishing, but in a lot of modern cases, if you've already begun the process of disclosure with a company that is a CNA, they may have you disclose your vulnerability via the CNA-defined process they disclose on the CVE website. Having this process handled by the company effectively folds disclosure and publishing into one big step. Some researchers have found that this is not always the case—sometimes the initial disclosure happens, and then any request for CVEs needs to be followed up with through the defined responsible CNA contact. Very large corporations may have separate teams responding to disclosures and requests for CVEs, so plan for variances and assume in every disclosure that CVEs need to be specifically requested.

A CNA-sponsored CVE

The first step you'll need to take is to consider if you need (or want) to use a CNA to disclose the vulnerability. Let's say, for our example, we reached out to the team managing Ecom-o-matic, and they shared with us that they belong to the parent company Logitech and that we'd need to work with Logitech to work on any security findings. With our initial disclosure out of the way, we'd want to determine if Logitech is listed as a company that is a CNA authority that can reserve and publish CVEs. We can do this by visiting www.cve.org/PartnerInformation/ListofPartners and searching for the company Logitech. In our case, we're in luck because Logitech is listed as a CNA. As a rule of thumb, if there's a direct CNA tied to the corporation which owns the software, we must use that CNA for our disclosure:

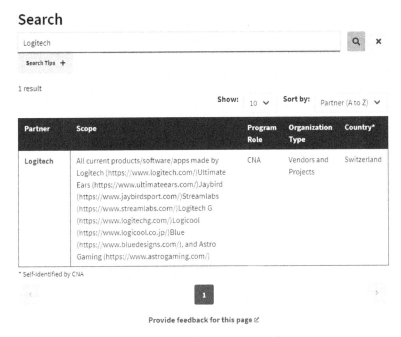

Figure 5.10 – CNA partner search

Now, if we click on the partner link, we can learn how the company Logitech would like to receive vulnerabilities from researchers. Usually, this includes a policy that will dictate how the vulnerability should be referenced, what products are in scope, and some type of contact form. In our case, we have the policy and the contact information, as shown in *Figure 5.11*:

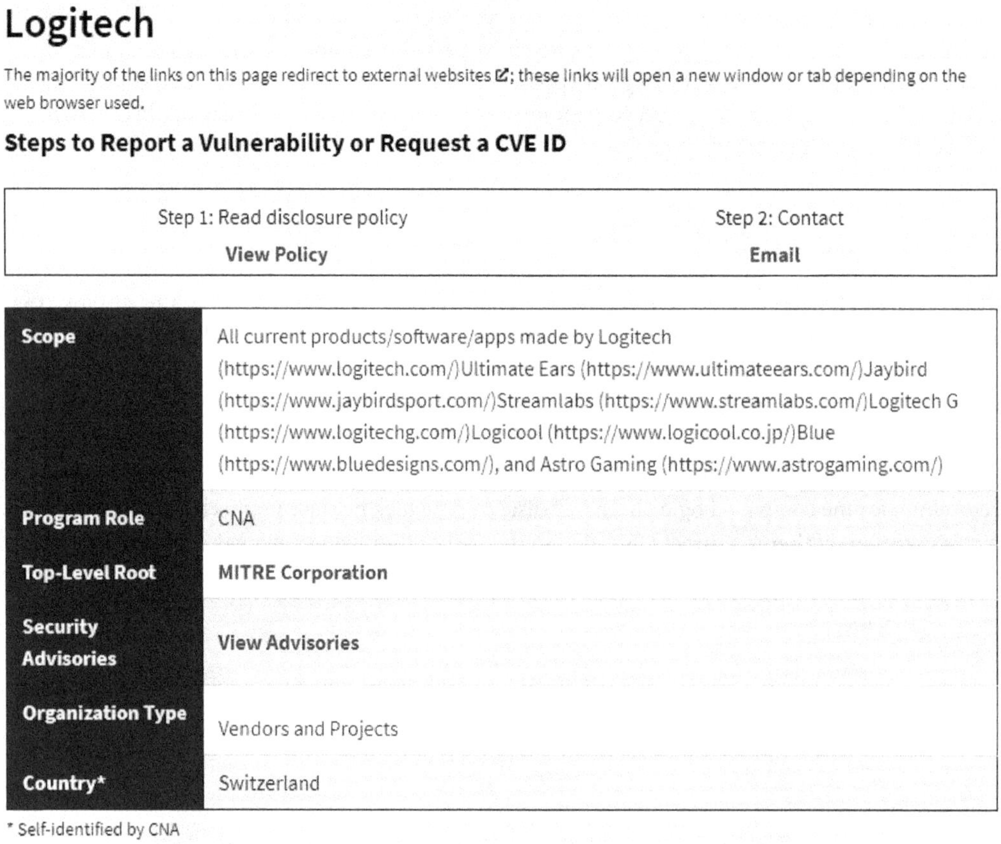

Logitech

The majority of the links on this page redirect to external websites 🗗; these links will open a new window or tab depending on the web browser used.

Steps to Report a Vulnerability or Request a CVE ID

Step 1: Read disclosure policy	Step 2: Contact
View Policy	**Email**

Scope	All current products/software/apps made by Logitech (https://www.logitech.com/)Ultimate Ears (https://www.ultimateears.com/)Jaybird (https://www.jaybirdsport.com/)Streamlabs (https://www.streamlabs.com/)Logitech G (https://www.logitechg.com/)Logicool (https://www.logicool.co.jp/)Blue (https://www.bluedesigns.com/), and Astro Gaming (https://www.astrogaming.com/)
Program Role	CNA
Top-Level Root	**MITRE Corporation**
Security Advisories	**View Advisories**
Organization Type	Vendors and Projects
Country*	Switzerland

* Self-identified by CNA

Figure 5.11 – CNA program details are listed for each CNA participant

If we click on the **View Policy** link in our case, we're directed to the policy, which happens to be hosted on the HackerOne platform. If you recall, HackerOne is a bug bounty platform that allows researchers to open security findings with an intermediate party that validates security research findings and can award money to researchers for reporting vulnerabilities, as seen in *Figure 5.12*:

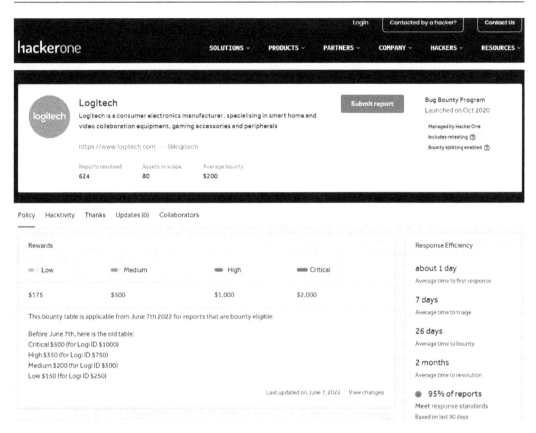

Figure 5.12 – CNA program policy links can take you anywhere,
including unexpected bug bounty program details

This is interesting for us. This likely means that we can share our findings through the HackerOne vulnerability platform. If our findings are valid, we can then collect a bounty for them. Logitech doesn't mention CVEs on this platform, but it's worth noting that HackerOne is a CNA as well, and as such, HackerOne can open CVEs on platforms with customers. It's unclear from the policy if this is how they handle software, and we'd really like a CVE to be opened. So, what might make the most sense to do next is set up an email to the contact listed in the CNA. In this email, we'll simply share that we found a vulnerability and would like to work with them to open a CVE and get advice on the next steps. For these scenarios, I advise using something like our initial disclosure—polite and short, maybe not sharing full details in the initial email. Here's how something like this might look:

Hello,

My name is {Name here}, and I recently discovered a security vulnerability in the application Ecom-o-matic. I contacted the EcomSolutions team directly to disclose this vulnerability, and they shared with me that their parent company handles all CVEs and vulnerability disclosures. I want to report this to you so that you can patch the issue before it is exploited by someone with malicious intent.

Details of the vulnerability:

Type: Cross Site Scripting

Related CWE: CWE-79

Version of software: 7.2.1

Feature where found: In the customer tab, in a text box labeled 'Comments'

I'd like to work with Logitech to open a CVE for this once it's been validated. I noticed on your disclosure form that your security policy directs to the HackerOne platform. Do you issue CVEs through the HackerOne platform for issues disclosed there, or is there another process involved with that? Once you provide the details on how to proceed, I'll be happy to provide detailed recreation instructions.

Thank you,

{{Name here}}

This cordial email should elicit a response, and usually, it's just a matter of waiting to hear back. If you don't receive an email from them, you could try again or attempt to submit the vulnerability via their HackerOne disclosure program. You should expect that each CNA program will have different policies and different requirements in disclosure. Sometimes they're short and sweet, while other times, they're much more involved.

So, what if our fictional software doesn't have a listed CNA? Well, we'll need to either open a CVE request through a CNA-LR or use an intermediate solution, as discussed in the previous section. Let's look at what that process looks like.

A CNA-LR-sponsored CVE

So, in this new scenario, let's say that our software isn't owned by a parent company, and during the disclosure process, we learn the company we're working with is the only company we'll be dealing with. If we go and look for a CNA for this company, we won't find one. That means we need to process vulnerabilities with a CNA-LR. We do this in two steps, first, the initial request for a CVE ID, and the second, a publication notification. Let's look at the first step now.

Requesting a CVE ID

CNA-LR options are great because they ensure you're working with MITRE or CISA directly and your vulnerability isn't being processed by another company that might have other motives or may reject or resell your research. To begin a CNA-LR request for a CVE, visit the following URL: `https://cveform.mitre.org`. You should be presented with a form as in *Figure 5.13*:

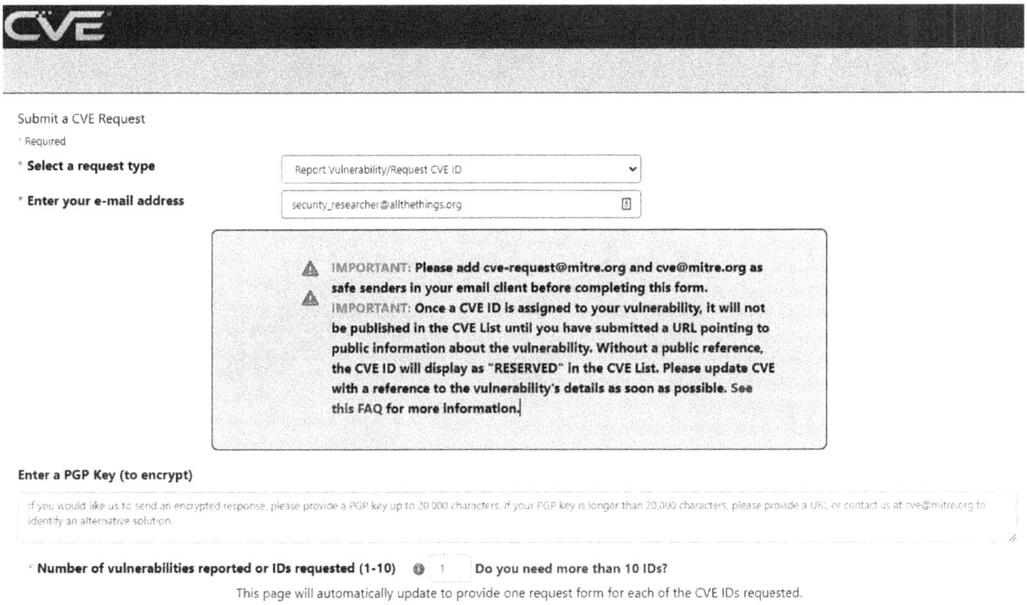

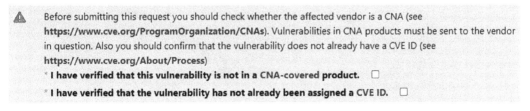

Submit a CVE Request

* Required

* **Select a request type**   Report Vulnerability/Request CVE ID ⌄

* **Enter your e-mail address**   security_researcher@allthethings.org

⚠ IMPORTANT: Please add cve-request@mitre.org and cve@mitre.org as safe senders in your email client before completing this form.

⚠ IMPORTANT: Once a CVE ID is assigned to your vulnerability, it will not be published in the CVE List until you have submitted a URL pointing to public information about the vulnerability. Without a public reference, the CVE ID will display as "RESERVED" in the CVE List. Please update CVE with a reference to the vulnerability's details as soon as possible. See this FAQ for more information.

Enter a PGP Key (to encrypt)

If you would like us to send an encrypted response, please provide a PGP key up to 20,000 characters. If your PGP key is longer than 20,000 characters, please provide a URL or contact us at cve@mitre.org to identify an alternative solution.

* **Number of vulnerabilities reported or IDs requested (1-10)** ⓘ 1   Do you need more than 10 IDs?

This page will automatically update to provide one request form for each of the CVE IDs requested.

Figure 5.13 – Start by selecting the request type, entering e-mail and optionally PGP keys for encryption

You'll need to submit your request type as **Report Vulnerability/Request CVE ID** and then submit your email address. Optionally, you can share a PGP key to encrypt your findings. Next, the form will ask you how many vulnerabilities you'd like to open. In our case, we'll just open one. Next, you'll be asked to agree that this is not a directly supported software product by a CNA and that there are no other CVE IDs open for the vulnerability. This is a great opportunity to go back and confirm that there is no CNA and that there are no published CVE vulnerabilities that you're aware of for the product you're reporting. Once you've confirmed both are true, we can begin filling out the vulnerability section, as depicted in *Figure 5.14*:

⚠ Before submitting this request you should check whether the affected vendor is a CNA (see **https://www.cve.org/ProgramOrganization/CNAs**). Vulnerabilities in CNA products must be sent to the vendor in question. Also you should confirm that the vulnerability does not already have a CVE ID (see **https://www.cve.org/About/Process**)

* **I have verified that this vulnerability is not in a CNA-covered product.** ☐

* **I have verified that the vulnerability has not already been assigned a CVE ID.** ☐

Figure 5.14 – Confirm that your vendor is not listed as a CNA and that it isn't already assigned a CVE ID

Next, we'll need to fill out the vulnerability type, the name of the vendor, and the version number:

Required

* **Vulnerability type** ⓘ

Cross Site Scripting (XSS)   ⌄

* **Vendor of the product(s)** ⓘ

ecommSolutions

Affected product(s)/code base ⓘ

* **Product**	* **Version**

7.2.1

Please enter the software versions affected. Please indicate a fixed version.

[-] Remove [+] Add

Figure 5.15 – Enter the type of vulnerability, the name of the
vendor, and the version number of the software

Our next section is optional; however, we advise that you fill this out so the CNA-LR has enough information to issue you a CVE number. This can also help improve the quality of vulnerability when it is eventually published. Here, you can define whether the vendor has confirmed the vulnerability, what the attack type is, what the impact is, and any affected components or vectors. Let's fill these out now to the best of our ability:

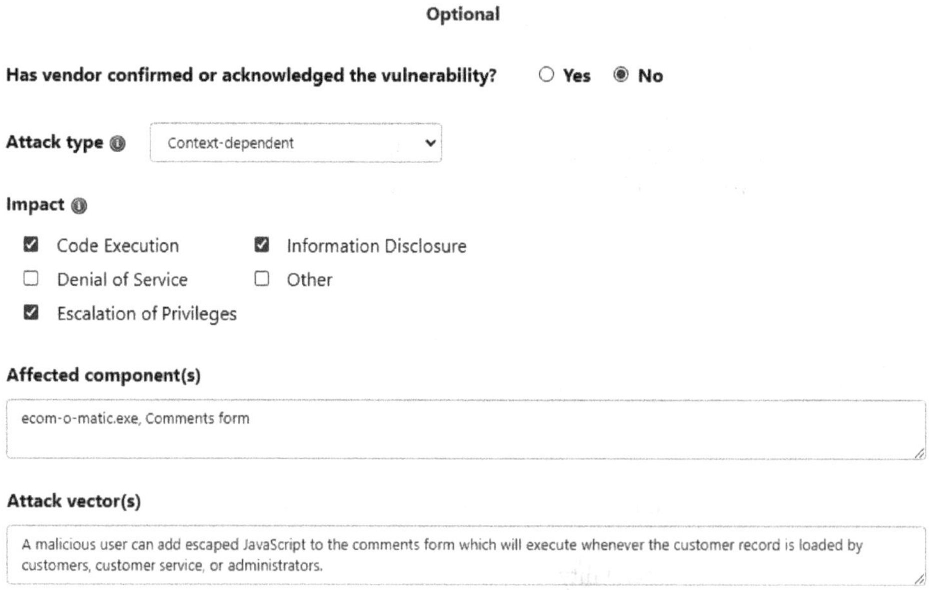

Optional

Has vendor confirmed or acknowledged the vulnerability?   ○ Yes   ◉ No

Attack type ⓘ   Context-dependent   ⌄

Impact ⓘ

☑ Code Execution   ☑ Information Disclosure
☐ Denial of Service   ☐ Other
☑ Escalation of Privileges

Affected component(s)

ecom-o-matic.exe, Comments form

Attack vector(s)

A malicious user can add escaped JavaScript to the comments form which will execute whenever the customer record is loaded by customers, customer service, or administrators.

Figure 5.16 – Define parameters related to whether the vendor acknowledged the
vulnerability, the attack type, impact, affected component, and attack vector

Next, we have the suggested description of the vulnerability for use in the CVE. This is one of the fields that usually trips people up, so let's spend some time talking about the format. There is a specific format MITRE is looking for here, and it's something all CNAs typically follow. If you spend some time looking through the formatting of past CVEs, you might pick up on the pattern. The pattern always includes the type of vulnerability, in which component it was found, the vendor, the name of the product, and the version. Additionally, information is also added, which clearly identifies how an attacker can do something malicious. MITRE provides a great template that contains this information:

- [VULNTYPE] in [COMPONENT] in [VENDOR] [PRODUCT] [VERSION] allows [ATTACKER] to [IMPACT] via [VECTOR].

Figure 5.17 – MITRE's suggested template for vulnerability descriptions

So, using the data we have so far, our vulnerability might look something like this:

XSS in the customer comments in EcomSolutions' Ecom-o-matic v 7.2.1 allows remote authenticated users to run arbitrary JavaScript by visiting the customer details page.

It doesn't need to be perfect; often, the CNA-LR will make changes where they see fit, but it's a good idea to get something close to what they're asking for to reduce friction where possible. For an excellent overview of the type of formatting and other examples, see this source for the preceding template and more examples: `http://cveproject.github.io/docs/content/key-details-phrasing.pdf`.

Our next field will be related to the discoverer or credits of this finding. If you'd like to be credited with the discovery, here's where you'd share that. The next piece of information you should share references to materials related to the software (in the form of URLs and links) and resources that are related to your findings if already published. Finally, there's a field you can submit that allows for any additional information you feel is important:

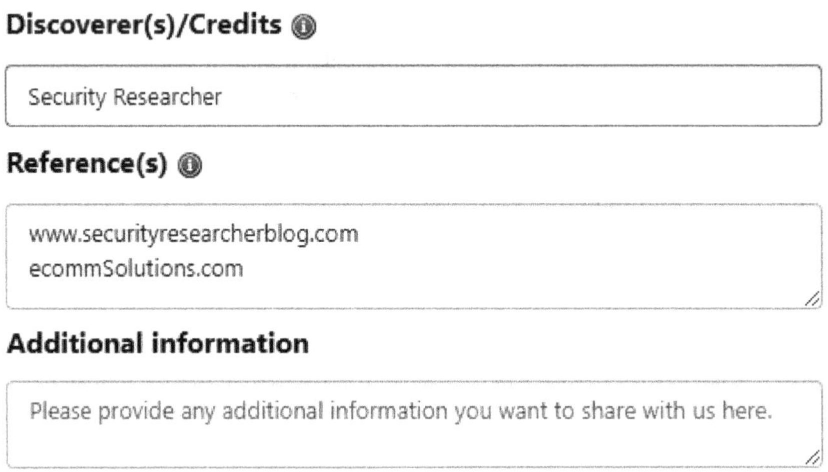

Discoverer(s)/Credits ⓘ

> Security Researcher

Reference(s) ⓘ

> www.securityresearcherblog.com
> ecommSolutions.com

Additional information

> Please provide any additional information you want to share with us here.

Figure 5.18 – Final fields include who should be credited, any references, and additional information

We suggest you take a moment to go back over what you just inserted into the record and double-check everything before submitting it to the CNA-LR. Once you feel you've got the best possible representation of your research, click **Submit Request**.

CVE number reservations are eventually distributed to researchers, the vulnerability request is rejected with comments, or additional information is requested. All these communications are shared over email. In most cases, it can take up to 8 weeks to hear back from a CNA-LR, but it's not unheard of to wait much longer. While we've covered it in this chapter and others, reserving a CVE number does not mean that your CVE is published; only once you have the number can you then submit another request to publish. Let's review the publication submission steps now.

Notify CVE about a publication

Once you've received your reservation via email, you can publish your vulnerability to the database, and to do that, you'll need to fill out a separate form at `cveform.mitre.org`.

Note about publishing

CVE publishing requires that something has been made public about the vulnerability and its subsequent details. Public means that it's been put somewhere on the internet where it can be referenced by the CNA-LR. In our case, this could be a simple post on a blog you run yourself where you share the details, a published submission of an exploit on PacketStorm, or a disclosure from a company's patch notes where the vulnerability was resolved. In any case, something needs to be public before this next step can be executed.

We'll start by selecting **Notify CVE about a publication**, filling out your email address, and optionally submitting a PGP key to encrypt your communications:

Figure 5.19 – Publishing requires a similar form to be filled out,
which requires your contact reason and request type

Once finished, you'll have just a few pieces of information to fill out. There is the **Link to the advisory** field, which would be either a blog post you've written about the vulnerability, a vendor disclosure, or a third-party publication on the vulnerability. You'll need to submit the reserved CVE IDs that were sent to you in the **CVE IDs of vulnerabilities to be published** field and any additional information about the disclosure and the date it was published:

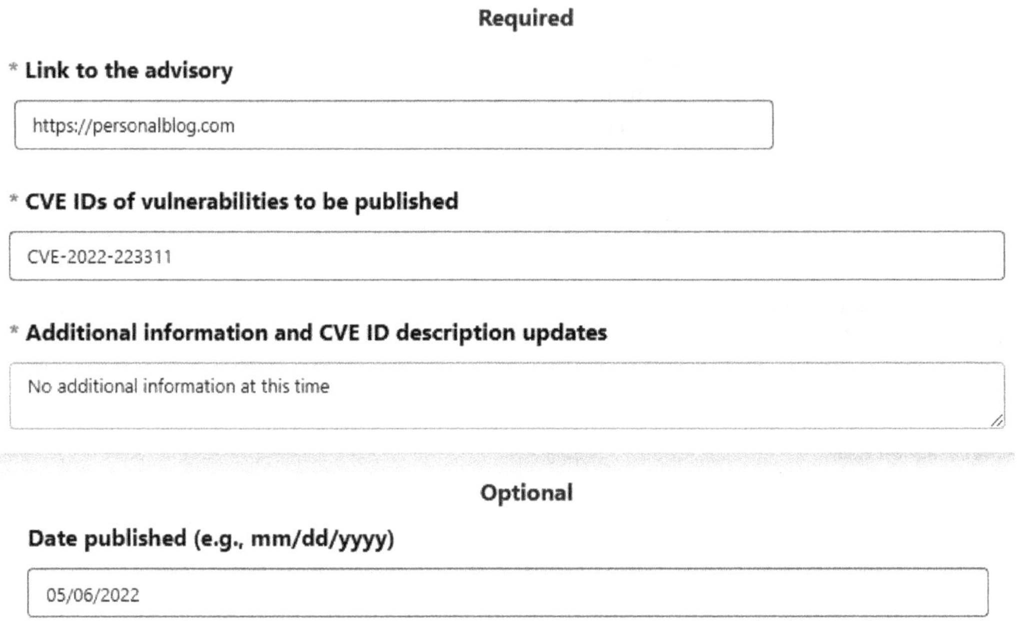

Required

* **Link to the advisory**

> https://personalblog.com

* **CVE IDs of vulnerabilities to be published**

> CVE-2022-223311

* **Additional information and CVE ID description updates**

> No additional information at this time

Optional

Date published (e.g., mm/dd/yyyy)

> 05/06/2022

Figure 5.20 – The publishing step requires less information, but you must have the
advisory (or publication information), the CVE ID, and any additional updates

Once complete, you can submit and will need to wait once again until you're notified by MITRE that your vulnerability was published. This can take a few days and usually happens much faster than the original reservation step. It's rare, but sometimes MITRE will ask for more information if the resources or advisory information does not meet their standards.

In the previous section, we talked a little bit about intermediate CNAs, which are vendors or people who run programs that can open CVEs. Let's briefly touch on that now.

CNA intermediate sponsored CVE

If working with a CNA-LR seems like work you'd like to avoid, you could explore a simpler submission process with a vendor such as Snyk, VulnDB, or other options that can offer monetary benefits such as the ZDI. Each of these programs has specific attributes that should be considered to see if they fit with your disclosure method. In our hypothetical example, let's think about the possible attributes our software might have:

- Is it an OSS: No

- Is it a software library: No

- Is it vendor-supported software: Yes

- Is the code hosted in the GitHub repository: No

- The approximate number of users: 2,000

So, in our case, it's not open source, a software library, or stored on GitHub, so that eliminates options such as huntr.dev and Snyk as they focus on OSS. As we have a low number of users at just 2,000, the ZDI might not be interested in our research. Our only option would seem to be VulnDB. We would need to then look up VulnDB and its unique submission guidelines. In this case, VulnDB has a simplified form requesting a title, summary, and a reference advisory:

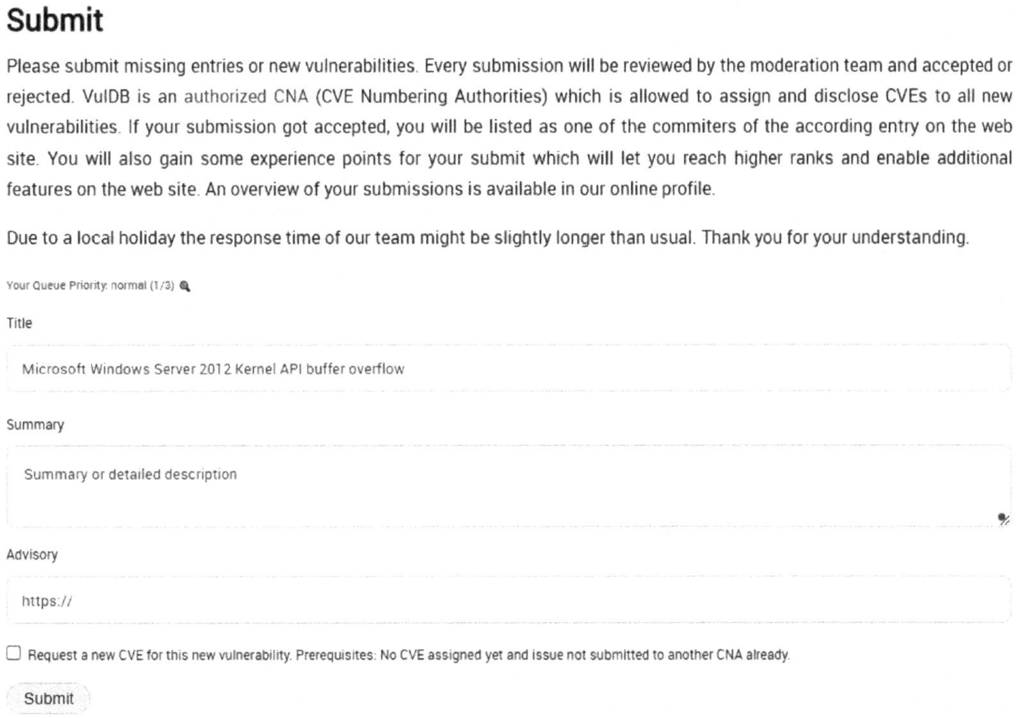

Submit

Please submit missing entries or new vulnerabilities. Every submission will be reviewed by the moderation team and accepted or rejected. VulDB is an authorized CNA (CVE Numbering Authorities) which is allowed to assign and disclose CVEs to all new vulnerabilities. If your submission got accepted, you will be listed as one of the commiters of the according entry on the web site. You will also gain some experience points for your submit which will let you reach higher ranks and enable additional features on the web site. An overview of your submissions is available in our online profile.

Due to a local holiday the response time of our team might be slightly longer than usual. Thank you for your understanding.

Your Queue Priority: normal (1/3) 🔍

Title

> Microsoft Windows Server 2012 Kernel API buffer overflow

Summary

> Summary or detailed description

Advisory

> https://

☐ Request a new CVE for this new vulnerability. Prerequisites: No CVE assigned yet and issue not submitted to another CNA already.

Submit

Figure 5.21 – VulnDB's vulnerability form is much smaller and
requires fewer details than using the MITRE CNA-LR

Submitting vulnerabilities to these products and programs ultimately does help these products enrich services that they, in turn, sell to customers. If that's something you're aware of and are OK with supporting, these programs might be right for your submission needs.

Closing this part of the chapter, you should have an excellent baseline knowledge of how to submit CVEs to CNAs, CNA intermediates, and should be CNA-LRs. Each has its own set of considerations to make, and which route you select may impact how much work and coordination you'll need to do.

Summary

In this chapter, we spent time developing our understanding of publishing vulnerabilities to databases. We explored the benefits of publishing vulnerabilities while contrasting that with historical publishing, which had a large impact on security research. We then discussed selecting the right vulnerability database, where we talked about CVE and CVE-adjacent publishers called CNAs. We discussed software that isn't eligible for publishing vulnerabilities and exploitation databases and their relationships with CVEs. Finally, we went over some practical examples of publishing vulnerabilities in three different ways. You now should have a good grasp of the process of publishing vulnerabilities. What if, though, during the publishing process, something goes wrong? Well, in the next chapter, we're going to talk about something we briefly mentioned in this chapter called vulnerability mediation, where we'll talk about how things can go wrong and who can help get your vulnerability disclosure and publishing back on track.

Further reading

- The BlueBorne whitepaper - `https://info.armis.com/rs/645-PDC-047/images/BlueBorne%20Technical%20White%20Paper_20171130.pdf`

- ISC Advisory on MiCODUS MV720 GPS Tracker - `https://www.cisa.gov/uscert/ics/advisories/icsa-22-200-01`

- VulnDB - `https://vuldb.com/`

- Snyk - `https://snyk.io/`

- Huntr.dev - `https://huntr.dev/`

- ZDI - `https://www.zerodayinitiative.com/`

- 0day.today - `https://0day.today/`

- ExploitDB - `https://www.exploit-db.com/`

- PacketStorm - `https://packetstormsecurity.com/`

- CNAs database - `https://www.cve.org/ProgramOrganization/CNAs`

- CVE request form - `https://cveform.mitre.org/`

- CVE description phrasing guidance - `http://cveproject.github.io/docs/content/key-details-phrasing.pdf`

- Assigning CVE IDs - `https://www.youtube.com/watch?v=JQYq-mxLo-U`

Vulnerability Mediation – When Things Go Wrong and Who Can Help

In the summer of 2021, German researcher Lilith Wittmann found herself entangled in a criminal investigation after disclosing security findings. The ruling political party of Germany at the time, the **Christian Democratic Union** (**CDU**), was using mobile applications to collect public opinion information for an upcoming election. With her organization, the **Chaos Computer Club** (**CCC**), Wittmann responsibly disclosed the vulnerability to the CDU, the Federal Office of Information Security, and the Berlin Data Protection Commissioner. Wittmann claimed that the vulnerability was so simple it was difficult to even call it a hack. The vulnerability exposed data on half a million German citizens and thousands of election workers. After the disclosure, the CDU initiated a criminal investigation of Wittmann and began reporting to the media that they were victims of data theft and were working with police to bring justice for this breach of privacy. Wittmann disclosed the fiasco on Twitter where she promptly received attention and resources from other researchers. Thankfully, Wittmann was never charged with a crime; once media outlets began reporting on the story, the charges were dropped by the CDU. Her organization released a notice stating that the CCC would no longer disclose security vulnerabilities to the CDU given their hostile response.

In this scenario, a relationship between a researcher and an entity quickly developed into criminal accusations, with the political party claiming sabotage of an upcoming election. While the CDU eventually apologized to the researcher, the damage had been done—security researchers told them they wouldn't release future vulnerabilities to the organization. As shown by this vulnerability disclosure, researchers disclosing vulnerabilities can quickly invite chaotic and hostile responses even when the researcher has the best of intentions.

In the previous two chapters, we learned about some basic guidelines on how to disclose and publish vulnerabilities. In this chapter, we'll talk more about mediating parties that can help you avoid unfortunate situations such as the one Wittmann ran into when disclosing a vulnerability. These resources can keep tensions low, and your name anonymous, and ultimately can help in legal scenarios.

In this chapter, you'll learn about the following:

- Mediation in disclosure
- The kinds of disputes that might arise during the disclosure process and which ones are a good fit for mediation
- Being equipped with resources and tools on suggested mediation organizations and how to choose the right one

These outcomes will be presented through the following main topics in this chapter:

- The basics of vulnerability mediation
- Resolving disputes through vulnerability mediation
- Mediator resources

The basics of vulnerability mediation

In our introduction, we learned about the vulnerability disclosure that Lilith Wittmann brought to a political organization. Unfortunately, while Wittmann took the correct route of communicating with the organization about the vulnerability, it's impossible to know how that organization perceived it. Miscommunication or misperception through online communication is one of the most common risks associated with your initial disclosures of any vulnerability. Language is expressed through words, body language, facial expressions, and even tone of voice. Because we can't see each other's facial expressions or body language, it's easy to misinterpret someone's tone or intentions. In addition, tensions can be exacerbated by differing native languages and cultural differences between both parties. All of these factors can contribute to a breakdown in communication and make it difficult to diffuse tense situations.

Therefore, if you find yourself working with a vendor who has previously been hostile, indignant, or is ignoring you, a mediating party who can help you disclose the vulnerability is beneficial. First, let's discuss precisely what vulnerability mediation is.

What is vulnerability mediation?

Vulnerability mediation extends the concept of coordinated vulnerability disclosure, focusing on an impartial third party representing a common interest. As we've discussed on the vulnerability life cycle in *Chapter 1, An Introduction to Vulnerabilities*, when a researcher finds a new vulnerability, they have a few options for what to do next. Often, researchers will work with the vendor to patch the issue and prevent exploitation. This process we introduced in *Chapter 4, Vulnerability Disclosure – Communicating Security Findings*, is called responsible disclosure, and it's generally considered the best practice when disclosing vulnerabilities. In most cases, a researcher will directly contact the vendor and work with them directly to resolve the issue, as in *Figure 6.1*:

Figure 6.1 – Direct disclosures are typically made between the researcher and the vendor

Vulnerability mediation is the process of resolving disputes that may arise during the disclosure of vulnerabilities with a third party during the vulnerability disclosure process. This third party usually works as a communicator, having both private and group conversations between the vendor and researcher, as depicted in *Figure 6.2*:

Figure 6.2 – Mediated disclosures take place with a broker that
manages communications and expectations

As introduced by the example of the vulnerability disclosure that opened this chapter, vendors are not always receptive to vulnerability disclosures. In these cases, mediation can normalize relations between the researcher and vendor, understand disagreements, and formulate a resolution plan.

Ultimately, mediation provides a structured way for parties to communicate and reach an agreement. In most mediator relationships, the researcher communicates with this impartial actor. In most cases, a mediator can help keep your name anonymous if you believe you'll be working with a hostile entity, help you diffuse hostile scenarios, and give you legal assistance if needed.

Types of mediators

The primary type of mediator is **organization-based mediators**, who are generally considered the best choice for getting help with disclosures. These organizations are typically run by volunteers, academics, and full-time employees who want to help improve software and hardware security. They often have relationships with companies willing to accept reports and can help protect the researcher's identity if needed. Additionally, these organizations often provide resources such as legal assistance if a company threatens legal action against the researcher.

While we've discussed bug bounty programs in the previous chapter, *Vulnerability Publishing – Getting Your Work Published in Databases*, they also can operate as mediators. Bug bounty programs are run by companies who want to improve their security posture by crowdsourcing vulnerability reports from the public. These programs typically have clear guidelines about what types of vulnerabilities they're looking for, how researchers should submit reports, and what rewards they can expect.

An uncommon source of mediators would be private individuals acting on behalf of a researcher. These mediators typically shield the researcher from any liability. These can comprise other researchers, lawyers, academics, and individuals who may or may not have experience in mediation.

Finally, most enterprises use legal staff in their mediation between one enterprise and another. Retaining legal services for most researchers is not affordable and, as such, is typically only used by larger vendors in dealing with disputes.

When to consider mediation services

There are many reasons why researchers might want to use a mediator when disclosing vulnerabilities. Not every relationship between vendors and researchers ends in hostility. Savvy researchers know that mediation helps protect researchers from various problematic disclosure liabilities. Researchers may use mediators to avoid going through proprietary vendor-specific vulnerability programs. These are not ideal for all researchers, and mediation can help researchers who want to avoid signing contracts or NDAs.

In other cases, working with a vendor might not be worth the researcher's time and effort. For example, it can be frustrating for researchers when companies don't have clear policies about vulnerability disclosure or ignore reports altogether. In these cases, going through a mediator can help get your report to the right people and increase the chances of getting a response by offloading a lot of the legwork to another party.

If these are not factors you'd usually consider, when to engage in mediation services can be difficult to ascertain. However, it's typically best to consider a third-party mediation service when tension between parties builds, and disputes about your research begin to form. Many different types of disputes might arise during the disclosure of vulnerabilities. Some of these common disputes include the following:

- Vendors refuse to action vulnerabilities for unclear or unstated reasons
- The disclosure represents multiple impacted vendors, with one vendor claiming the other won't action vulnerabilities
- Individuals disagree on how to fix or patch a vulnerability
- Vendors misrepresent the truth
- Vendors fail to meet timelines and promises of remediation
- Vendors don't communicate or stop communicating with researchers

As a researcher, inevitably, there will be a point where your research meets a scenario that seems difficult to navigate. If it does, consider initiating a coordinated disclosure with a mediator. Recentering the conversation about your research with an impartial party can help immensely. So, what are some of the common benefits that disclosure brings?

Benefits of vulnerability mediation

If you're unsure of whether you should embark on reaching out to a mediator, there are distinct advantages. While mediation is more lengthy than an immediate resolution, certain benefits outweigh the inconvenience and are often the prime reason some researchers only disclose with mediation help. Some of the benefits include the following:

- **Improved communication**: In many cases, a mediator can help improve communication between the researcher and the entity. This is helpful in situations where the entity is unresponsive or has a language barrier. For example, if an entity is not responding to a researcher's attempts to disclose a vulnerability, the researcher can contact a mediating party. The party can then reach out to the entity on the researcher's behalf and try to establish communication. If both parties are receptive, the mediator can help facilitate conversation and keep things cordial. A mediator can also help keep both parties calm and focused on resolving the issue. Escalating tensions can cause inflammatory language, and communication through a mediating party can prevent things from escalating.

- **Increased chances of getting paid**: In some cases, a mediator can help increase the chances of getting paid for your research. This is especially true with bug bounty programs and zero-day brokers who buy vulnerabilities, which they then disclose to vendors.

- **Protection from legal action**: Mediators can help protect researchers from legal action. This is particularly helpful when working with companies that might threaten legal action against researchers who disclose vulnerabilities without permission. This protection can include anonymity for the researcher and invoking legal services where necessary.

- **Brand recognition**: You, as a researcher, might not have an established name in the security research community and, therefore, have little brand recognition for the company you're contacting. Using a mediation service will help legitimize your research since mediators often validate research before disclosing it and often use names commonly associated with security research work. For example, Carnegie Mellon offers programs that offer instant name recognition and increased authority to your reporting. This can help add credibility, build healthy amounts of pressure, and create a dedicated focus on fixing vulnerabilities.

- **Objectivity**: Mediators can provide an objective third-party perspective on a situation. For example, if you're unsure whether to publicly release information about a vulnerability, a mediator can help you weigh the risks and benefits of doing so.

> **Note**
>
> With all these benefits in mind, please note that when working with mediators, the expectation is that you will allow them to lead the process and instruct you on what to do and when to do it. Acting outside of the guidance provided by the mediator is strongly discouraged and can cause even deeper divides in any vendor relationship.

Now that we understand what vulnerability mediation is, when to engage a mediator, and its key benefits, let's discuss the primary process and show a practical example of a mediation system in action.

Resolving disputes through vulnerability mediation

Resolving disputes through mediation is relatively simple once you've located and initiated contact with a mediator. Let's briefly review the primary process and steps vulnerability mediation takes.

The vulnerability mediation process

The process of vulnerability mediation can vary depending on the specific dispute. However, there are generally three basic steps involved in mediation:

1. One of the involved parties in the dispute initiates contact with a mediator, and the researcher typically starts this. The mediator can agree to or reject involvement in the disclosure at this point.

2. Once the mediator has agreed to take the disclosure case, the mediator collects contact information for the target organization. The mediator will often review and validate claims made by the researcher during this time as well. With their contacts and validated information, they then begin the communication process, reaching out to either party to discuss timelines and set expectations around resolution.

3. The mediator helps the parties reach an agreement on resolving the dispute. The mediator then monitors the progress of the resolution and concludes their involvement once they see all potential issues resolved or resolved to the best of their abilities.

Mediators will vary in their sophistication depending on who you ask for help. With that said, as there is a need for quality mediation, better systems have emerged to help meet this need. One excellent example is the **Vulnerability Information and Coordination Environment** (**VINCE**), provided by **The Computer Emergency Response Team Coordination Center** (**CERT/CC**).

We like VINCE because it has a lot of great features. Think of VINCE as a private email and calendar system that helps organize information related to vulnerability disclosures. As with most vulnerability reporting systems, VINCE requires a researcher to develop a disclosure report first so that they can get up to speed on the impacted systems (see *Figure 6.3* for example). During this disclosure VINCE's system allows the researcher to stay anonymous to the vendor, and VINCE will not publish or share your information as you step through its process:

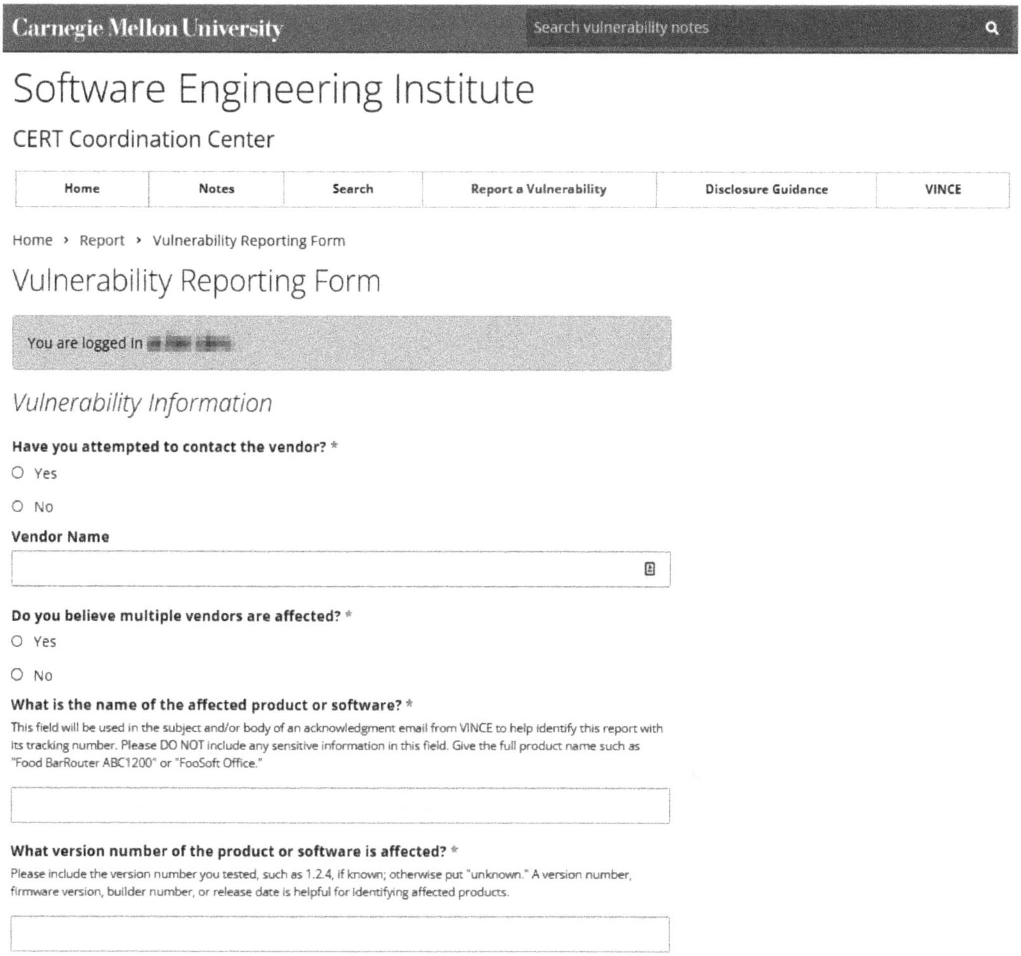

Figure 6.3 – The initial submission form for VINCE

After submitting the initial vulnerability information, the data gets assigned an ID and a representative from CERT/CC who will drive the process. Once you have assigned resources in the VINCE system, you'll receive communications from CERT/CC, who will ask for additional information. Typically, these are details about the vulnerability, contact information for the company, and anything else they might need, as shown in *Figure 6.4*:

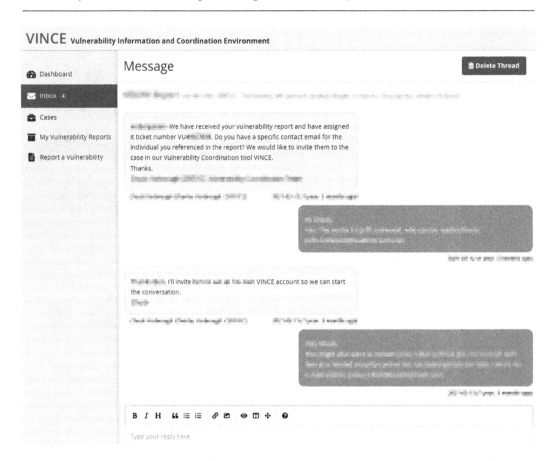

Figure 6.4 – Communication portal in VINCE where you can have private discussions with CERT/CC

Once the mediators have begun talking with the vendor, they help set realistic timelines and offer tested and effective messaging to define the parameters for expectations on closing the vulnerability. Vendors, mediators, and researchers collaborate in a message thread with an expected disclosure date. Depending on the severity of the vulnerability, CERT/CC may decide to publish vulnerability disclosures themselves or leave that to the discretion of the researcher given the dates provided. All the information is displayed on the VINCE dashboard for your convenience, as shown in *Figure 6.5*:

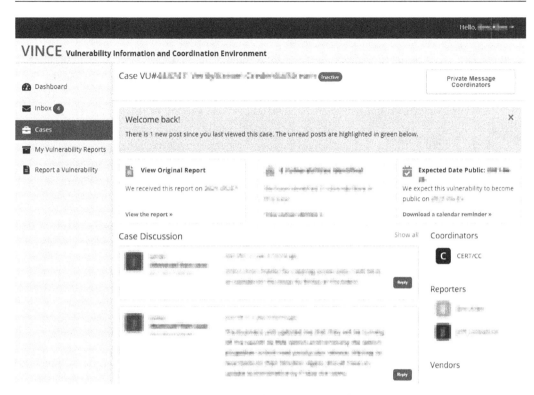

Figure 6.5 – VINCE has a comprehensive dashboard with all information relevant to the case

The cases available to you in VINCE are all prefixed with a **VU** number, and VINCE conveniently keeps the communication, documents, and parties involved all in one place. Once CERT/CC has completed mediation between the parties, the report is closed and saved in your dashboard for later review.

Most mediation resources are not this comprehensive or organized since most operate over email. Although your specific needs for mediation call for the work of CERT/CC, we strongly suggest you utilize the VINCE system.

Now that we understand how disclosure works and have reviewed this process with the CERT/CC resource VINCE, let's talk through other resources we can use if we're looking for specific help in mediation.

Mediator resources

Unfortunately, when it comes to resources available to the public, there isn't a comprehensive collection of resources related to mediation. However, there are three major mediating organizations you should consider researching first. These are considered part of a **Computer Emergency Response Team** or **CERT**. CERTs are primarily popular in the United States but can be found in other parts of the world. With that said, even if you are in a country outside of the United States, if there are components in your research serviced in the United States, using one of these three resources is likely the best avenue through which to seek help. Let's discuss the three most notable organizations now.

> **Note**
>
> CERT is an acronym used by various governmental organizations, such as the Community Emergency Response Team and the Correctional Emergency Response Team. These are often confused with one another, as they both deal with emergencies and teams.

The CERT/CC

The **CERT/CC** is a center that helps to coordinate the response to computer security incidents. The CERT is a part of Carnegie Mellon University's **Software Engineering Institute** (**SEI**). The SEI works with the US Department of Defense and other government agencies. The CERT/CC is one of seven divisions within the SEI.

The CERT program began in November 1988 in response to the Morris worm incident. This worm caused significant damage to computer systems across the internet. CERT/CC was created to help coordinate the response to future incidents and to provide information about security risks.

Since its inception, the CERT/CC has responded to thousands of incidents. These have ranged from small-scale denial-of-service attacks to large-scale worms such as Code Red and Nimda. The CERT/CC has also worked with law enforcement agencies on several investigations.

In addition to responding to incidents, the CERT/CC works on several proactive projects. These include developing security metrics, researching new attack techniques, and working with vendors to improve the security of their products.

The CERT/CC is part of the more considerable effort to improve computer security. Other organizations, such as the **US Computer Emergency Readiness Team** (**US-CERT**) and the **UK National Cyber Security Centre** (**NCSC**), play essential roles in this effort and are inspired mainly by CERT/CC.

As discussed in our previous section on *Resolving disputes through vulnerability mediation*, the best resource for tapping into the CERT/CC mediation program is VINCE. This service will work for most disputes and provides the easiest way to collaborate with the mediators at CERT and a problematic vendor. Here are the links you can use:

- **VINCE**: `https://www.kb.cert.org/vince/`
- **The CERT/CC**: `https://www.kb.cert.org/vuls/`

The US-CERT

The US-CERT is a team that coordinates the response to computer security incidents in the United States. They also provide guidance on best practices for disclosure. The US-CERT is part of the Department of Homeland Security and began operations in 2003 in response to the 9/11 terrorist attacks on the United States. Since its inception, the organization has increased its focus on cybersecurity. The US-CERT mission is to secure the nation's cyber infrastructure by working with partners to prevent, detect, and respond to cyber threats while protecting the citizens of the United States and the world. To carry out its mission, the US-CERT focuses on the following objectives:

- Collecting and analyzing information about cybersecurity threats and vulnerabilities
- Sharing information with partners about cybersecurity threats and vulnerabilities
- Developing and disseminating cybersecurity guidance
- Coordinating the response to computer security incidents
- Providing incident handling assistance to victims of computer security incidents

The US-CERT also operates the National Cyber Awareness System, a platform for sharing cybersecurity information with the public. The National Cyber Awareness System includes a website, email subscription service, and social media accounts, all of which can be used to inform the public about vulnerabilities. In addition, the US-CERT works with many partners in the public and private sectors, including the following:

- Federal, state, local, and tribal governments
- Law enforcement agencies
- The intelligence community
- Critical infrastructure owners and operators
- The research community
- The software development community
- Internet service providers
- Vendors of cybersecurity products and services

The US-CERT aims to improve the nation's cybersecurity posture by working with these partners to prevent, detect, and respond to cyber threats. In the case of vulnerability disclosure, the US-CERT works directly with product vendors to coordinate the disclosure of vulnerabilities. This includes working with vendors to develop patches or alternative solutions. The US-CERT also disseminates information about vulnerabilities and threats through its public website, mailing lists, and social media accounts. As a result, the US-CERT is an excellent partner that can help mediate security vulnerability disclosures or, at the very least, connect you to resources best suited to your specific needs. Here is the link you can use:

- **The US-CERT**: `https://www.cisa.gov/uscert/`

The Industrial Control Systems Cyber Emergency Response Team (ICS-CERT)

The **ICS-CERT** is a division of the US Department of Homeland Security. The ICS-CERT's mission is to reduce risks within the industrial control systems environment. One way that the ICS-CERT accomplishes this mission is by working with vendors and researchers to coordinate the disclosure of vulnerabilities in industrial control system products and components.

When a security flaw is discovered in an industrial control system product or component, the ICS-CERT works with the vendor or researcher to coordinate the disclosure of the vulnerability. This coordination includes developing a plan for how and when the information about the vulnerability will be made public. The goal is to provide users and organizations enough time to patch or mitigate the vulnerability before attackers can exploit it.

The ICS-CERT also guides users and organizations on how to handle vulnerabilities. This guidance includes information on what to do if you believe your organization has been targeted by an attacker and tips for protecting against future attacks.

Suppose you are a vendor or researcher who has discovered a security flaw in an industrial control system product or component. In that case, you can contact the ICS-CERT to coordinate the disclosure of the vulnerability. Here is the link you can use:

- **The ICS-CERT**: `https://www.cisa.gov/ics`

Other CERT organizations

There are many different mediation organizations available to researchers. CERT programs are available globally, and over 75 member organizations are in different countries. One of the best ways to look up your country to see whether there is a participating CERT program is through the **Forum of Incident Response and Security Teams (FIRST)** team directory, as shown in *Figure 6.6*:

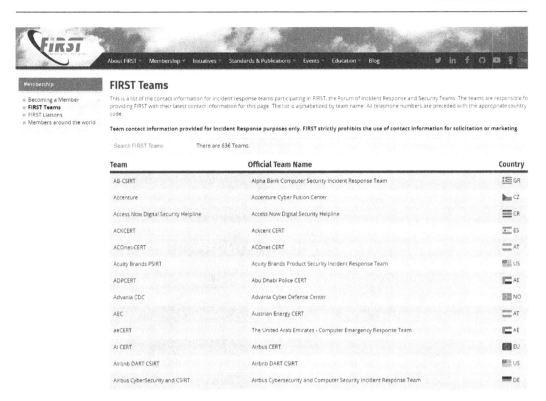

Figure 6.6 – The FIRST team directory can help you find other CERTs

While FIRST is a great organization to turn to, it will not handle vulnerability disclosures. *A FIRST team is not necessarily a CERT, but CERTs are usually FIRST teams.* Keep that in mind as you review their team directory; CERTs will usually be delineated with the acronym *CERT*. Here is the link you can use:

- FIRST team directory: `https://www.first.org/members/teams/`

Bug bounty programs

Bug bounty programs were discussed in our chapter regarding the disclosure process, *Chapter 4, Vulnerability Disclosure – Communicating Security Findings*. Typically, the programs operate as a mediation service, another possibility when seeking mediation resources.

While most bug bounty providers operate under a model where bounties are paid out for specific scopes, there are alternatives. For example, the Open Bug Bounty platform follows the ISO standards on coordinated ethical disclosure and allows researchers to submit bugs about websites that do not participate in the program; see *Figure 6.7* for their statics and compliance statements. While excellent, the Open Bug Bounty program is limited in scope and only allows for reports on specific classes of vulnerabilities on web applications:

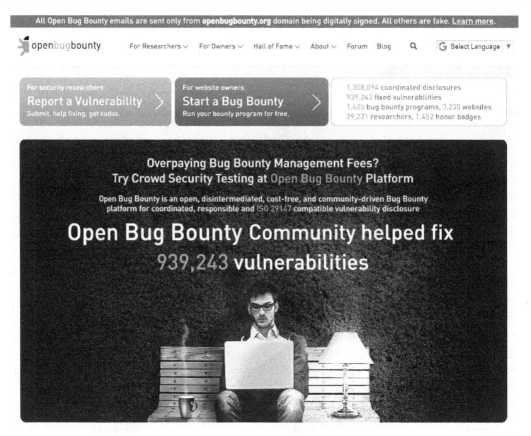

Figure 6.7 – OpenBugBounty is ISO 29147-compliant, a unique feature for a bounty program

Here is the link you can use:

- Open Bug Bounty: `https://www.openbugbounty.org/`

Legal support

Disclosing vulnerabilities can trigger litigation, and researchers risk legal trouble. When legal risks begin to form, security researchers often turn to the **Electronic Frontier Foundation** (**EFF**) for support. The EFF is a nonprofit organization that fights for civil liberties online, with a focus on protecting the rights of hackers and security researchers.

The EFF has helped many hackers who have been threatened with legal action for disclosing vulnerabilities. In many cases, the EFF has represented hackers who found a security flaw in software programs. The software company threatened to publicly sue the hacker if they disclosed the flaw.

The EFF intervened and helped negotiate a resolution that allowed the hacker to disclose the vulnerability without fear of legal retaliation. The EFF is committed to protecting hackers who engage in vulnerability disclosure. By doing so, they help make the world a safer place for everyone. Here is the link you can use:

- The EFF: `https://www.eff.org/`

Other mediation options

Mediators do not always come in the form of official organizations. There aren't any rules that stipulate who can be a mediator. For example, researchers can use the following if they are otherwise unable to use an organizational resource:

- A lawyer who is familiar with cybersecurity and information law

- A professor or researcher specializing in cybersecurity or information security

- An ethical hacker or security consultant who has experience with vulnerability disclosures

- Any other neutral third party you feel could help facilitate communication and understanding between both parties involved in the disclosure process

It's important to note that anyone can mediate, regardless of background or experience. However, do note that using mediators with no experience may cause the mediation to be more elongated and troublesome than when using an experienced mediator. The key is finding someone you trust and feel comfortable with to guide you through the process. Clearly understand your objectives and what you want and need out of a mediator and engage with an organization or person that represents your interests and goals.

To close the topic of mediation resources, you should now recognize the key mediating organizations used by researchers and how to find international organizations and other ancillary resources.

Summary

Disputes during disclosure can be challenging to resolve. However, mediation can be a helpful tool for resolving these disputes. Mediation can help improve communication between parties, prevent future disputes, and build trust between parties. Many different organizations can help if things go wrong during disclosure. When choosing a mediation organization, it is essential to consider the specific dispute that needs to be resolved, the parties involved in the dispute, the location, and the mediation's cost. Acting quickly is essential but choosing the proper method of acting is also important. The best way to act will depend on the specific dispute and the parties involved.

Using mediation is considered one of the best disclosure practices. In our next chapter, we'll review one final avenue of last resort, often perceived as one of the worst practices in disclosure – self-publishing complete disclosures.

7
Independent Vulnerability Publishing

Within hours of publishing his research titled *Many of Talkspace's Clients Susceptible to Fraud* on his private blog, Jackson Jackson received a letter from Talkspace. Talkspace's legal council informed him that he would face legal consequences if he didn't remove the post about their company on his website. Jackson complied with Talkspace's request but went to the media with his story. TechCrunch picked up the story, where Jackson was described as a security researcher who had discovered that he could use company coupon codes to sign up for and use Talkspace for free by searching for specific terms on Google-indexed websites. He then shared that he could sign up for Talkspace using promo codes that belonged to other companies who had paid for the service. Zack Whittaker, the reporter who published the story with TechCrunch, framed the legal notices as the latest in a string of examples of researchers being threatened by large tech companies.

While it is very accurate that security researchers (and even members of the press) are increasingly seeing legal threats against their disclosure of security research, is the outrage in Jackson's case warranted? In Talkspace's letter to Jackson, they shared that they took issue with specifically worded issues in the blog post regarding Talkspace's clients being robbed. Associating Talkspace's clients with robbery and fraudulent actions did not sit right with Talkspace, and they sent Jackson a cease-and-desist notice.

Security researchers are a lot like the press because they share details about their findings and report them to the public. But, unlike the press, some researchers find their voice vis-a-vis passionate blog posts and sometimes speculative statements about their research. In addition, security researchers often work from a place of limited perspective as an outsider looking in, which causes many security researchers to fill their knowledge gaps with assumptions and hypotheses.

When the communication process breaks down with vendors, researchers may find themselves looking for alternative methods for sharing their research with the community. That's where independent vulnerability publishing comes in and is often used when the vendor and the researcher cannot reach a consensus or if mediation between the two parties has failed.

Wrapping up our section of chapters that have covered vulnerability research, disclosure, publishing, and mediation, we'll close with a discussion on **independent vulnerability publishing**. You may recall we discussed vulnerability publishing related to independent disclosure in *Chapter 4, Vulnerability Disclosure – Communicating Security Findings*, and *Chapter 5, Vulnerability Publishing – Getting Your Work Published in Databases*. However, we wanted to take some extra time to discuss independent publishing since its presence has been and will continue to be a vital tool researchers can use to disclose findings to the public when vendors will not. Additionally, we'll continue our review of Jackson's dispute and research disclosure with Talkspace and discuss how it likely fell under one of the six risks you should avoid to prevent legal action being taken against you. Finally, we'll share a checklist that distills this chapter's advice into an easy-to-follow set of bullet points.

In this chapter, we're going to discuss the following items:

- Independent publishing for vulnerabilities and inherent risks

- How to best represent yourself and ways you can help prevent being on the receiving end of a legal notice

- The six scenarios that researchers need to avoid in independent publishing

- How to independently publish a disclosure

These outcomes will be presented through the following main topics in this chapter:

- Independent disclosures and their place in the vulnerability life cycle

- The benefits of independent publishing

- The risks of independent publishing

- How to independently publish while avoiding risks

> **Note**
>
> Before we begin this chapter, let's be clear about something. It is not the advice of this author or the publisher that you should take any actions to publish a vulnerability disclosure on your own. When deciding whether you should disclose a vulnerability, have an honest conversation with yourself about your goals. What are you trying to accomplish with this disclosure? Have you exhausted the possibilities through mediation or working with a publisher who will assume the risk on your behalf? Take care and much caution when considering whether there might be better ways to accomplish what you want without disclosing this vulnerability yourself. We will explore exactly how to do this while minimizing any risks you may encounter, but even with those risks minimized, there are inherently still risks at play that you alone will assume if you accept these risks and publish a vulnerability disclosure independently. Consider this warning seriously before you act.

Independent disclosures and their place in a vulnerability life cycle

In traditional full disclosure, once a researcher discovers a new bug, they report it to the company or organization responsible for the software in question. The company or organization then assesses the bug to determine whether it's a valid security issue and if so, they work on developing a fix. Once the fix is ready, they coordinate with the researcher to release it publicly, along with an announcement detailing the issue and how to mitigate it.

This process works well when all parties involved are cooperative and transparent. Unfortunately, not everyone, especially from the vendor side, meets those basic tenets of having a functional, intact, rational vulnerability disclosure program. Sometimes companies will sit on vulnerabilities for months or even years without patching them. In some cases, this is due to a lack of resources on the company's part. But in others, it's because the company doesn't want to acknowledge that its software has a security flaw. To combat this, as a researcher, you could initiate a mediation with the company you have grievances toward, as described in *Chapter 6, Vulnerability Mediation – When Things Go Wrong and Who Can Help*. However, what if the company doesn't come to the negotiation table? Maybe they do, and the mediation fails, and neither party is satisfied with the outcome. If this happens to you, independent disclosure might be the last step in your series of actions to notify the public.

An interesting element that may drive researchers to independent publishing is that some vendors might not accept vulnerability disclosures without first entering a legal agreement with the researcher. An excellent example of such a case is when the security vendor modzero disclosed minor issues found inside CrowdStrike's Falcon **endpoint detection and response (EDR)** agent on August 8, 2022. CrowdStrike's Falcon agent is like advanced anti-virus software that monitors events and halts malicious activity. To be effective, though, the agent must be installed on the computer so it can monitor the system. In the disclosure by the security researchers, they found that they could uninstall the software in a way that allowed a researcher to bypass the security protections meant to stop the software from being removed. When Modzero disclosed the vulnerability, they were directed to use the HackerOne platform to disclose vulnerabilities. As discussed in *Chapter 4*, bug bounty programs often have terms of service and conditions. Modzero found the terms unacceptable (especially under a **non-disclosure agreement (NDA)**) and wanted to disclose the vulnerability directly to CrowdStrike. After several back-and-forth discussions over almost 3 months, Modzero released its exploit code on its blog because CrowdStrike was unwilling to accept the security findings without Modzero signing an NDA.

As a security researcher, it's essential to remember that if you're sharing your research and the disclosure process is uncomfortable or unreasonable, you should share it with the community. If the consensus is that the practices are so bad that it causes outrage in the research community, the vendor might change its policies and improve research outcomes. After Modzero published its report, several other researchers' stories came to light about their bad experiences, and ultimately, CrowdStrike began fixing the vulnerability (even though it claimed no responsibility) and promised it would take an introspective look at these policies. Sadly, when vendors create challenging scenarios like these, it erodes trust in them as cooperative parties in future disclosures.

In response to these practices, some researchers have started independently publishing their findings, much as Modzero did. In short, this means that the researcher writes a report detailing the issue and publishes it online. Unfortunately, this is usually done after many months have passed since the original disclosure and the vendor has failed to respond.

In these independently published vulnerability disclosures, researchers might release **proof-of-concept** (**PoC**) code or exploit steps so that others can replicate the issue. However, if the vulnerability is at high risk of harming the user or operating environment, the researcher may only state that the vulnerability is present or show end-exploitation states. Overall, the goal is to put pressure on the company by making it clear that the vulnerability exists and that it's only a matter of time before someone with malicious intent finds and exploits it.

With all this said, it's essential to understand that independent disclosure shouldn't involve finding a vulnerability and publishing said vulnerability. Instead, it would be best if you attempted to first work with the company, informing them of the problem. If a coordinated disclosure is impossible, the company has stopped cooperating, or worse, mediation with a third party failed, then it's overdue for public disclosure. In addition, most **computer emergency response teams** (**CERTs**) recommend that vendors should be given a 45-90 day window of time to respond and resolve the vulnerability.

Overall, independent publishing can be a powerful tool to prompt vendors to patch vulnerabilities. However, it also comes with its share of risks. These risks might include criminal and civil liabilities, which can cause governments to prosecute you or where vendors attempt to sue you. We'll discuss these risks in more detail later, in the *Risks of independent publishing* section. But first, let's look at the benefits of independently publishing your findings.

The benefits of independent publishing

One of the key benefits of independent publishing is that it pressures the company to act. For example, if a researcher publishes a report on a severe security issue and the company does nothing, it reflects poorly on them. As a result, customers may take their business elsewhere, and other researchers may be less inclined to work with the company in the future. Vendors know that, and it prompts them to act. While the security community has long suspected that publishing vulnerabilities like this can cause better vulnerability responses, it was studied in the 2010 research paper titled *An Empirical Analysis of Software Vendor's Patch Release Behavior: Impact of Vulnerability Disclosure*. According to the research and analysis conducted by Ashish Arora, Ramayya Krishnan, Rahul Telang, and Yubao Yang of Carnegie Mellon University, vulnerabilities were patched much faster. They found that vendors were two and a half times more likely to patch the software, and on average, disclosures caused patching to occur 35 days earlier than if it wasn't disclosed to the public.

In addition to these benefits, independent publishing also allows researchers to control the timing and narrative of the process. For example, as we discussed in *Chapter 4*, it may be prudent to give the company time to patch the issue before publishing anything. But in other scenarios, getting the information out as quickly as possible may be more critical so that users can protect themselves. With independent publishing, you can do what you feel is best based on your information.

It's not uncommon to hear stories from researchers where a vendor downplayed the severity of their reported findings, undercutting valuable research or not giving them credit for their work outright. When researchers independently publish, they can choose what to include in their reports and how much detail to include. Independent publishing can also allow you to decide whether you'll use your full name or a pseudonym if you publish a demo to show how alarming your discovery is and what the impact is, and even share exploit code if you wish. But if you independently publish your disclosure, you can ensure that people know the issue and have all the information they need to understand and mitigate it.

Finally, independent publishing allows you to establish yourself as a credible security researcher. Provided your research is accurate, thoughtful, and follows generally observed best practices, it can be beneficial if you're hoping to break into the information security field. With that said, watching what you publish in your disclosures is essential. Let's now review some of the risks involved in independently publishing your research.

Risks of independent publishing

Independent publishing of vulnerabilities can be a great way to bring attention to your findings and ensure that people are aware of the risks. But it's important to weigh the risks and benefits before deciding.

Researchers can face a range of legal consequences related to independently publishing research. For example, if you release PoC code or exploit steps along with your publication in the United States, you could violate copyright law or the **Computer Fraud and Abuse Act (CFAA)**. Software code, for example, is covered by copyright law. As a result, you may be sued for copyright infringement if you publish a vendor's code as part of your PoC without permission.

In contrast, the CFAA also prohibits unauthorized access to computer systems. It's often used to prosecute hackers who break into systems or steal data. But it has also been applied to researchers who release PoC code or exploit steps. That's because releasing this information could be seen as aiding and abetting someone else to hack a system.

Committing crimes isn't the only thing you need to worry about in independent publishing. For example, simply writing about companies in a negative way (if not done correctly) can trigger viable legal threats against you through defamation lawsuits in civil cases.

In addition to the legal risks, independently publishing research can damage your reputation if it isn't done in line with the best practices. For example, suppose you disclose a vulnerability well before it's been patched, and there was no forewarning. In that case, you could be accused of putting users at risk—or even be liable for damages associated with your disclosure. Another possible risk is publishing sensitive information, such as working PoC code, which exposes identifiable information about the vendor's customers, and you could be accused of irresponsibly disclosing the issue.

That said, independent publishing can be a powerful tool for researchers who want to ensure that their findings see the light of day. Moreover, when used responsibly, it can help to hold companies accountable and protect users from serious security risks.

We should note that while some of these risks sound daunting and potentially dangerous to the well-being of a researcher, legal consequences are often few and far between. We liken it to the dangers of operating a motor vehicle. Yes, it can be scary, and bad things can happen; however, if you're well-prepared and safely operate the vehicle, risks are significantly reduced. Therefore, the most important thing you can do as a researcher is to be aware of the risks and avoid them as much as possible.

With these risks in mind, let's take some time to discuss how you avoid these risks and how to independently publish a vulnerability while avoiding six of the most common risks researchers face when disclosing a vulnerability independently.

How to independently publish while avoiding risks

When a researcher begins their first vulnerability disclosure through self-publishing, it's not uncommon for them to be nervous about what they should do. Unfortunately, we likely haven't improved the nerves of anyone who read our opening disclosure on the risks in this chapter. Usually, researchers new to independent publishing are worried about getting in trouble or angering the wrong people or any negative impacts their research might have on their lives.

Recently, while discussing vulnerability publishing with colleagues and other researchers, one (anonymous) researcher quipped that publishing vulnerabilities in the United States is protected under the free-speech constitutional amendment. This suggests that these activities are protected under law, and saying true things about a company is legally allowed if you didn't enter a binding agreement with that company not to say these things. They likened vulnerability publishing to leaving a bad review for a business on Google, Yelp, or something similar—say, one of your local restaurants. If you had a bad experience, and the restaurant didn't try to make it right (or even if they did), you can say whatever you like about it; in the United States, it's your right to do that.

Following the restaurant analogy, the reviewer is free to say whatever they like. Still, if those things are not accurate or falsified in some capacity, and the business can suggest that the review led them to suffer losses to their business, they can pursue legal action against you. Of course, the restaurant can also sue you for just about anything, but it doesn't necessarily mean they'll win.

Let's go back to our opening story about Jackson Jackson and his blog post on Talkspace. Unfortunately, we do not have the contents of his original blog post. Still, in the letter he shared online, the Talkspace lawyer referred to specific parts of the published content and quoted them directly. These sections referenced that Talkspace was not doing any validation concerning their clients, that their enterprise clients were being robbed, and that Talkspace's clients are susceptible to fraud. Based on this information, it's not a stretch to see why Jackson Jackson received a legal notice from Talkspace.

As an outside security researcher, Jackson found coupon codes and unique entry websites, allowing him to obtain free services. His opinions on his research should have said just that—*sticking to the facts*. Instead, he likely does not have any unique insight into how clients are being billed for services and if Talkspace is or is not doing validation. These passionate conclusions were neither appropriate nor validated with evidence or proof, as referenced in the press release after the legal notice was sent to Jackson.

How exactly do you avoid these risk factors? We'll get to that, but first, let's spend time defining how to prepare against the six most common risks researchers face.

Avoiding the common risks in publishing

There are six general things a researcher can get in trouble with independently publishing and disclosing vulnerabilities to the public in the United States. Please note that these cases are specific to the United States. However, your outcomes and risks will likely vary depending on which country you publish your research in. For example, it's technically against the law in Japan to share factual information that might damage a company under its strict defamation laws. So be sure to consult any laws enforced in your respective region.

Breach of contract

Many companies have strict confidentiality agreements that employees, contractors, and others must sign before accessing company information. These agreements typically prohibit the person from disclosing company information to anyone outside the company. As a result, researchers have been sued for breach of contract after publishing information they agreed not to disclose.

When doing research, you may find yourself bound to contracts that stipulate limitations on research and disclosure. As a researcher, it is important to read the contracts you sign and be very mindful of what you can and can't say. Unfortunately, this advice is something many researchers learn the hard way. It isn't uncommon for experienced researchers to avoid software that must be acquired through signing contracts or NDAs. If you break a contract, be prepared for the consequences. These are solemn legal agreements that can result in severe repercussions if violated.

Violation of the Computer Fraud and Abuse Act

The CFAA is United States legislation that prohibits unauthorized access to protected computers. The CFAA has been used to sue researchers who have accessed company systems without permission.

Servers are expensive, software is expensive, and researchers may not want to invest in purchasing the software themselves; they may look to borrow instead. In addition, many researchers will test their software on servers they do not own. This is generally accepted if you have explicit permission from the server's owner or have entered into an agreement through a bug bounty program.

If you do not have permission to test the resources, it could be argued you're committing a crime, and legal action could be taken against you. Therefore, you should only access systems you have been authorized to access and test.

Copyright infringement

The **Digital Millennium Copyright Act** (**DMCA**) is a United States law that makes it illegal to produce or distribute any technology, device, or service designed to bypass measures controlling access to copyrighted material. It also criminalizes the act of circumventing these measures, even if there is no actual infringement of copyright.

The DMCA has been used to go after researchers who have published PoC code. For example, in 1999, the DMCA was wielded like a weapon against hackers who posted copies of the **DeCSS** decryption program used to decrypt DVDs. Eventually, higher courts decided that posting the DeCSS program and code was ultimately a form of protected speech in the United States, but that was only after the parties of the suit had drained the defendants of resources.

To avoid being accused of copyright infringement, you should only publish PoC code that you have written yourself. If you do use someone else's code, be sure to get permission first.

Using vulnerabilities for criminal purposes

This one is simple—don't do it. If you find and exploit a vulnerability for criminal purposes and then disclose it, that's called **double dipping**, and it's a bad idea. When authorities or the vendor inevitably find out, you will likely end up dealing with both criminal and civil cases filed against you. This type of scenario does not often happen, but when it does, it makes headlines because it's such an egregious misuse of the researcher's powers.

Defamation

Defamation is the act of knowingly or unknowingly making false statements about people or organizations that cause harm to their reputation. In the United States, the constitutional provision of the First Amendment to the United States guarantees the freedom of speech. Still, if the thing you're saying is false and harms another party's reputation, that party can file a civil lawsuit against you for defamation. There are two types of defamation in the United States: *libel* (written statements) and *slander* (spoken statements).

Defamation typically falls under libel, where the researcher incorrectly states that a specific product is vulnerable when it's not in the publication they share. These public statements can result in a lot of wasted time and effort on the part of users who follow up on the report only to discover that there was no issue in the first place. Ultimately, improperly validated vulnerabilities can cause many problems for researchers, so when you publish your research, be careful and demonstrate facts and evidence for your claims. Avoid speculation, and make it clear what your opinion is and what the facts are. Companies who seek legal action against you for incorrect statements may reference that you've committed libel in a way that caused the expenditure of resources in human capital and damaged profits.

Researchers have been sued for defamation after making false or unsubstantiated statements about companies or their products. Defamation doesn't stop at products, though. Think back to our opening discussion about Talkspace, where the researcher made specific statements about the company robbing its clients. It took no umbrage at his factual claims about being able to submit codes to claim access to services without paying for them. While what was said about Talkspace might have been true, it wasn't backed by evidence and was, therefore, speculative.

To avoid being sued for defamation, you should only make factual statements. Be 100% positive about what you're saying before you say it, and be able to back it up with evidence. If you don't know, don't speculate. Stick to the facts.

Failing to give notice

Immediate publishing of any vulnerability with no warning is controversial, and obviously, we have stated repeatedly in this book so far that you should give vendors plenty of notice before publicly sharing vulnerabilities in their products. We'll repeat it: do not disclose vulnerabilities directly with no initial notice to the vendor. As a researcher, you should err on the side of caution and give the company reasonable time to patch the issue before going public. Ensuring you're transparent, helpful, and communicative to the vendor will help avoid any potential legal repercussions down the road and create a better reputation for all future security researchers working with the company.

How to independently publish a vulnerability

There are a few different ways to publish independently. The simplest way is to write a report that includes your findings and your (redacted) interaction with the vendor and suggested fixes and post it online. You can use a personal blog or hosted website that allows people to publish content, such as Medium. The report doesn't necessarily need to be limited directly to general findings; researchers can also choose to release PoC demos, original exploit code, and anything else they think would be helpful to the content consumer.

If you don't have a personal blog you can publish to but would like to, we suggest you utilize GitHub Pages. GitHub Pages is a free and accessible way to set up an independent blog through a developed software repository. Then, using a simple templating language such as Jekyll, you can build something that looks professional and polished for the excellent price of zero dollars:

Sample blog post

Each post also has a subtitle

Posted on February 28, 2020

This is a demo post to show you how to write blog posts with markdown. I strongly encourage you to take 5 minutes to learn how to write in markdown - it'll teach you how to transform regular text into bold/italics/headings/tables/etc. **[Read More]**

Tags: test

Flake it till you make it

Excerpt from Soulshaping by Jeff Brown

Posted on February 26, 2020

Under what circumstances should we step off a path? When is it essential that we finish what we start? If I bought a bag of peanuts and had an allergic reaction, no one would fault me if I threw it out. If I ended a relationship with a woman who...

[Read More]

Tags: books test

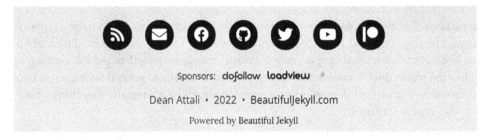

Sponsors: *dofollow* **loadview**

Dean Attali · 2022 · BeautifulJekyll.com

Powered by Beautiful Jekyll

Figure 7.1 – An example of a Jekyll-formatted GitHub page

You can check out some of the 1,000-plus themes they have on GitHub using the GitHub topic *Jekyll-theme* here: `https://github.com/topics/jekyll-theme`.

Another popular option with researchers that meets the independent publishing bar is submitting the report to a **security mailing list** or security forum. Unfortunately, this medium is not as used as it once was, and some of the most iconic mailing lists have been shuttered. For example, **Bugtraq**, one of the most popular mailing lists, shut down after 27 years in 2021 after several changes to the platform. However, despite the dwindling popularity of the method, it continues to be a rich source of relatively unfiltered commentary on security research. Arguably, some of the best research is still found through these forums, encouraging researchers to discuss vulnerabilities.

The best possible resource for getting started with security mailing lists is **SecLists** (`http://seclists.org`). It's a website published by Gordon Lyon, the creator and maintainer of the prevalent network scanning tool Nmap. Reviewing the site, you'll be shown a series of several mailing lists, their archives, and information about the lists, as seen in the following screenshot:

Figure 7.2 – SecLists.org has several mailing lists you can subscribe to and browse

If you're interested in using a mailing list such as the ones found on `SecLists.org`, take some time to explore the ones that interest you and get a good feel for how they operate. You might find one that fits your particular use case much better than another.

> **Note**
>
> Security mailing lists often have rules that must be abided by to ensure your research is shared with the subscribers. While security mailing lists are usually loosely monitored and moderated, they are still managed by administrators who typically decide what can and cannot be published on the list. Ensure you review the rules before submitting anything.

Finally, one viable option might be getting the media involved. Unfortunately, this is often seen as a last resort, as getting reporters interested in a story can be tricky unless it's incredibly explosive. One way to overcome the potential disinterest that mainstream media outlets usually express is by working directly with a technology-focused media company, such as TechCrunch, which reported the story that opened our chapter. Other media entities, such as Ars Technica, Wired, Dark Reading, Tom's Hardware, and The Verge, are excellent sources that regularly publish stories about researchers and their work. It's not unusual for a story to first make it to one of these outlets, and if interesting enough or the developments that come from the story are of public interest, the mainstream media will mirror the story.

With a better understanding of where these vulnerabilities can be published, let's cap off our discussion on publishing with a checklist you can follow to double-check your work before you hit the **Submit** button.

A before-you-publish checklist

We've spent much time discussing a specific method of publishing vulnerabilities. But, again, we did this to help you understand that when you independently publish vulnerabilities, you inherently take on risk. If this risk is acceptable to you, we hope you follow this advice if you decide to publish your research. To help condense this into a more easily consumed format, we've created a checklist that can help limit any risks or liabilities you might face. While following this advice will help avoid the risks with the independent publication of vulnerabilities, this will not completely protect you from risk, even if everything you share is factual and justified with plenty of evidence. Returning to our analogy of the unfavorable restaurant review, a business owner can pursue legal action against you for whatever reason they choose to; this also applies to any research you publish on a company or its products. It doesn't mean they'll win, but the resulting legal battle will likely drain your resources. So, with that out of the way, here's that checklist:

- If applicable, review any contracts you or your company may have entered through a security disclosure program or directly with the vendor.
- Double-check that the company or a researcher has not already published the vulnerability.
- Inform the vendor of your intent to publish within a clearly communicated timeline.
- As you're writing, check for facts. Humor and snark are okay, but if your disclosure includes assumptions without evidence about the company, their interactions with you, or the vulnerabilities themselves, you may find yourself getting letters from lawyers in short order.

- Remove any private information about the company or its users if discovered.

- Remove any code or specially licensed content from your disclosure.

- Give credit where credit is due. If you had help from other research or blogs, make sure you mention that and credit other researchers for their contributions.

- Have someone you trust proofread your disclosure for correctness, grammar issues, potential bias, missing evidence, and factual correctness.

- Publish the vulnerability disclosure.

- Optionally, let the vendor know where they can review your disclosure.

If you're unsure how to create your initial disclosure in the form of a blog post, we provide a template in *Chapter 10, Templates, Resources, and Final Guidance*, that you can use to get started with your independently published disclosure.

Well, this closes our chapter on independent publishing. Let's review what we've covered.

Summary

In this chapter, we discussed the topic of independent vulnerability disclosures. We first examined where these fit into the vulnerability life cycle and why you might want to use this method to share vulnerabilities with other researchers and, more importantly, the public. Next, we discussed the various benefits and risks inherent in these disclosures. We then examined six key things that typically get researchers in trouble when they decide to self-publish and helped share key strategies to avoid these stumbling blocks. Next, we briefly explored the mediums used to publish research and finally reviewed a checklist you can customize and use to hopefully limit your risk when you decide to publicly share information about vulnerabilities. Throughout this book, we've shared real stories about researchers finding and disclosing security risks to companies, which is a valuable way to learn how to do this yourself. In the next chapter, we'll examine disclosures in even greater depth (with sometimes anonymized content), contrasting them to what we've learned, and extract critical insights from the successes and failures.

Additional reading

- Talkspace threatened to sue a security researcher over a bug report, TechCrunch – `https://techcrunch.com/2020/03/09/talkspace-cease-desist/`

- GitHub Pages – `https://pages.github.com/`

Part 3 – Case Studies, Researcher Resources, and Vendor Resources

The objective of this section is to provide resources for vulnerability disclosure. This includes information on case studies in which real-world researchers succeeded or failed in their work. We then turn the tables and speak to vendors about working with security researchers. We close this section with useful templates and research resources.

This section comprises the following chapters:

- *Chapter 8, Real-World Case Studies – Digging into Successful (and Unsuccessful) Research Reporting*
- *Chapter 9, Working with Security Researchers – A Vendor's Guide*
- *Chapter 10, Templates, Resources, and Final Guidance*

8

Real-World Case Studies – Digging into Successful (and Unsuccessful) Research Reporting

Throughout this book, we've discussed stories about security researchers discovering and disclosing vulnerabilities. We've also talked about how these stories often follow a similar pattern: someone finds a security flaw, tells the company responsible for the affected software, and then (if all goes well) the company releases a patch to fix the problem. In other cases, there are complications. For example, the researcher and the company might disagree on whether the flaw is a problem. The company might not be responsive to the researcher's disclosure. Or, as in some of the most famous cases, the company might try to silence the researcher through legal means.

It's lovely when disclosures are received well, and everything gets patched up quickly and cleanly. However, conflicts between researchers and vendors are common even with expanded awareness and investment in security. These conflicts can often devolve into scenarios that expend resources such as time, money, and patience. This can jeopardize meaningful relationships between companies and security researchers. This chapter aims to help you learn about these problems by telling stories about researchers and the challenges they have faced in the past. Finally, we'll reflect on what might have been learned from these experiences and discuss possible improvements that could be adopted in future interactions with vendors.

Due to the sensitive nature of these interactions, we'll be anonymizing all the impacted researchers and companies. These stories cannot explicitly be discussed for various reasons, some of which will be clear as we explore them. However, by reviewing these vulnerabilities, we should better understand how researchers report and respond to vendors, likely problems in disclosures, and ways we can ensure better outcomes in our research.

To recap the upcoming content, in this chapter, we're going to discuss the following:

- We'll explore five case studies of vulnerability research and disclosure

- We'll reflect on lessons learned in each case

- Finally, we'll briefly discuss possible opportunities for using this information to improve our research outcomes in the future

These case studies will be presented through the following main topics in this chapter:

- Case study 1 – are we there yet?

- Case study 2 – contract clause

- Case study 3 – tough customers

- Case study 4 – large corporations and you

- Case study 5 – I'd like to speak to your manager

Case study 1 – are we there yet?

In this case, we'll explore vendors who are uncooperative with responsible disclosure policies, elongated disclosures, and how one slight error in your publishing can delay your publication by months.

In 2020, a vulnerability researcher was engaged by a company to run a typical in-depth security review that they often received. This software consisted of a web application, a fat client, and server applications. During the application security review, the researcher found several unique vulnerabilities that needed to be reported to the software vendor who built and serviced the product. Some of these vulnerabilities were rated as high risk, and the parent company that requested the security review was concerned.

The researcher prepared a report of their findings and delivered it to their employer. Their employer, in turn, shared these findings with the vendor that had built the software and got their employer in touch with the vendor. The was is a multi-billion-dollar company with a responsible disclosure program and a security team responsible for attending to vulnerabilities. The security researcher reviewed their program and shared the vulnerabilities per the requirements of the responsible disclosure policy.

The vendor began to share with the researcher's company and the researcher that the vulnerabilities would be prioritized and fixed. The two parties agreed to follow up in a few weeks to determine the next steps after the development team had time to review the product. Weeks passed, and the researcher checked back in with the vendor. The vendor shared that they didn't know when the vulnerabilities would be fixed, but that they'd update the researcher and associated contact.

Several months passed before the researcher reached out to the vendor for updates. The request was met with no response for some time, so the researcher tried again. After several more attempts, almost an entire year after the initial disclosure, the vendor responded and shared that the product would no longer be updated or supported. The vulnerabilities would never be fixed.

The researcher was disappointed by the outcome. The researcher decided to publicize their findings to increase awareness of the risks associated with using this software, which was being actively sold while it was unsupported.

The vulnerabilities were eligible for CVE publication under the rules outlined by MITRE, and the researcher began to review their options. After collecting all the required information about the vulnerability, the researcher requested six vulnerabilities, which MITRE assigned to the researcher a month after they were requested.

The researcher notified the vendor of their intention to publish the CVEs and provided them with the details. The vendor asked for additional time to resolve the issues they said they wouldn't resolve but didn't commit to a date or timeline. As a show of good faith, the researcher allotted 3 additional months before publishing. Once again, after checking in with vendors and waiting for a response, the researcher didn't receive any update. They proceeded to publish a public blog post on their findings and then requested the publication of the CVEs from MITRE.

To the researcher's surprise, their initial request for publishing was declined by MITRE. Instead, MITRE shared with them a generic canned response that said the following:

The CVE Team needs a public reference URL that contains the minimum required information for the vulnerability covered by the vulnerabilities you wish to disclose. Please provide such a reference. If you do not have one, a quick way to create your own reference is for you to post your entire form-submission information containing the minimum data requirements to https://gist.github.com as a public gist. You can use any other hosting resource (e.g., a blog or the http://seclists.org/fulldisclosure mailing-list archive or http://pastebin.com).

Please do not hesitate to contact the CVE Team by replying to this email if you have any questions or to provide more details.

The researcher emailed them, puzzled, asking questions about why they might need a published disclosure since one was provided in the publishing. After a few weeks, the researcher had not heard back from MITRE, so they began a new publishing request. After a few days, the request was sent back again, stating there was no public reference to the materials and the researcher.

The researcher emailed again, asking what they might be doing wrong. Eventually, 5 weeks later, MITRE wrote back with a canned response, once again stating that they didn't receive their requested materials:

Thank you for the submission, regarding publishing the [CVEs], a publicly accessible reference that details the vulnerability is still required. Since one was not provided in a timely manner, the service request [service request ID] is being rejected. Please feel free to resubmit at your earliest convenience.

Please do not hesitate to contact the CVE Team by replying to this email if you have any questions, or to provide more details.

The researcher was confused. They consulted with other industry peers, who thought it might make sense to open individual vulnerability publishing requests for each one of the vulnerabilities. However, they thought submitting all of them (as defined as an option on their website) would be the most efficient way of troubleshooting this problem since MITRE didn't appear to have anyone answering emails. Instead of submitting all five of the vulnerabilities, which they initially tried to submit with one publishing request, they made five specific vulnerability publishing requests, one for each vulnerability.

After this submission attempt, the researcher received four approvals and one denial. On reviewing the denial, the researcher noted in their blog materials that the rejected vulnerability had the incorrect CVE ID attributed. As a result, they revised their published content. They then resubmitted the vulnerability report to MITRE, closing out this process which took almost two years to complete from start to finish.

Lessons learned

This case study is an example of the challenges faced by security researchers when working with vendors who seem able and willing to intake research but fail to deliver on their promises of ensuring that their products are secure.

In this case, the researcher eventually published their vulnerabilities by MITRE after a long and frustrating process of the vendor misleading the researcher about their efforts. Reflect for a moment on how this highlights how easy it could be for security researchers to become discouraged and give up when faced with hurdle after hurdle. two years is a long time to focus on just a small set of vulnerabilities discovered in just a few days of testing.

Additionally, this highlights some challenges the CVE program has faced since its adoption. Since writing this, vulnerability reporting has increased yearly, sometimes by daunting numbers, in the last several years. The team working on this project is constantly flooded with requests—in 2021, on average, 56 vulnerabilities were published (not counting those requested) per day by researchers. The CVE program has automated pre-configured e-mails where it can, but sometimes, as discovered in this study, they are not always helpful or informative.

Possible improvements

The researcher did the right thing by reporting the vulnerability to the company, but a possible improvement could have been pursued if the researcher had worked with a mediator. In addition, working with a mediator can help establish accountability for a vendor who isn't sticking with their promises or timelines. If the vendor fails to work with the mediator, it's reason enough to disclose your findings and not drag out the process over the course of two years.

Finally, the researcher should consider another improvement: breaking their findings into individual disclosures. The MITRE team is very busy, and the automated way they handle some requests can result in confusion, and resubmission can potentially cause even more work to flow into the CVE disclosures inbox.

Let's now explore our following case study, which explores how contracts constrain researchers.

Case study 2 – contract clause

In this case study, we'll explore how vendors build contracts and **non-disclosure agreements** (NDA) that bind researchers in ways that researchers cannot sometimes expect.

In 2021, a researcher was asked to do a security assessment on a data analysis platform used at the company at which they were employed. The product was licensed and serviced by a vendor who sold the product to the organization.

When the researcher was asked to review the application, the business had already started to use the product. It was deployed with no sub-production environment directly on the internet, meaning any changes or work done to the platform would happen in a live environment. The researcher was keenly interested in not doing testing, which might disrupt the operations of the software. Therefore, they devised that they would test the application in an environment that they set up according to the specifications in the vendor's documentation. The researcher built their environment with a trial version that the researcher found published on the vendor's website. The researcher did their best during the review to understand the use cases and replicate that in their testing environment after a lengthy review with their employer's users.

During the security review, the researcher found several vulnerabilities that helped exploit the software to allow a remote takeover of the machine it was installed on. While this vulnerability was limited to authenticated users, authentication itself was a problem. The vendor used default usernames and passwords, and this was paired with single-factor authentication. This was especially problematic because this software was designed to be used over the internet as a public web application.

The researcher made initial reports internally to the business owners who used the software, but the vendor primarily serviced the software. Therefore, the researcher, in turn, was asked to work with the vendor to resolve the problems. The researcher obtained support contact information from the internal business owner and contacted the vendor. The vendor initially replied to the researcher's email but was uninterested in the findings. The researcher followed up over several months but received very little information from the vendor outside of confirming that they had received the vulnerability report and were investigating it.

Eventually, after several requests, the vendor told the researcher that they didn't consider their work a vulnerability. They reasoned that it was unlikely that someone would use their software this way because their users were not typically hackers. The researcher found this claim bizarre and reiterated that this vulnerability could lead to a compromise of all the interconnected systems. While hackers might not be the primary users, they most certainly would be interested in the data contained in the system, especially seeing it was publicly accessible from the internet.

After this failed interaction, the researcher decided that the vulnerability should be mediated since there was a disagreement; they didn't feel they could resolve it independently. The researcher opened a case in the CERT VINCE program, and the mediating coordinator contacted the vendor after the researcher had supplied the initial information. Once the mediator reached out to the vendor, it quickly became apparent that they refused to speak with the mediator. They immediately escalated the matter with the company the researcher worked with.

Unbeknownst to the researcher, the contract for services that was originally signed when the software was initially acquired had included language that explicitly stated that vulnerabilities related to the software were not to be disclosed to any third party. While the software itself is something you can download, install, and use, the contract signed by the company that had purchased these rights to use the software essentially made it impossible for the public to know about the vulnerabilities without a breach of contract between the researcher's organization and the vendor.

The vendor wasn't happy that the researcher wanted to disclose the vulnerabilities, so they began messaging, which alerted several internal teams about a breach of contract with the disclosure of findings. In their request, they stated that any publication or shared knowledge about the vulnerability would be considered a breach of contract under the terms that both parties had agreed to. To remediate this violation, the company demanded that the messaging be retracted from CERT, and no further disclosure or discussion was made on the vulnerability. The researcher was notified to remove the communications from CERT by his employer.

The vulnerabilities were not get published to the public and are likely still present in the software, which large corporations use to gain insights into their data. As a result, the knowledge of these vulnerabilities will likely stay within the confines of those who initially found them until another researcher discovers and reports them.

This is a case where ethical considerations conflict with business interests. The researcher found themselves in a difficult position because their employer had agreed to terms that prevented them from disclosing the vulnerabilities. On the one hand, they wanted to help protect people who might be affected by these vulnerabilities, but on the other hand, they were bound, by proxy, to an agreement signed by their employer. Ultimately, the researcher complied and did not disclose the vulnerabilities.

Lessons learned

This case study is an excellent example of how vulnerabilities and their publication can be stifled by NDAs and contracts that you may not be aware of as a researcher. Unfortunately, it isn't uncommon to hear that some enterprises make deals such as these to get reasonable prices for software licensing.

As unsettling as this might be to discover as a consumer, this is a reality that researchers deal with often. For example, information security conferences are no strangers to research disclosure obstructions. There have been many cases where researchers couldn't present research at a conference. For example, vendors block research releases via this medium by coercing conferences to cancel their speaker's presentations and threatening various parties with litigation. In rare cases, vendors have even physically detained researchers in hotel rooms to prevent them from speaking out about their research.

Thankfully, the coercion this researcher faced was not of a physical sort. The legal threats subsided after the researcher pulled their disclosure from CERT. However, this research was not published, and the flaws found in this software likely exist today. This is a scary reality, and it's one that we, as an industry, need to change.

Possible improvements

There, unfortunately, was not much the researcher could do outside of perhaps referencing any contracts to prepare themselves for this type of possible outcome. It might have been possible for the researcher to have published the vulnerabilities as an independent researcher by remaining anonymous or using a pseudonym. This strategy has possible issues, though. It's feasible to say that the researcher initially acted in good faith and disclosed the vulnerability. However, if the vendor chose not to act, any disclosures after that interaction may have been tied back to the initial reporter, even if the information was disclosed anonymously. For some researchers, it's a losing scenario that jeopardizes their employment.

Beyond consumer protections, which arguably should be provided by the government, there isn't much recourse for consumers of software, who sometimes agree to contracts they might not even understand. It might be advantageous to speak with procurement partners and help establish a vulnerability disclosure clause in new contracts that acquire software rights. This clause could establish basic expectations of the company's rights for recourse if a vulnerability is found in the product and if the vendor decides not to act. If a vendor is unwilling to accept this kind of clause, it may indicate how they might respond to future security reports.

With this case study behind us, let's explore the subsequent case study, which defines the consequences when researchers and vendors communicate poorly.

Case study 3 – tough customers

Let's now review issues concerning the vulnerabilities found previously in older versions of code, poor communication, and how public disclosure can cause quick remediation from the vendor but may impact software users.

In late 2017, a security researcher aimed at a popular software application that organizations use to facilitate online commerce. The researcher specialized in reverse engineering security patches and finding flaws in remediations. They began their investigation by looking for publicly known vulnerabilities patched on the platform.

Focusing on one recent vulnerability that the vendor had allegedly fixed, the researcher believed there might be flaws in the implementation with their initial review. After more digging, they found that the patch technically only addressed one attack vector while leaving another one unpatched. They decided to try to exploit this incomplete patch which, if successful, would allow the researcher to take over user accounts and steal information such as credit card data.

After a few hours of experimentation, they were successful in their attempt and were able to exploit the vulnerability. The researcher was confident that this vulnerability would be valuable to the vendor and hoped to receive compensation for their work. This researcher found the appropriate contacts for the vendor and began initial communication. In that initial communication, the researcher didn't share all the details and was intentionally vague, hoping to entice the vendor to render some type of award to the researcher. This strategy backfired.

First, the vendor didn't believe the researcher and believed the researcher was trying to extort money out of them for something they thought they had successfully patched. The vendor had previous experience of these kinds of interactions with researchers and didn't want to fall victim to a possible scheme from a criminal. The researcher and the vendor spent a few days going back and forth over email, exchanging hostilities until, eventually, the vendor told the researcher that they couldn't recreate the issue with the information provided and, therefore, would not be working on a fix or rewarding the researcher.

Unfortunately for our researcher, in their communications to the vendor, they provided technically incomplete proof-of-concept exploits. This made it impossible for the vendor to verify the claims of the researcher and resulted in miscommunication between the vendor and the researcher. Worse, the researcher prefaced this research with a request for a financial reward. As a result, the vendor didn't take the researcher seriously and had sufficient reason to dismiss the claims made by the researcher.

In our case, though, the researcher did not think this was an acceptable response from the vendor, so they decided to go straight to the public with the findings. First, they published a blog post detailing the flaw and how it could be exploited and provided compelling video evidence of the exploitation in action. Then the researcher emailed technology-focused news outlets to inform them of this serious issue and how the vendor allegedly didn't care.

The story gained some traction and was populated on several popular technology blogs and news sites. Unfortunately, the vendor was made aware of the media stories through requests for comments on the story from a technical reporter.

In reviewing the blog post by the researcher, the vendor discovered that the publication had all the details the vendor previously didn't have in their communications—this allowed them to recreate the issue. As a result, the vendor quickly released a patch for the flaw and urged their clients to patch it as soon as possible. However, the researcher's work and explicit information on exploiting the vulnerability resulted in the compromise of several businesses that used the application, resulting in uncalculated damages.

Lessons learned

This case study is an excellent example of how communications can break down in highly detrimental ways. This petty, unnecessary conflict resulted in end users having their information stolen by criminals who took the researcher's pre-made exploit information and immediately weaponized it.

Without a doubt, both parties should have communicated better. Unfortunately, the researcher was vague and unclear about their initial concerns, and the vendor was dismissive and made assumptions they shouldn't have. If either party had been more patient or understanding, this situation could have been avoided altogether.

However justified the researcher felt the moment that they disclosed the vulnerability, they also kept the vendor in the dark as to their intentions of sharing it with the media. As a result, the media helped amplify the story and increased negative attention, resulting in the theft of personal information such as credit card numbers, home addresses, and passwords. However frustrated you may be, this is not a pattern to emulate; the researcher made the scenario exponentially worse through their actions.

Possible improvements

It's important to remember that we can't always control how others communicate, but we can control our actions. Researchers are already seen as hostile disturbances; perhaps this case helps solidify some of those views. Arguably, the researcher could have been clearer and provided more details to the vendor. Conversely, the vendor could have been more understanding and responsive to the researcher's concerns instead of initially being defensive and dismissive. In the end, better communication could have helped prevent this situation from escalating.

As an improvement, we should also be very cognizant that as researchers, we must take care in how we share our findings. Providing pre-made exploits to the public when there are no known patches available is downright reckless, dangerous behavior that should be avoided. CVE disclosures do not require in-depth details.

In the end, while this scenario wasn't necessarily something the vendor was entirely at fault for, they likely could have improved their handling of vulnerabilities too. Many vendors do this by outsourcing their intake of research with a bug bounty program, which communicates that they are willing to work with researchers and reward them for their work. As a prerequisite, the researchers must demonstrate the vulnerability and communicate the risk before benefiting. However, as discussed in *Chapter 7, Independent Vulnerability Publishing*, some researchers do not care for bug bounty programs. As such, the vendor should also account for possible exceptions and be flexible in their research intake.

In the following case study, we'll discuss how researchers might encounter large entities that can assign and publish their own vulnerabilities.

Case study 4 – large corporations and you

This case study explores working with a large corporation that is a CVE issuer and the potential issues you may encounter in working with large organizations.

In 2019, a researcher unexpectedly came across a vulnerability they weren't looking for. While reviewing other software for potential vulnerabilities, they noticed something odd about the software running on their research environment, which appeared to be a rather severe vulnerability in a software product operated by a multi-billion-dollar organization.

The researcher responsibly disclosed the issue to the organization. The organization was grateful for the report and quickly began working on a fix. However, due to the organization's size and scope, fixing the issue and deploying the patch took several months. In the meantime, the researcher continued to look for other potential vulnerabilities and found a second related issue.

Again, they responsibly disclosed this finding to the organization. However, this time, instead of being grateful, the organization became defensive and began asking questions about why the researcher was looking at their software in the first place. They demanded to know what purpose the research had, threatened legal action, and ultimately asked the researcher to sign an NDA before they would provide any further information about the vulnerability or the fix.

The researcher was caught off guard by this response and didn't know how to proceed. They wanted to help the organization fix the issue but didn't want to sign an NDA that would limit their ability to discuss their findings.

In this case, the researcher began to review the possible avenues they might have for publishing the vulnerability. When reviewing options, they discovered that the company was a **CVE numbering authority (CNA)**. The researcher reviewed the corresponding CNA disclosure policy and the publication information supplied by the vendor's security team—they noted that the email for disclosing CVEs was very different from the email they had been corresponding with.

With this new information, the researcher began copying all correspondence to the email address associated with the vendor. This vastly improved the communication and got the security department of that organization involved in patching this problem, which was initially just worked on through the software development teams.

Since the vulnerability was reported to a CNA, the researcher just needed to wait for the patch to be released and for the research to be published. After the vulnerability was published, the researcher was a bit surprised to see that no acknowledgments were attributed to their work, despite having emails that showed correspondence with the security team. On further review, the CVE reference materials downplayed the severity of the findings, essentially undercutting their work.

Unfortunately, the researcher disengaged with the vendor and decided to cut their losses and not continue the correspondence with the vendor or pursue further research with the company. After all, their program offered no financial rewards, appeared hostile even though they were CNAs, and actively undercut the research without thanking the researcher for their contributions, which made the vendor's product more secure.

Lessons learned

This case study is an excellent example of how a CNA shouldn't handle security disclosures. There are a few key points to take away from this story. The first we think is to ensure that you review your options when disclosing vulnerabilities. Attempt to determine whether the company is a CNA or not and whether they understand their policies. Finally, always review disclosure policies before submitting any information about potential vulnerabilities.

The second point would be to be wary of NDAs. You'll often be asked to sign these when you begin trying to work with a company to close risk. In many cases, they are simply a way for the company to buy time while determining how to mitigate the risk. If you sign an NDA, make sure it is limited in scope and time. You don't want to be bound by an agreement that prevents you from discussing your work or findings in the future.

Finally, it's best to keep in mind that working with large corporations can be frustrating. Still, it is essential to remember that they often try to protect their reputation and may not be as responsive as you would like them to be. This isn't always the case, and it's all too common for researchers to be burned out by working with vendors that are unresponsive, dismissive, and undercut their findings, which ultimately improve a product that they're not directly responsible for. It's imperative to remember that not all companies are created equal—while one may be unresponsive and difficult to work with, another may be incredibly helpful and appreciative of your efforts. It's essential to keep this in mind when pursuing research and disclosures, as it can help you maintain a positive attitude even in the face of difficulties.

Possible improvements

A few things could have been done differently in this case study to improve the outcome. The first is that the researchers should have started initially by determining who would be best to contact about the vulnerability, which was well-defined in the policy they used as a CNA. As a result, the researcher ended up spending time talking to people who were ill-equipped to work with them and asked the researcher to sign an NDA, which would have stifled their disclosure to an ever-greater degree.

The second is to take the time to understand how CNAs work and what their policies are regarding attribution and disclosure. This would have helped avoid misunderstandings about how the researcher's work would be used and credited.

Finally, an improvement the vendor could have possibly made to prevent disenfranchising researchers is to ensure they thanked researchers publicly for their help and stuck to the facts. In *Chapter 7*, we advised researchers to avoid editorializing their disclosures, which goes for vendors too. Stick to the facts; people operating in good faith will find it hard to fault you.

In our final case study, we'll explore incompetence and how sometimes escalation in your disclosure can lead to healthier outcomes.

Case study 5 – I'd like to speak to your manager

This case study explores dead ends and rampant miscommunication between people who receive and process information from researchers.

In 2017, a researcher reviewed a software product used by non-profit organizations as part of a security review of one of their clients. The software was used to determine how the non-profit organizations allocated funds to projects and included sensitive banking and fundraising information.

During their research, they found a way to take over any system account by exploiting a weakness in the platform's configuration. The researcher quickly contacted the organization, which hired the researcher to test the software. The company got the researcher's contact information for the software vendor so they could work with them to notify and hopefully get a fix for the vulnerability. In speaking with support engineers, the researcher was informed that the company already knew about the vulnerabilities and that they were fixed in the latest software version. They advised the researcher to talk to their client about upgrading the software.

The researcher then spent time developing a report and a summary of actions for their client to take, including upgrading the outdated software version. Their client was very confused, though, because they had upgraded to the newest version of the software a couple of months before the researcher looked at it.

The researcher got back in touch with the company, and in speaking with the same person they initially talked to, they asked why they advised an upgrade when they were already at the latest version. The customer support person apologized and said they were confident that the vulnerabilities were fixed. They would return any details to the developers and get them fixed in an upcoming release. The researcher then sent all the details to the person they talked to and set a reminder to follow up in three months for the next release of the software.

Once three months had passed, the researcher again reached out to the same support person who shared that the vulnerabilities had been fixed before. The support person was happy to report that the vulnerabilities would be fixed in the next version—after the version scheduled to be released in a couple of weeks. The researcher knew, after all, three months was a pretty short period for intaking vulnerability findings and then delivering a patch to customers, so once again, they set a reminder to follow up.

At the subsequent follow-up, the researcher, talking again to the same person they had initially met and disclosed the vulnerabilities to, was informed that the vulnerabilities were indeed fixed, and all the changes would be in the release notes of the software. The researcher contacted the client and shared the good news, and the client scheduled the software upgrade. The researcher wanted to ensure the vulnerabilities were fixed and scheduled time with their client to confirm all the vulnerabilities were closed. Once the client had upgraded their software to the latest version, the researcher tested it, finding that every vulnerability originally reported was still present in the software. The researcher recalled that all the fixes would be in the change notes of the software. To the surprise of the researcher, the change notes had only one sentence in them:

There were no significant changes in this release.

Once again, the researcher called the vendor to inquire about this. The researcher, at this point, had been told the software was already fixed, then that it was going to be fixed in the next release, then the next, and when tested, it was not fixed. The same support engineer who had initially helped them explained that there might have been some confusion on their part about what was fixed or wasn't fixed. They shared, though, that they'd be back in touch after they contacted their developers.

Several months went by with no contact from the vendor. Eventually, the researcher reached out to the vendor once again and spoke with the same person, and this time, the support person apologized for not being in touch and shared that next month's upgrade was the upgrade where all the fixes they had promised before would be in the software.

Going through the motions of working with their client and upgrading to the latest version about a month later, the researcher found that no vulnerabilities had been patched, much like the last time they had reviewed the software. Understandably, the researcher was very frustrated and felt that the customer support person they had been working with was being dishonest or incompetent. The researcher decided the next step would be to open a request for a CVE, share the numbers once they were reserved, and then inform the company that if the vulnerabilities were not patched in the next 90 days, they would release the information publicly. Once the researcher received their CVE reservations, they scheduled a call to discuss the situation. Speaking with the same support engineer, the researcher explained their frustration at being lied to and promised fixes that never materialized. The support engineer once again apologized and said they would do better in the future and, once again, reiterated that the vulnerabilities would be fixed in the next version.

The researcher then asked to speak with the manager of the employee. They shared they believed that the support engineer was trying their best, but it was not resulting in the outcomes needed to resolve the situation, and escalation was the thing that was needed. After some reluctant discussions, the support engineer passed their manager's contact information to the researcher. The researcher constructed an email to the manager explaining the situation, their frustration with the inaction of the vendor, and how the vulnerabilities would be disclosed in the coming weeks.

The manager responded within a day, asking to speak on the phone. After discussing with their employee, the researcher discovered that the vulnerabilities were never passed to the right people. The support engineer gave the reports to the operations teams, who ran anti-virus scans on servers with the software installed and claimed that there were no vulnerabilities. The manager who understood the issue followed up several times over the next few weeks with questions about potential mitigations and workarounds for their customers. Finally, after several weeks of back-and-forth, the manager committed to a date when the researcher would test the software again to verify that the vulnerabilities had been fixed before the next upgrade would go to the client—all well before the deadline the researcher shared on when they'd publish their findings publicly.

The researcher followed up with the manager on the agreed-upon date, verifying that all the vulnerabilities had been fixed. They thanked the manager for their time and efforts in patching the software and preventing a public disclosure with no mitigation. While this situation had a happy ending, it's easy to see how things could have gone very differently, especially if the researcher hadn't been persistent in following up with the vendor.

Lessons learned

This is one example of communication going desperately wrong. Our researcher made the mistake of assuming they were talking to the right people. It turned out that the support engineer had a very basic set of skills, couldn't interpret the technical research, and didn't know how to respond appropriately. If the researcher had gone directly to the manager, they could have avoided all the frustration and wasted time.

In this case, it's also important to note that the researcher gave the vendor a lot of chances to fix the problems before going public. They went above and beyond in trying to work with the vendor and only escalated when it was necessary. However frustrating, it's often the best approach when dealing with vulnerabilities—ensuring that you give the vendor a chance to fix the problem before going public but be prepared to go public if they don't act.

It's good to trust and be patient, but if the first one or two outcomes are not to your liking or are not correct, sometimes it's good to involve more people who might be able to unravel the complexities and be of more use to you and your goals. Therefore, asking to speak to a manager, in this case, was precisely the thing that was needed to help correctly communicate the findings.

Possible improvements

A few things could have been done differently in this case study to improve the outcome. The first is always to ensure you're working with more than just one person, if possible, to broaden the possible expertise of your audience.

Another possible improvement is that the researcher could have escalated sooner when it became clear that the support engineer wasn't helping. This escalation, if conducted earlier, would have saved a lot of time and ensured that the researcher's client received patches sooner.

Finally, setting dates for specific disclosure when initially working with a vendor is advised. While it's terrific for a researcher to talk with a vendor and understandably wait for a patch, vendors do not consistently deliver. Outlining your plan to the company first stating that you will disclose your findings in X number of days can draw particular attention to the matter. An event such as this might cause people to involve their managers, escalating the scenario without the intervention of a researcher. Overall, though, the researcher did an excellent job of trying to work with the vendor before escalating.

Hopefully, you found these five case studies insightful. Now, let's close out the chapter with a quick summary and recap of what we learned.

Summary

In this chapter, we spent time considering five case studies that dug into vulnerable software disclosures, which had their share of problems and casualties of circumstance. The takeaway for your own research and disclosure journey should be that things don't always go to plan. It's essential to rise above the sometimes unscrupulous or incompetent behavior exhibited by vendors in these scenarios. In each case discussed, some kind of communication breakdown led to a less-than-ideal outcome. In some cases, the researcher made assumptions about who they were talking to and their expertise level. In other cases, the vendor didn't act even after being given multiple chances, or worse, was hostile to researchers.

To protect your work and to make an impact, it's essential always to remember a few key things:

- Always communicate with vendors professionally while being firm on what you expect from them
- Consider mediation at the first signs of difficulty or delays
- Give vendors a reasonable amount of time to fix the issue before going public
- Have a solid plan for disclosure, including deadlines and backup plans
- Be prepared to follow through on your disclosure plans if there is no cooperation from the vendor

With these things in mind, you'll be in a much better position to handle any situation during your future adventures in research disclosure.

In the next chapter, we'll shift our focus to providing advice directly to software manufacturers and vendors to help them understand better why researchers might be contacting them and how to represent their business interests best and positively leverage the research.

9

Working with Security
Researchers – A Vendor's Guide

When Barnaby Jack gave his infamous 2010 Black Hat talk, he left his audience cheering and stunned. With a flair for showmanship, he presented an exploitation technique for **automated teller machines (ATMs)** named **Jackpotting**. Using malware that targeted vulnerabilities found in standard ATMs, he executed a live demo of this technique for an audience of security practitioners and hackers. In his demo, he remotely triggered a vulnerability that hijacked the ATM displays and triggered a graphical representation of a jackpot animation from a slot machine while spewing vast amounts of currency onto the stage.

Before his death at age 35, he had demonstrated up-and-coming research that detailed vulnerabilities in medical equipment such as insulin pumps and pacemakers. Barnaby Jack's life and work were nothing short of incredible. Through his curiosity, he developed special abilities and skills that gave him something like modern-day superpowers over technology. He could get ATMs to spit money out practically on command. He could cause people to spontaneously have heart attacks or cause diabetics to suffer from hypoglycemic shock by transmitting specially crafted radio signals. Think for a moment about how incredible it is that someone did these things and instead of selling this research or abusing this knowledge for personal gain, they shared it to improve the world around them. Much like many researchers, Jack found fulfillment in making the world better and safer by gaining a deep understanding of technology and its various shortcomings.

Throughout this book, we've spent time talking a lot about vendors who create software. As you read through this material, you might find yourself at this point in your career in various roles related to operations, development, or even security at a company like this. Despite the negative coverage of vendors throughout this text, vendors employ practitioners who (generally) want to do good work concerning the products they support. With that said, most vendors and the people who work with them do not understand what a security researcher is, what they do, or what motivates them. Security researchers are the proverbial superheroes in technology, and like most fictional universes, the heroes are often misunderstood—and even vilified—by those who do not understand them. Similarly, vendors' fundamental misunderstandings about security researchers can lead to vendors fostering a negative association with them. This negative association can lead vendors to miss critical opportunities to build productive relationships and capitalize on the security expertise researchers are willing to offer to organizations.

This chapter provides a vendor's guide for talking to security researchers about vulnerability disclosures. First, we aim to clarify what a researcher is in relation to a vendor. Next, we'll discuss the importance of building healthy relationships with researchers as this can help ensure that disclosures are handled responsibly and promptly. We will then offer guidance on communicating with researchers, including tips on responding to disclosure requests and providing feedback on proposed fixes. Finally, the chapter provides an overview of the different disclosure policies vendors can adopt along with recommendations on crafting an effective policy for your organization.

So, to summarize the upcoming content in this chapter, we're going to do the following:

- Define security researchers by exploring their characteristics, skills, and motivations
- Reflect on how organizations can collaborate with researchers constructively to build better, more secure products and services
- Clarify the best path to build trust with researchers, outlining the things to do and avoid
- Explore how to craft an effective, responsible disclosure policy while examining a complete example policy that could be used to model your own

These outcomes will be presented through the following main topics in this chapter:

- What is a security researcher?
- Harnessing researcher resources
- Building trust and collaboration with researchers
- Crafting a responsible disclosure policy

Let's start our chapter with an examination of what a security researcher is now.

What is a security researcher?

You might have a pretty good idea if you've read this book, starting at *Chapter 1, An Introduction to Vulnerabilities*, through to this sentence. To recap, though, a security researcher is someone who looks for vulnerabilities in software and systems. Researchers may be working on their research entirely independently or as part of a team. Researchers have varied educational backgrounds, some with no formal education to some of the brightest minds in academia. Companies employ researchers to research their products and software; some are professional bounty hunters and others work for organizations that focus on commoditizing security research. We believe that to communicate and build relationships with researchers effectively, you must first attempt to understand them. One of the ways we can grow our understanding of researchers is by understanding their common characteristics, what skills a researcher might have, and what motivates them. So, let's begin by examining the common researcher characteristics.

The characteristics of a researcher

It is generally believed that some of the most successful researchers share key characteristics: they are creative, curious, and persistent. These characteristics complement each other and help researchers understand the things they're looking to master. Starting with creativity, we'll explore what makes security researchers tick by discussing these characteristics.

Creativity

The best information security researchers can think about abstract problems in unique ways. They can see patterns where others see chaos and they can devise new ways of accomplishing goals outside of predetermined workflows. This creativity is expressed in their ability to look at a problem from different angles and to find new and innovative solutions.

This creativity is also evident in the way that they approach their work. They are constantly testing their new ideas and envisioning new ways of approaching old problems. This willingness to experiment and try new things allows them to find the best solutions to complex challenges.

Curiosity

The best information security researchers are also insatiably curious. They want to understand things and take a head-first approach to explore challenges. These traits allow them to push the boundaries of possibilities and discover weaknesses in logic.

Thinking back to some of the most explosive research conducted in the last decade, it usually came from humble beginnings. It's not unheard of for a researcher to seek a greater understanding of technology through the in-depth review of a **Request for Comments** (**RFC**), a ratified **Institute of Electrical Electronic Engineering** (**IEEE**) standard, or tomes of research published before them. They navigate through waters of uncertainty and often come out of this curiosity on the other side with a comprehensive understanding of how something works. This curiosity leads to mastery of the subject matter.

Persistence

The most gifted researchers are determined. Researchers might have a common sentiment that it isn't that something isn't possible; it's just that it isn't possible at that point in time. As a result, they'll return to scenarios repeatedly, if given the ability, and will only typically give up on something after many constant failures.

This persistence and determination are essential for researchers since they will face many setbacks when their ideas don't work. They need to be able to pick themselves up and keep going after each failure to eventually find success. This determination can be seen as a form of resilience, another essential trait for researchers. If in ample supply, this persistence often separates the best information security researchers from the rest. They constantly push themselves to improve and never give up when challenged.

These characteristic traits of researchers alone don't amount to a security researcher. Good researchers have a wide variety of skills and knowledge on technical subjects. Let's discuss these now.

The skillset of a researcher

Successful researchers will need to have a solid foundation of various skills. The best researchers deeply understand how technology is tied to and used in connection with computing systems. They may excel in studies and disciplines that heavily focus on logic, such as mathematics. Additionally, they may have communication skills, including writing, speaking, and influencing others. Let's talk about these skills now.

Technical skills

The best information security researchers have strong technical skills. They can understand complex systems and have a mastery over programming languages and development tools. These technical skills vary but commonly consist of several of the following categories:

- **Reverse engineering**: The ability to understand how software and hardware work without access to the source code or design documents.

- **Cryptography**: The ability to understand and exploit cryptographic algorithms.

- **Programming**: The ability to write code and, most importantly, understand how it is written in one or more programming languages.

- **System operations**: The ability to understand how administrators configure computer systems and how to exploit those configurations.

- **Networking**: The ability to understand interconnected systems that communicate with each other using a variety of standards and protocols. This may include an understanding of physical mediums and ethereal mediums such as radio operations in wireless networks.

Analytical skills

Often, researchers have an adept ability to identify patterns where others cannot. They should be able to quickly analyze large amounts of data. This analytical set of abilities is also helpful when troubleshooting problems in their research. Researchers often need to identify the root cause of conditions quickly to understand possible alternatives.

Communication skills

While not always the case, excellent researchers may possess or develop a penchant for sharing their work, often to further their own research or the research of others during their careers. Often, this leads researchers motivated by the desire to improve security to become involved in efforts related to informal education about their findings. These communication skills can surface in the style of Barnaby Jack's flashy Black Hat presentation or more muted forms of intellectual exchange. Researchers with these skills may also have the innate ability to communicate effectively with a broad demographic.

You might conclude that researchers have a high level of intelligence and subversive traits that allow them to question and challenge generally accepted norms of use. For example, some researchers might be tempted to use their skills for criminal purposes, while others might use their skills to solve complex problems or better society. To help us better understand why researchers do what they do, we'll need to examine the motivations of a researcher.

The motivations of a researcher

Like all humans, a researcher's behaviors are driven by their motivations, which are influenced by cultural, social, and personal factors. Many different motivations can drive researchers to engage in their work. Some of these motivations may be more personal, such as a desire to contribute to the advancement of knowledge or to make a difference in the world. Let's explore these now.

Discovery

The need for discovery is a powerful motivator for many researchers. The challenge of finding something new, or uncovering something that has been hidden, can be a motivating factor for many people. The need for discovery can also be a motivating factor for researchers trying to find new ways to solve problems. For example, a researcher trying to find a new way to exploit a software program may be motivated by the challenge of finding a new way to do something.

Competition

The need for competition is another common motivator for researchers. The challenge of being the best, or the first to find something, can motivate many people. In some pockets of the greater information security community, competitive researchers who study exploitation and defense techniques can be found in **capture-the-flag competitions**, which pit some of the brightest minds against each other for cash prizes awarded to the best hackers. Similarly, other researchers may joust and rush to be the first to reverse engineer a security patch, revealing otherwise hidden vulnerabilities.

Knowledge

The need for knowledge is another common motivation. Researchers want to know how things work and are often driven by the desire to understand the world around them. The need for knowledge can manifest in different ways for different people. For example, some researchers may want to understand how a particular system works, while others may want to understand how a particular attack works.

Recognition

The need for recognition is another common motivator for researchers. The satisfaction of getting credit for their work, or having their work recognized by their peers, can be a motivating factor for many people. Some researchers do this to improve their reputations, while others may leverage their research for career or other professional opportunities.

Power

It could be argued a darker influence that researchers are influenced by is power. Some researchers derive immense pleasure through gaining control of the world around them or influencing it to their desires. These motivators are often present in **hacktivism**, where people hack to demonstrate their social, ethical, religious, or political views or to force their views upon others.

Money

Money is also a common motivation for many researchers. The desire to earn a good income, or the need to support oneself or one's family, can be an influential motivating factor. Given this ability, researchers can make an income much higher than average worldwide salaries for their work. This income can be provided through lawful methods, such as working as a dedicated researcher for an organization or as a bug bounty hunter. Conversely, researchers can also pursue ethically questionable methods of selling vulnerabilities to brokers or navigating a path of outright criminal activity.

Helping others

The need to help others is another motivation that can be seen in some researchers. The desire to make the world a better place, or to help others, can be an influential motivating factor for some people. This motivator might surface in ways that aid their ideologies. For instance, a researcher who believes in social justice might try to find ways to help people oppressed due to their views or because of who they are. However, there is a fine line between helping others and abusing power.

For example, a researcher may be concerned with privacy and research mobile applications that violate users' privacy. Discovering these issues and delivering this information to the public so that the public can make more informed decisions is an excellent example of helping others. However, it may not be considered helpful if this private information is weaponized or exploited, causing human rights abuse by, say, authoritarian governments that seek to oppress minorities.

Now that we have a basic understanding of what makes researchers who they are, let's spend some time discussing how organizations could possibly benefit from working with these talented individuals.

Harnessing researcher resources

Forward-thinking organizations know they can improve their security posture by harnessing the power of security research. Now that we have a relative understanding of what security researchers do, their characteristics, and what they're motivated by, let's talk about how organizations can use these attributes to benefit them.

With the competitive landscape of zero-day exploits and their high monetary value, some researchers might be more inclined to sell their findings rather than share them directly with a vendor organization. These researchers usually have a few routes they can take. They could share their research with an unknown amount of effort directly with a vendor with no promise of reward, exploit the vulnerabilities themselves, or sell them to brokers. If a researcher contacts a vendor organization, take this as an excellent sign that the researcher is operating in good faith.

As discussed in *Chapter 4, Vulnerability Disclosure – Communicating Security Findings*, security researchers have generally been advised to reach out to companies if they find their research intersects with a business and its products. Well-meaning researchers motivated by more constructive purposes should be welcomed in an organization. After all, they hold the key to discoveries that could improve security posture.

One of the best things a company could do to welcome and encourage researchers to work with a company is to have a public **responsible disclosure policy** that is easy to find and inclusive and seeks collaborative relationships with researchers. Unfortunately, most vendors do not have a process to receive and manage incoming reports of vulnerabilities. Vendors who do not have such policies risk abandoning an opportunity to work with researchers. Researchers may associate a company without such policies with past negative experiences, frustration, and a feeling of devaluation, which they might have experienced with other companies without such policies. Feelings such as these could lead to the researcher going public without even contacting you, resulting in complete disclosure (less optimal) or perhaps reselling their findings to a receptive party.

A coordinated disclosure process can help to address these issues. These policies state how researchers should report vulnerabilities they discover and how the organization will handle these reports. By establishing clear policies and procedures, organizations can ensure that disclosures are managed responsibly and in a timely manner. In *Chapter 4*, we advise researchers to seek security disclosure policies and see them as a positive sign of a company's willingness to work with them.

> **Warning**
>
> While implied here, it's worth calling out directly. When a vendor decides to be non-communicative, dismissive, or threatening to researchers, vendors create scenarios where they lose control over the vulnerability. Well-meaning researchers are offering vendors something of value—*control over how the narrative unfolds*. Researchers may turn to other methods that can expose vendors to risks, liabilities, and a possible loss of revenue depending on the scenario. You should avoid this and seek more favorable outcomes with reasonable policies and coordinated disclosure policies that take control of how things unfold.

In many cases, a responsible disclosure policy might be found on a vendor website, usually under a *security* hyperlink. However, newer methods, such as the file format specification on vulnerability disclosures **RFC9116** from the **Internet Engineering Task Force (IETF)**, suggest that companies should include a text file in their website's root directory named security.txt. This text file should include information such as the email address that a researcher should use to initiate contact, encryption keys that could be used to encrypt email communications, a copy of the policy, and a security acknowledgments page. This simple text file could be as brief as the following example:

```
# Our security address
Contact: mailto:security@example.com

# Our OpenPGP key
Encryption: https://example.com/pgp-key.txt

# Our security policy
Policy: https://example.com/security-policy.html

# Our security acknowledgments page
Acknowledgments: https://example.com/hall-of-fame.html

Expires: 2021-12-31T18:37:07z
```

Figure 9.1 – An example of what the RFC9116 standard looks like when implemented

Adopting standards such as these can help make security policy easier to find and it signals to security researchers that you want to work with them to improve your products. In the *Crafting a responsible disclosure policy* section, we'll discuss what should be included in such a policy.

Harnessing the power of vulnerability disclosures from researchers can create a win-win situation for both companies and researchers. Companies can benefit from improved security and trust for the security research community and researchers can gain recognition and rewards for their work.

It is also important to remember that disclosure is a two-way street. In addition to receiving reports of vulnerabilities, vendors also need to provide feedback to researchers on the proposed fixes. This feedback should be timely and constructive, considering the researcher's perspective.

A vendor who effectively manages researcher relationships or makes a thoughtful effort to build meaningful, collaborative relationships can reap many benefits. In addition, when these relationships are managed effectively, relationships with researchers can offer considerable benefits with a low investment cost. These include early detection and prevention of attacks, improved product security, perceived inclusion and transparency, and increased customer trust.

Now, let's dive into the standard things you should and should not strive to do when building these collaborative and meaningful relationships that can bolster your products' security and harness the resources of a researcher's work.

Building trust and collaboration with researchers

Vendors who first encounter a security researcher might be apprehensive about the researcher's motivations. Unfortunately, this often leads organizations to take missteps in working with researchers. They might avoid all contact, thinking any communication will result in an attack or public disclosure. They might try to buy the researcher's silence with a bug bounty and a mandatory non-disclosure agreement. Worse, they might threaten legal action against the researchers. These suboptimal responses can damage the potential of creating opportunities to calmly control the scenario while creating positive outcomes for you, your customers, and the researcher.

To create positive outcomes, we must first examine missteps when working with researchers and how we can avoid them. Let's explore this topic now.

Avoiding common relationship missteps

We'll now spend some time discussing the common ways a vendor can damage a potential relationship with a security researcher. While this is not the most exhaustive list, these are the common themes we observed while speaking with and interviewing researchers who actively engage with vendors.

Don't be dismissive

When working with researchers, it is essential to remember that they are experts in their field and have many valuable insights. Unfortunately, many vendors make the mistake of dismissing reports without even looking into them or brushing off researchers as *hackers* that are just trying to break things. Dismissive behavior shows a lack of respect for the researcher and a lack of understanding of what they do. Remember that these individuals are trying to help make your software more secure and should be treated as collaborators, not possible criminals. It is rare for criminals to contact you directly with an offer to improve your software. Remember that these individuals are subject matter experts trying to help you make your products more secure, sometimes without the promise of benefits.

Don't make assumptions

It is vital to avoid making assumptions about what a researcher is looking for or why they are contacting you. For example, many companies assume that all researchers are interested in financial gain and will only work with you if you offer them a bug bounty. In some cases, this might be true, but this is most certainly the exception and not the rule. Many researchers are simply interested in helping make the internet safer and will work with you even if you can't offer them anything monetary in return. Making assumptions about someone's motivations can often lead to tension and mistrust, so it's best to avoid doing this altogether.

Don't ignore reports

One of researchers' most common complaints is that vendors simply ignore their reports. This leaves the researcher feeling unappreciated for their contributions, often leading to them losing interest in working with that vendor altogether. Radio silence from vendors may also generate resentment from the researcher, causing them to disclose their findings to the public and usually share their experience with the company not being responsive. Ultimately, this could lead to consumers questioning the quality of the software that is sold, perhaps asking if the vendor truly cares about the safety of their product.

To avoid this, vendors need to take every report seriously. Taking reports seriously means responding to the researcher promptly, acknowledging their reports, and promising to review them. If found valid, communicate with the researcher, acknowledging their work, thanking them for their submission, and taking action to fix the identified issue. These actions show that the company values the security of its product and is willing to work with researchers to ensure that it meets consumers' expectations.

If a company ignores reports or takes too long to address them, it frustrates researchers and gives them little incentive to continue working with the company. Furthermore, this could jeopardize the security of the software and damage the company's reputation. This terrible outcome can be easily avoided by following up on reports promptly, even if it's just to offer a quick thank-you and say that your team is currently investigating the issue.

Don't stop communicating

Researchers and vendor collaborations have often fallen apart due to communication struggles where vendors do not return emails for status updates. Just because a researcher has submitted a report, doesn't mean their job is done. Often, researchers will want to publish their research and, as such, will monitor your progress on remediation of their findings.

For example, researchers will often continue to communicate with the vendor throughout the vulnerability mitigation process to offer additional information, provide examples of how the vendor can implement security issues, recreate the issue for developers, and even retest once the vulnerability has been mitigated. In many cases, researchers will also help your teams understand the root cause of the issues and offer recommendations on how to prevent similar issues from happening. These insights from subject matter experts can be an invaluable resource for improving your product's security posture overall by helping your staff to understand their areas for improvement.

If a researcher reaches out to you after filing a report, be sure to respond promptly and keep them in the loop on the status of their report. Once you've addressed the reported issue, let the researcher know what actions you took and whether their report helped resolve it. This feedback is essential to maintain a good relationship with researchers and to encourage them to continue working with you in the future.

Don't take too long to fix the issue

Once you have received a report, you must act on it promptly. Researchers are often quite frustrated when they find an issue and report it, only to have the vendor take months or even years to fix it. Elongated periods of remediation show researchers that you're not prioritizing security. Deprioritizing this work can make the researcher feel like their work is pointless and, ultimately, leaves the vendor's products vulnerable for an extended period. Instead, commit early to a timetable that aligns with the best industry practices for patching (e.g., 30 days for high-severity vulnerabilities, 90 days for medium severity) and communicate this with the researcher.

If you cannot fix an issue within the committed timeframe, reach out to the researcher and explain the situation. In most cases, they will be understanding and may even work with you to help come up with a solution. However, if you repeatedly fail to meet deadlines or do not keep the researcher updated on your progress, they will likely lose faith in you and go public with their findings.

Don't take reports personally

It's important to remember that when a researcher submits a report, they are not trying to attack you or your company. Most researchers that are explicitly reaching out to you are driven by motivations around improving the security of products. If you receive a vulnerability report, try to take it constructively and use it as an opportunity to improve the product's security. It's not uncommon for researchers to receive unconstructive commentary from embarrassed vendors as the vulnerability has somehow wounded their pride. Nevertheless, researchers want to help you and you should accept that help when offered. The alternatives are far worse.

Don't lead with dishonesty

This is rare but something we have observed. Vendors may misrepresent their positions, plans, and abilities to appear stronger than they are or make a researcher disappear. Unfortunately for vendors, researchers rarely ever go away, and their traits of persistence will follow vulnerabilities to their conclusion. If they find they've been lied to throughout the process, don't be surprised that a researcher will lose faith in your company and as a result go public with their findings, which will undoubtedly feature details about how you misled them.

Don't start with litigation

Classic examples of communication between vendors and researchers often start with a legal threat. If a researcher reaches out to you looking to work with you, sometimes without a clear benefit, they are likely not good candidates for this heavy-handed approach. This is not the way to open a dialogue and will only further damage the relationship. If a researcher feels like they are being threatened, they are likely to stop communicating entirely and will take their story to the media. While specific scenarios warrant the use of lawyers or law enforcement, it might not be best to start the conversation through the imminent notice of a threat.

Now that we've covered some of the things not to do when working with researchers, let's talk about what you should do to build positive relationships.

Building positive vendor-researcher relations

With the fundamentals of what we shouldn't do under our belt, let's talk about things that can help strengthen a relationship and harmonize a researcher's work and a vendor's efforts to build and service great products.

Be timely and gracious

As we mentioned earlier, one of the most important things you can do when working with researchers is to respond to their reports promptly. Behavior and practices such as these show that you appreciate their work and take their concerns seriously. Consider for a moment that it took the researcher time and effort to prepare the report, submit it, and wait for a response.

When you first receive a report, you must quickly acknowledge receipt and thank the researcher for their work. Immediately, this sets the tone for future interactions and shows that you value their contributions. You can do this by sending a simple response such as *"Thanks for sending this over. We appreciate it. We'll take a look and get back to you within a few days."* Follow this with an offer to have the researcher directly respond with any additional questions.

If a report requires additional investigation, a response can be given. Let the researcher know that their input is valuable and appreciated, even if you can't provide a detailed response at that moment. This type of communication goes a long way in building trust and rapport.

Setting expectations

One of the things we advised earlier to researchers, in *Chapter 4, Vulnerability Disclosure – Communicating Security Findings*, regarding the disclosure of vulnerabilities is to set expectations with vendors they're working with. This goes for the vendor as well; scenarios where researchers become disengaged are often due to an unseen mismatch of expectations. As a vendor, you should set realistic expectations with the researcher on what you can and cannot do. These expectations should be framed within a communicated timeline.

For example, if a researcher reports a critical issue that needs to be fixed immediately, let them know the next steps and when they can expect to hear back from you. On the other hand, if a researcher reports an issue of low severity or something that cannot be fixed immediately, let them know so they do not become frustrated waiting for a response.

Another critical thing to remember is that not all researchers are familiar with the inner workings of a company. As such, explaining any delays in response or why a particular issue cannot be fixed is essential. Setting expectations and regularly meeting with them along the way will undoubtedly create trust and build a rapport with the researcher.

Keeping lines of communication open

As we mentioned earlier, one of the best things you can do as a vendor is to keep lines of communication open with your researchers. This means being available to answer questions, provide updates on progress, and discuss new ideas.

A great way to keep lines of communication open is to have a dedicated contact for researchers, whether an individual or a team. This contact should be easy to reach and responsive to inquiries. Additionally, this contact should be empowered to make decisions and act on behalf of the researcher.

Depending on the severity of the issue the and resources available to both the researcher and vendor, another way to keep communication lines open is to host regular meetings or calls, one on one or with a group. These can be used to update researchers on the progress of their reports, answer any questions, or discuss new ideas.

Fix the issues promptly

Once you have received a report, it is vital to act promptly. Researchers are often quite frustrated when they find an issue and report it, only to have the vendor take months or even years to fix it. Vendor inaction makes the researcher feel like their work is pointless and leaves the software vulnerable for an extended period. If your company cannot fix the issue immediately, or within a reasonable timeline, keep the researcher updated on your progress and set realistic expectations. The researcher may have shared their expectations on when they wish to communicate their findings.

Offer rewards and acknowledgment

While not all vendors have the same resources, one way to incentivize researchers is through financial rewards. One of the key motivators for researchers is recognition of their efforts and monetary benefits. More prominent vendors have succeeded with a bug bounty program or private arrangements with individual researchers.

Through researching content for this book and examining positive relationships between vendors and researchers, we heard of some novel stories where sometimes vendors might offer paid speaking engagements. This involves having the researcher talk to company employees about security research.

Rewards don't necessarily need to come from money or employment. Instead, some researchers will find appreciation through gifts of goods of various value, including things such as boxes of snacks, beverages, t-shirts, hats, and mugs.

Hiring or paying a researcher isn't necessary, though. Non-financial forms of incentives can be just as effective in motivating researchers. For example, public recognition of a researcher's work is a great way to show appreciation and encourage future engagement. Acknowledgment could occur in a blog post, a social media shout-out, a running list of security contributions, or even a simple thank-you email where a vendor shares their support.

Other unconventional ways to build relationships and incentivize researchers are by providing access to new features or products before they are released to the public and asking for their input on the product's security. This type of early access can be very motivating for researchers and it shows that you value their input.

Successful vendors who build uniquely valuable relationships with researchers employ several methods, if not all. But, if you think back about what motivates researchers, rewarding researchers with money, goods, and, most importantly, acknowledgment ticks many boxes.

Be transparent

Another essential thing to do when working with researchers is to be transparent. Transparency means being honest about the state of your software and openly sharing information about security issues. Through this transparency, you can show that you are committed to working with researchers, which helps build trust between you and them. Additionally, it is crucial to keep the researcher updated on your progress in fixing the issue. Involving them throughout the remediation process will help them feel like they are making a difference and encourage them to continue working with you.

Acknowledge autonomy

Researchers have autonomy and part of maintaining solid vendor-researcher relations is respecting that. Acknowledging a researcher's autonomy shows that you respect their work and are willing to work with them rather than against them. One way to do this is to allow researchers to choose how their names are listed in public reports. If a researcher prefers to be anonymous, honor that request. Additionally, try to give researchers control over when and how their report is published. Giving researchers a say in the process shows that you value their input and want to work collaboratively.

If there are disagreements between a researcher and vendor, acknowledge that the researcher has a different perspective and try to see the issue from their point of view. Also, acknowledge that the researcher can do and say what they choose. For example, a common source of conflict is when a researcher should publish their findings. A vendor may wish for the researcher to stay silent until a fix is in place or never release or publish their research. On the other hand, researchers may feel that disclosing the finding is in the best interest of public safety. In this case, without a legal arrangement, it's important to remember that the researcher has the final say in whether to disclose their findings and can act how they see fit. Impeding this autonomy sets a bad precedent, and researchers will likely publish their research along with any torrid details of how you may have tried to suppress their research.

It is often in the vendor's and researcher's best interest to agree on publishing before any work is done. But if that's not possible, try to understand the researcher's position and remember that they are likely acting in good faith.

We now have a good set of principles of what to do and what not to do when working with researchers. However, as stated in our earlier section on harnessing researcher resources, building a responsible disclosure policy is one of the best ways to establish good relationships. Applying what we now know will anchor our policy constructively, building positive relationships. Let's now explore what these policies look like and how to create one.

Crafting a responsible disclosure policy

A responsible disclosure policy is a set of guidelines that dictate how a company will handle reports of vulnerabilities. For example, the policy should state who can report an issue, how they should do so, and what information should be included in the report. It should also define what issues will be considered for disclosure and what timeline the company expects to follow for patching vulnerabilities.

There are many ways to formulate a disclosure policy, but all policies should aim to strike a balance between the need to protect users and the need to give researchers the credit they deserve.

A responsible disclosure policy can help to build trust between a company and the security research community. It can also improve the overall security of a company's products by ensuring that all reports of vulnerabilities are taken seriously and addressed promptly.

Building trust with researchers is often bookended by a company policy that reflects a collaborative, respectful, transparent spirit that rewards researchers with the things they want most and refrains from punishing them. Having a disclosure policy can set expectations for how you want researchers to work with you and what type of information you need from them. Policies such as this help to avoid misunderstandings and unnecessary conflict in the vendor-researcher relationship.

There are a few key components that should be included in every responsible disclosure policy:

- A clear statement of the company's commitment to security and privacy. The policy should show that the company is serious about protecting its users and data.

- A description of what types of vulnerabilities will be accepted under the policy.

- A clear statement that the company does not condone illegal activity, such as hacking, without permission. If permission is meant to be granted in this document to researchers, this statement might include a scope of what is permitted.

- An outline of the process for submitting a report, including contact information for the appropriate team. Researchers should know who to get in touch with and how to submit a report without having to jump through too many hoops.

- Excellent disclosure policies typically have an authorization section that states that researchers do not need to fear prosecution as they share their findings with the company.

- The best policies include timelines for responding to reports and addressing vulnerabilities. Researchers should know when to expect a response and when the issue will be fixed.

- After the issue is addressed, include a statement about what type of information will be shared with the researcher. For example, this might include information about when the fix will be released or whether the researcher will be credited in any public disclosures.

Remember that your policy should balance being welcoming to researchers and protecting your company's interests. It's also important to remember that your policy is not set in stone. You can adjust it as needed, based on feedback from the researcher community.

With an understanding of the core tenets of the responsible disclosure policy, what it does, and what should be included, let's spend some time examining an example policy.

An example policy – Acme Logistics' responsible disclosure policy

There's a lot that a responsible disclosure policy might contain. Still, in most cases, the best policies are accessible to non-legal experts, consist of just a few pages, and clearly define the parameters of a researcher's relationship with the company. In our following example, we'll examine the fictitious policy of **Acme Logistics**, a company with a functional responsibility disclosure policy that delivers on the best practices discussed earlier in this chapter. Note the author's notes will appear in italics to bring additional context to the sections you're reviewing.

Introduction

An introductory section should open every disclosure policy. It should reflect the values of the representing organization. This section should take a committed, concerned, and receptive tone.

At Acme Logistics, we value the safety of our customers and citizens above all else. Therefore, we have implemented strict measures to protect sensitive information, and we value any contributions to make these investments more valuable to those we serve. The purpose of this document is to provide a framework for security researchers when conducting research activities, such as scanning for vulnerabilities or testing software for bugs. This policy describes how to securely contact us with any vulnerability reports and gives guidelines for how and when research should be disclosed by the researcher if desired. We encourage all researchers to contact us to report potential vulnerabilities in our systems, and we look forward to working with researchers to help close unforeseen gaps in our systems.

Authorization of use

This section is meant to affirm a position that if security researchers are acting in good faith, they can expect not to face legal consequences for their actions through seeking prosecution or civil damages.

If security researchers follow the guidelines in this document, we will authorize research within the *Guidelines of use* and *Scope guidance* sections of this document. Researchers must make every effort to adhere to these restrictions and to contact us if their research begins to deviate.

Acme Logistics promises to help resolve any issues researchers find and will not pursue punitive legal action against them. If another company files legal actions against you for your actions that were authorized by adhering to this policy, we will reveal this authorization upon the researcher's request.

Guidelines of use

Guidelines of use should outline to researchers what they must do to remain authorized to conduct research.

Compliance with this policy entails that you adhere to the following principles in your research and you pledge to do the following:

- Notify us using the methods disclosed in the policy concerning any security vulnerability or risk discovered during your research

- Provide Acme Logistics with reasonable amounts of time to remediate any vulnerabilities and risks before public disclosure or publishing to vulnerability databases such as MITRE's CVE list and the **national vulnerability database (NVD)**

- Adopt a zero-harm method of research that aims to avoid creating events of system degradation

- Refrain from violating users' privacy in a way that assumes their identity or exposes passwords or other private information in ways that could be considered unsafe

- Do not sell vulnerabilities or information related to systems and services we offer to third parties such as vulnerability brokers

- Do not use unnecessary exploitation techniques that cause damage or undue burdens on the support staff of Acme Logistics

- Refrain from using deception through social engineering of Acme Logistics employees or customers of Acme Logistics

As such, security testing, which will be considered strictly off-limits, covers techniques such as:

- Social engineering

- Denial-of-service attacks

- Bruteforce password guessing

- Use of unstable exploitation packages, which are known to cause system instability

Through your research, if you believe that you have come across or observed any sensitive information, such as trade secrets, financial data, personally identifiable information, financial information, or anything considered proprietary, research must cease, and you must notify Acme Logistics immediately. Under no circumstances should you disclose or share information about details or contents under penalty of violating adherence to this policy.

Scope guidance

This section covers the scope of what interconnected systems can be tested (if any) if they adhere to the policy.

Our policy limits research to what is defined as *in-scope* for testing and evaluation. The scope of researchable assets that are internet-facing includes the following domains:

- `*.acme-logistics.com`
- `*.acme-mail.com`
- `*.acme-delivery.com`

Services and hosts discovered while reviewing these in-scope hosts will also be considered in scope. This policy also applies to our commercial product offerings of software and our open source contributions to various development libraries.

Any other discovered resources that may hold affiliation with Acme Logistics will be considered out-of-scope. If you wish to discuss assets that are not in scope, please do so by emailing us at `security@acme-logstics.com` before conducting testing and research. If a particular system is not in scope that you think merits testing, please get in touch with us to discuss it first. We will increase the scope at our discretion to the entirety of this policy or through an ad hoc explicit agreement with the individual researcher.

Reporting a vulnerability

This section describes how you would like to receive research reporting. In this section, ensure you clearly define what you expect and need from a researcher to verify their findings.

We accept vulnerability reports at our general security email address, `security@acme-logistics.com`. In your reporting, there is no expectation that the researcher must be involved with further discussion of any disclosers, and as such, reports may be submitted anonymously. If you decide to share contact information with your reporting, we will acknowledge receipt of your reporting within 14 calendar days of the submission date.

Information submitted under this policy will only be used for defensive purposes to mitigate or remediate vulnerabilities. If your reporting impacts a third-party partner of Acme Logistics, we may share your research with the impacted third party. In our communications about vulnerabilities, we will not share your name or publish content about your work unless permission is explicitly given to Acme Logistics.

It is our expectation that your report must clearly describe the vulnerability, the risk it poses, and locations where the product can be seen as vulnerable. Your reporting should also include recreation instructions with screenshots and evidence where appropriate.

Researcher response expectations

This section helps the researcher to know what to expect from your organization after they send their research to you. This information should be aligned with realistic operational considerations that are strictly followed.

We commit to you, the researcher, a dedicated policy of ensuring that your research is treated seriously and that you should expect the following timelines for any research you share with us:

- We will acknowledge your vulnerability report within 14 calendar days of the submission date. In this acknowledgment, you should expect a date of when the research will be examined and verified by Acme Logistics.

- We will be transparent about our efforts to verify your report, requesting assistance and additional clarification if your contact information was initially shared with us.

- Once your report has been verified, we will determine the severity of your findings using the **Common Vulnerability Scoring System** (**CVSS**). If the risk is rated as *informational*, it will not be actioned and you will be informed of this action.

- Once the severity has been determined, we will work with you in building an effective remediation plan that will include expected dates of resolution.

- This process of acknowledgment, verification, and planning for remediation should be executed in no more than 60 calendar days.

- We will remain open collaborators and respond to any inquiries or requests for updates within 14 calendar days of their initial submission.

Researcher award and acknowledgment expectations

Researchers often want to know specifically how they'll be acknowledged by the company, when they can publish their research, and if any awards will be given to them for their contributions. It's essential to state timelines they can expect for publishing their research and whether they'll be acknowledged. Hold yourself accountable here, giving the researcher permission to publish if the organization fails to meet its policy. Researchers respect this immensely.

Acme Logistics is cognizant of the time and resources researchers expend in reviewing our products to make them safer for our customers. With this in mind, we endorse the publishing of all research to third-party vulnerability databases or public websites, provided that the researcher allows for the following time periods to pass:

60 days, which is inclusive of the initial process of acknowledging the report, verifying it, and planning remediation steps, along with the following:

- 30 additional days for resolving critical-risk findings
- 60 additional days for resolving high-risk findings
- 90 additional days for resolving medium-risk findings
- 180 additional days for resolving low-risk findings

This time allotment will provide Acme Logistics ample time to respond and remediate the vulnerabilities following our internal policies. Acme Logistics reserves the right to request additional time extensions depending on the extent of the work up to one additional time for a period equal to the initial requested time. If Acme Logistics does not fulfill its commitments, the researcher is welcome to publish their findings as they see fit, without repercussions.

We request that in any information disclosure, please consider limiting information in a way that does not explicitly disclose the vulnerability.

All research disclosures will be acknowledged in release notes. In addition, before publishing, we will confirm whether you would like us to redact your name or any other information regarding your research. Acme Logistics, as a policy, does not award financial rewards for research. However, in exceptional circumstances impacting the organization, Acme Logistics has awarded company apparel, unique plaques commemorating research, and the occasional one-time award payment for beneficial research.

Feedback and questions

In this section, the organization caps off the policy with a sincere thank you, an invitation to inquire for more information, and a request for feedback on the policy.

Thank you very much for reviewing our policy, and if your research includes our resources in the future, we look forward to building a more secure future for our product and organization with your help. If you have any questions related to this policy, they can be submitted through our general security mailbox at security@acmelogistics.com. In addition, we welcome suggestions for improving our policy. If you see opportunities for us to improve this policy, please let us know how we can build a better relationship with you and the greater information security research community.

Concluding thoughts on effective policies

We hope this example policy has clarified what something might look like at your own company. We modeled this policy after current policies throughout the United States that have built effective structures of expectations for security researchers. Feel free to copy this and modify it as you build your policy. However, as you navigate creating your policy or improving one, seek guidance on this policy at a leadership level. Policies published unilaterally by a security department are rarely effective without the support of people in leadership roles. Seek guidance and adoption from executives who may see possible risks or legal departments wishing to limit the organization's liability. These actors can help weigh in and improve the responsible disclosure policy to best align with your organization's goals and ensure its adoption company-wide.

With our goal of reviewing a responsible disclosure policy out of the way, let's now summarize what we've learned from this chapter.

Summary

In this chapter, we've spent time reviewing security research through the eyes of a company that might not know much about what a security researcher is. First, we helped further understand a security researcher's characteristics, skills, and motivations. We then explored how we might harness the expertise of a researcher to help an organization improve products and services by making them more secure. We then covered some of the most common ways to build trust with researchers and the things that should be avoided that may destroy an otherwise productive relationship. Finally, we explored an example of a responsible disclosure policy modeled from several policies in use by large organizations, governmental agencies, and non-profit organizations. As we close this chapter and move forward to our final chapter in this book, we will spend time providing templates for researchers to use in their communications with vendors and vulnerability databases. Finally, we'll touch on some final references and recommendations and close our book with a note of encouragement from the author.

10
Templates, Resources, and Final Guidance

Throughout this book, we've reviewed and built knowledge about vulnerabilities, their life cycle, and how to get started researching. Then, we reviewed the methods used to communicate and publish vulnerability disclosures. Next, in our edge cases, we discussed how we could seek mediation help from third parties and how to publish vulnerabilities on our own. Afterward, we explored several real-world scenarios highlighting the difficulties researchers face. Finally, we discussed disclosures from a vendor's perspective and how to best build collaborative relationships.

I sincerely hope you've enjoyed these materials. My wish is that they have bolstered your understanding of how simplistic research can transform into published vulnerabilities. Now, armed with this knowledge, you should be well equipped to begin your own journey and face potential challenges.

This final chapter is meant to supplement this book with additional resources, such as research templates, communication templates, and organizational resources, which will help you manage and keep track of the vulnerabilities you discover. Finally, the closing section offers you some final words of encouragement from the author.

So, to summarize the upcoming content, in this chapter, we're going to review the following:

- Vulnerability research test case templates

- Email communication templates

- Templates and resources for publishing vulnerabilities and reserving CVEs

- Organization resource templates

- A closing statement that reflects on the challenges of this work

In this chapter, we'll review templates that can be used to help you in your research as you aim to organize your research, communicate it to vendors, and then publish vulnerabilities. These outcomes will be presented through the following main topics in this chapter:

- Research test case templates

- Vendor communication email templates

- CVE templates

- Organizational templates

Let's start this chapter with research test case templates, specifically exploring the systemization of the *OWASP Testing Guide (v 4.2)*.

Research test case templates

As our chapter introducing research covered, we don't need to look too far for research test cases. In *Chapter 3, Vulnerability Research – Getting Started with Successful Strategies*, we discussed and showed how to create your test cases in **CherryTree**. Our test cases could contain a small database of test notes, descriptions, and statuses. We wanted to prepare you for the most common kinds of web application testing you might have through the adoption and systemization of the *OWASP Testing Guide (v 4.2)* within the CherryTree application. As seen in the following screenshot, we've organized all test cases into a system of categories that can be sequentially tested. We have included information about the test case and the testing methods outlined by the best industry experts and have added testing note sections you can check off as you complete your test cases. We encourage you to take this template and make it your own:

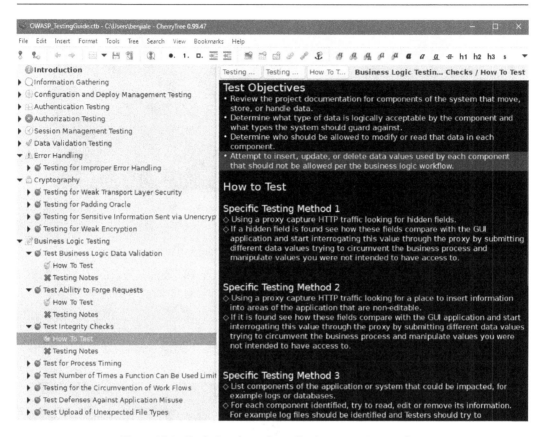

Figure 10.1 – Exploring the web application test suite template

Here's how you can grab a copy of this template and start getting your template configured to your liking.

We'll be using Linux for this example; however, you can use Windows or macOS to do this. We'll need to clone the following repository with this command:

```
git clone https://github.com/BallinBallen/OWASP-Testing-Guide-
Cherry-Tree-Template.git
```

Alternatively, you can visit the repository directly in a web browser. Download a copy of the template here: https://github.com/BallinBallen/OWASP-Testing-Guide-Cherry-Tree-Template.

To use the template, open the `CherryTree` file with CherryTree. If you're using something such as Kali Linux, you can expect this program to be preinstalled on the operating system, as seen in *Figure 10.2*:

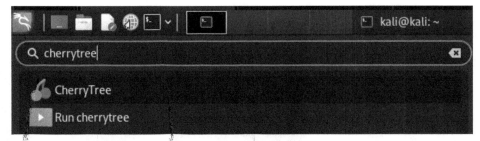

Figure 10.2 – Opening CherryTree

> **Note**
>
> If you're using a Windows, macOS, or another Linux operating system, you can download and configure CherryTree by visiting the GitHub repository where the application source and builds are kept: `https://github.com/giuspen/cherrytree`

Once CherryTree is open, let's locate the file you just cloned from the first command, as seen in the following screenshot:

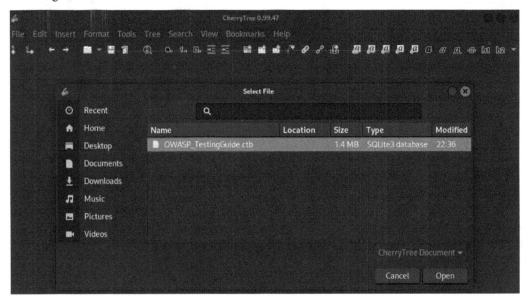

Figure 10.3 – Opening the template

Once open, start by reviewing the introduction, which covers primary usage and advises the tester to use the template to craft specific test suites that align with their goals, as depicted in *Figure 10.4*:

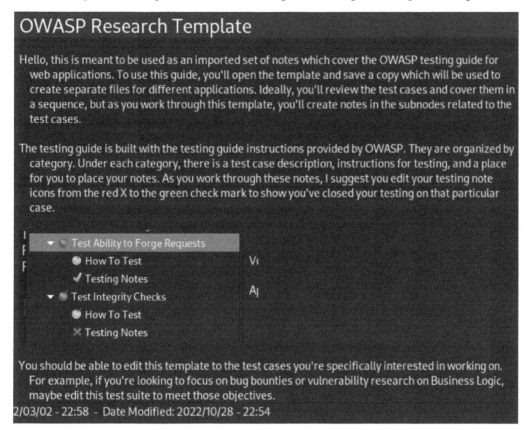

Figure 10.4 – The information page shares information on the use of the template

Next, we suggest you spend some time looking through the test cases to get familiar with what they look like and how they're structured:

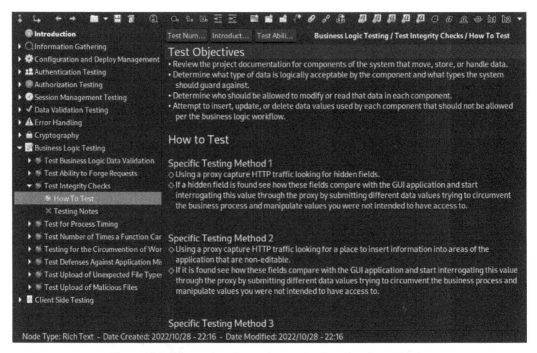

Figure 10.5 – Instructions for testing can be found under each test

Once you're ready to start using this template, save a copy of this set of notes to a separate file with a name representing the application you're testing. The testing notes are blank; the general workflow would consist of reviewing the test case and instructions and completing the test case notes.

If you're looking for a smaller, perhaps more condensed version of the OWASP templates, we suggest reviewing the OWASP checklist published by **tanprathan**. It's an excellent brief spreadsheet that covers all the specific low-level cases that might need to be executed. It does not, however, provide the tester with a place to keep research notes:

	Authorization Testing	Test Name	Description	Tools	Result	Rema
47						
48	OTG-AUTHZ-001	Testing Directory traversal/file include	dot-dot-slash attack (/), Directory traversal, Local File Inclusion/Remote File Inclusion.	Burp Proxy, ZAP, Wfuzz	Not Started	
49	OTG-AUTHZ-002	Testing for bypassing authorization schema	Access a resource without authentication? Bypass ACL, Force browsing //admin/adduser.jsp)	Burp Proxy (Autorize), ZAP	Not Started	
50	OTG-AUTHZ-003	Testing for Privilege Escalation	Testing for role/privilege manipulate the values of hidden variables. Change some param groupId=2 to groupId=1	Burp Proxy (Autorize), ZAP	Not Started	
51	OTG-AUTHZ-004	Testing for Insecure Direct Object References	Force changing parameter value (?invoice=123 -> ?invoice=456)	Burp Proxy (Autorize), ZAP	Not Started	

Figure 10.6 – Some testers prefer lighter documentation methods such as Excel spreadsheets

You can find this template in the following GitHub repository: https://github.com/tanprathan/OWASP-Testing-Checklist

While these research templates don't cover every case on every specific software, they should give you the right inspiration to build a test suite that works for you and the research you're looking to execute. Remember to create your plan, use these tools to build your execution plan, and then execute it.

With our test case templates out of the way, let's now look at our communication templates that are meant to help structure possible communications with vendors.

Vendor communication email templates

In our initial disclosure of vulnerabilities to vendors, we might run across various scenarios with undefined policies. In this section, we'll provide a few email templates that you can use to take and craft your email response.

An introduction email for a company with no security disclosure policy

In this example template, we'll introduce ourselves to a company with no defined security disclosure policy on its website/contact information. It's best to keep these brief, where possible, and not full of details outside of the fact you discovered something:

Hello,

My name is {researcher name}, and I am a security researcher. I recently discovered a potential vulnerability in your company's website/product. I wanted to reach out and let you know about it, as well as see whether your company has a process for handling such submissions.

I would be happy to provide additional details and work with your team to resolve this issue. Due to the sensitive nature of these findings, I'd like to submit this to your security team for initial validation. Is there a person or team who would be best suited to receiving this information?

I hope to hear from you soon. I'll follow up in 30 days if I have not heard from your team about our next steps. If you need any assistance or help, please reach out to me via email at {email address}.

Thanks,

{researcher name}

Once you've heard back from the vendor with an appropriate contact, or whether they wish to receive details directly, you could follow up with an email similar to the one we'll cover for the sample disclosure template with a security policy:

Hello,

I'm following up after getting your contact information from someone I had initially corresponded with. My name is {researcher name}, and I would like to share some of the vulnerabilities I discovered while reviewing the security of {software name}.

There are {vulnerability count} vulnerabilities in {software name}, specifically in the {version number} version. In the next section, I'll describe these vulnerabilities:

Vulnerability 1

{CWE mapping name and ID}

This vulnerability is found in the {where the vulnerability was found} section of the application. This weakness can result in {CWE impact description}, which may impact your customers {scenario how this vulnerability would impact the user}.

To recreate this vulnerability, you can follow these steps. I've provided screenshots to help illustrate a proof-of-concept.

{Recreation steps}

Vulnerability 2

{Additional vulnerabilities}

As part of my research, I plan to release {blog/publishing CVE} for which I'd like to receive any contributor credits when you fix and disclose this vulnerability to your customers. Additionally, I'd like to offer any assistance I can that will aid in helping fix this problem impacting {software name}.

I hope to hear from you soon. I know this is a lot to process, so I'll follow back up in 30 days if I have not heard from your team about our next steps. If you need any assistance or help, please reach out to me via email at {email address}.

Thanks,

{researcher name}

Let's now review possible communication strategies that can be used with an organization with a pre-defined security policy.

Sample disclosure template with security policy

In this email template, we'll set up variables for your contact information, vulnerability information, and vendor information in curly brackets. We aim to communicate in a friendly, collaborative way that includes our intentions and all the relevant, helpful information about our research:

Hello {vendor name department},

My name is {researcher name}, and I'm an independent security researcher. I recently became interested in your software {software name} and spent some time reviewing the platform's security.

This email is to inform you of the security vulnerabilities I discovered during my research. I'm sharing these with you because I'd like to help improve the security of your excellent software and reduce the chance of your customers being impacted by a criminal exploiting a security risk.

There are {vulnerability count} vulnerabilities in {software name}, specifically in the {version number} version. In the next section, I'll describe these vulnerabilities:

Vulnerability 1

{CWE mapping name and ID}

This vulnerability is found in the {where vulnerability was found} section of the application. This weakness can result in {CWE impact description}, which may impact your customers in {scenario how this vulnerability would impact the user}.

To recreate this vulnerability, you can follow these steps. I've provided screenshots to help illustrate a proof-of-concept.

{Recreation steps}

Vulnerability 2

{Additional vulnerabilities}

As part of my research, I plan {to release blog/publish CVE} for which I'd like to receive any contributor credits when you fix and disclose this vulnerability to your customers. Additionally, I'd like to offer any assistance I can that will aid in helping fix this problem impacting {software name}.

I hope to hear from you soon. I know this is a lot to process, so I'll follow back up in 30 days if I have not heard from your team about our next steps. If you need any assistance or help, please reach out to me via email at {email address}.

Thanks,

{researcher name}

Now, let's close these templates off with a couple of examples of reminder emails you could send as you follow up with the people with whom you've been communicating.

Attempting to reinitialize communication

In this email template, we'll send friendly reminders to the folks who may have already heard from you but have not responded to your initial emails. We suggest giving a full 30 days in most cases (unless the vulnerability is severe) to the vendor for following up. A reminder email could look something like this; note how we specifically inform the vendor that we intend to move forward with disclosure within 90 days:

Hello {vendor name department},

I'm following up on an email I sent you 30 days ago on {date}. I want to understand how your organization will handle the disclosure I sent you. As a reminder, there are {vulnerability count} vulnerabilities in {software name}, specifically in the {version number} version.

As previously disclosed, I plan on {releasing blog/publishing CVE} for which I'd like to receive any contributor credits when you fix and disclose this vulnerability to your customers. I'd also like to remind {vendor name} that I'm happy to offer any assistance I can that will aid in helping fix this problem impacting {software name}.

I hope to hear from you soon. Note that the best practices stipulate that 90 days should be afforded to any organization before research is published. If I do not hear from you, I will assume that your organization is comfortable with me releasing this research on {date – 90 days into the future}. If you need any assistance or help or have any questions, please reach out to me via email at {email address}.

Thanks,

{researcher name}

Sometimes, even after trying to work with the vendor, they are unresponsive. Ensure you still attempt to share updates on publication with them. We'll cover this in the following scenario.

Notification of pending publication with an unresponsive vendor

In this email template, we'll let our vendors know our plans on what they can expect for our research to be published:

Hello {vendor name department},

I'm following up on several emails regarding vulnerabilities in {product name}. There is a total of {vulnerability count} vulnerabilities in {software name}, specifically in the {version number} version.

As previously disclosed, I will disclose these findings {releasing blog/publishing CVE}. As previously shared, the best practices stipulate that 90 days should be afforded to any organization before research is published. However, because I have not heard from you, I have assumed that your organization is comfortable with me releasing this research on {date of release}. Therefore, I plan to release it through {method of publishing/blog/CVE, etc.}, which will be publicly accessible on this date or shortly after.

If you have any questions, don't hesitate to contact me via email at {email address}.

Thanks,

{researcher name}

While we can't cover every possible avenue, these templates should be helpful if you want to work directly with the vendor and would not like to enter into any mediation using a third party. This covers our section on vendor communications. We'll now talk about CVE templates in the form of acceptable blog posts that MITRE will accept for CVE descriptions and a bias-free example of self-publishing.

CVE templates

Publishing vulnerabilities can be pretty straightforward if you've already got your ducks in a row with disclosure. We'll now cover a CVE reservation template and a CVE disclosure template. The MITRE CVE project explicitly states that they need one of these two templates completed to correctly fill in the *Suggested description of the vulnerability for use in the CVE* section of the CVE form.

CVE reservation template

CVE reservations need to be kept to a minimum:

{Vulnerability type} in {component} in {vendor} {product} {version} allows {attacker} to {impact} via {vector}.

If the names of the labels are unfamiliar, we suggest you reference CVE's documentation on how to correctly fill in these attributes at the following URL: `http://cveproject.github.io/docs/content/key-details-phrasing.pdf`

CVE disclosure template

Self-published CVE disclosures can be simple and to the point. Here's a great example of what you'll need to communicate to stick to the facts and be brief for the MITRE team:

CVE-{RESERVED ID}: {Product Name} – {Component Name}

A vulnerability was discovered in the {Product Name} {version} and below for the {component name}. {Short description of flaw}, which {short description of the impact}.

To recreate the conditions for exploitation, do the following:

Step 1: {Initial recreation steps}

Step 2:...

To fix this issue, {define steps to fix issue}.

You don't need to get too fancy with these disclosures; remember, this is the bare minimum you want to submit to MITRE for proof of publishing. So, stick to the facts and don't hypothesize. If you wish to do a long-form write-up on this vulnerability, that's fine. Maybe though, for this, publish these two things separately, linking the long-form publication to your shorter submission for MITRE.

Now, we'll close our template section off with a section on organizational templates we can use to help create effective work tracking of research.

Organizational templates

Staying organized is so important, especially regarding research projects that produce vulnerabilities that need to be actioned. As you progress with your testing, we've noted that vulnerabilities that need CVEs will require tracking over months and sometimes years. Combine that with the fact you might be working on a series of applications over time, and not having a system can mean that details could get lost in the process. Of course, you might have systems of organization that work for you, but let's explore an option we strongly suggest and find very helpful in tracking research and vulnerabilities: **Kanban boards**.

Think of Kanban boards as consisting of tasks configured on *cards* and *columns*, indicating whether the task is to be done or completed. Kanban boards are sometimes represented physically with Post-it notes on whiteboards with lines to divide the columns, also called **swimlanes**:

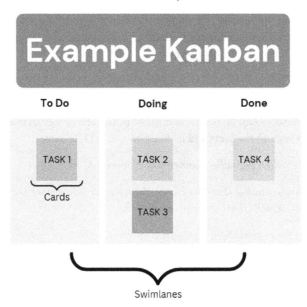

Figure 10.7 – A Kanban example

For this book, we're sharing four Kanban templates that can be used with the Trello software. **Trello** is a cloud-based software that can be used for free and we've made these templates public for anyone to use. Now, let's review the templates and how they work. While Trello is what we're using here, feel free to copy these same ideas and apply them to a physical board or another software, if you prefer.

Workspace

Trello has the concept of **Workspaces**, where similar Kanban boards can be stored and worked. In our case, we're going to build a Workspace and then add our templates to each Workspace. To build a Workspace, we will need to create a Trello account and select the **Create Workspace** option from the **Create** button dropdown at the top of the screen:

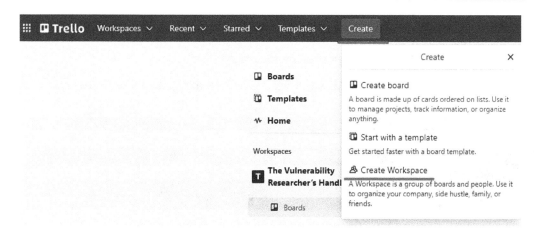

Figure 10.8 – Creating the Trello Workspace

Once clicked, the Workspace creation menu will appear. Set the Workspace name to something you'd prefer and add an optional type or description:

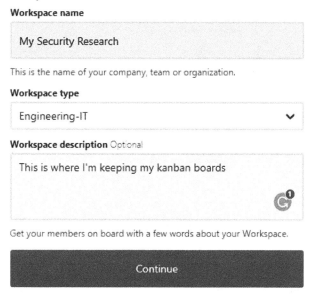

Figure 10.9 – The Let's build a Workspace window

Now that you've set up your Workspace, let's copy some boards over to it. We're going to start with the software research board. You can find the software research board used for this at `https://trello.com/b/4VVGFBky/software-research`.

Let's open this URL and visit the board, which should resemble the Kanban board depicted in the next screenshot:

Figure 10.10 – Exploring the template boards we need to copy

Once we visit the board, we'll just copy it to our Workspace since we can't make any changes to this template. What you'll need to do to copy the board is to click **Board Settings | More**, and then select **Copy board**, as seen in the following screenshot:

Figure 10.11 – Opening the More menu

Once you click **Copy board**, you'll want to give it the same title and select your own Workspace. You'll also want to change the default permission to make sure your research stays private. Click on the link that says **Change.** next to the text that says this board will be **Public**. Change this to **Private**, as shown in the following screenshot:

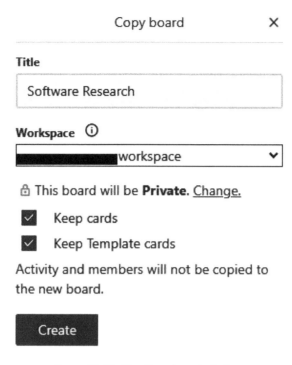

Figure 10.12 – The Copy board window

With your board copied, you can customize it to your liking. Before that though, let's talk a little bit about the board. The board has four columns, **Software To Research**, **Currently Researching**, **No Vulnerabilities Found**, and **Vulnerabilities Found**:

Figure 10.13 – Creating our first card with the provided template using the create from template button

As you plan your research, you should build up a backlog of items you'd like to research. We've created a template that helps you gather that information in one place. Let's create a new card on the **Software To Research** board by using the small icon on the right-hand side of the **Software To Research** column:

Figure 10.14 – Clicking the icon to add a card

Once we've clicked on this, a menu should appear titled **Card templates**, letting us select our only template. Click on this template to create a new card with the template:

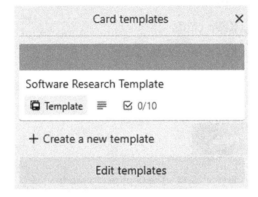

Figure 10.15 – The Card templates window

Once you've clicked the template, you'll be given the opportunity to name the card something other than **Software Research Template**. We suggest using the name of the software and keeping the checklists attached to the template. For this example, we'll use **Poodle Groomer 5000** as our research target:

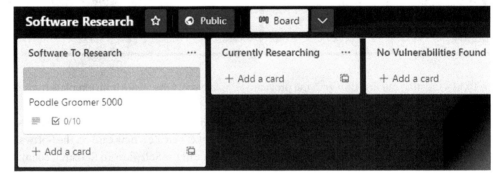

Figure 10.16 – Reviewing our first card

Now, let's click on our new card. On clicking **Poodle Groomer 5000**, we'll be greeted by a description field that we'll want to fill out, as shown in *Figure 10.17*:

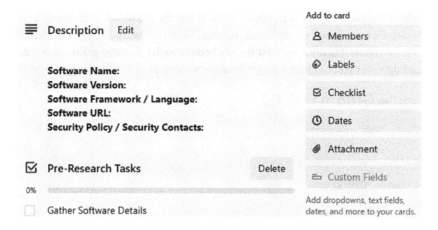

Figure 10.17 – The Description field for Poodle Groomer 5000

You'll notice as you're editing the card a set of checklists that we'll complete as we move through the research process, as shown in *Figure 10.18*:

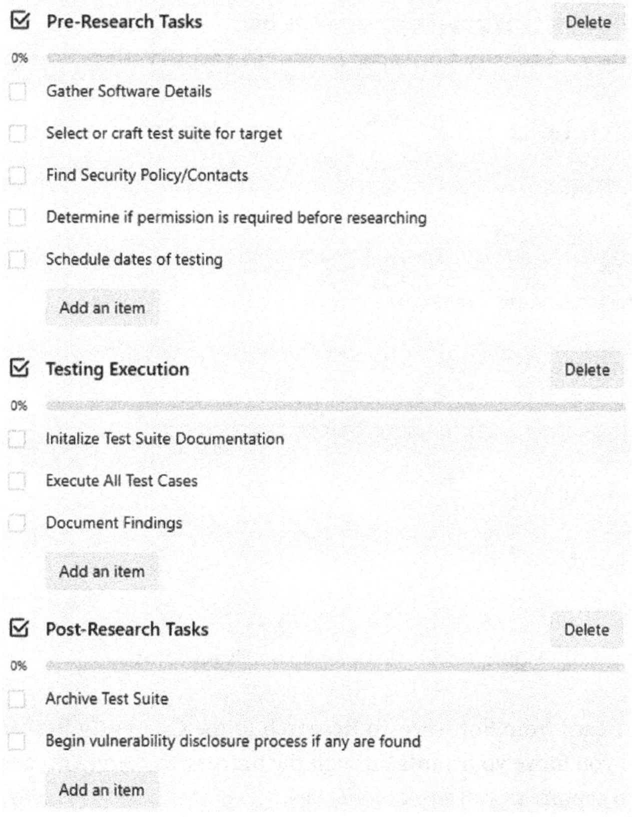

Figure 10.18 – Each swimlane has its own set of tasks in a checklist to track completion

Like with any checklist, you start at the top and execute the work as needed. Each checklist represents a phase in the task that needs to be completed. As you check off the items, you can then move the cards to the next swimlane. So, once our first list has been completed, we've gathered our details and set up our target dates for testing, which might look something like the following:

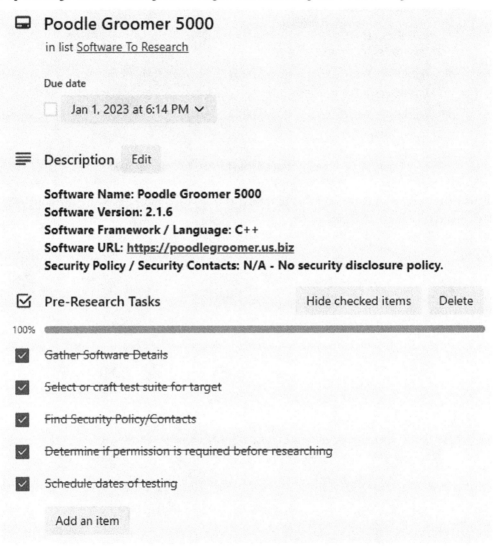

Figure 10.19 – Completing the listed items

We can then move our card from **Software To Research** to the **Currently Researching** swimlane. You can make edits, as you move your cards through the process, to comments and historical notes, which may be useful to capture as you work on the task.

There are three additional boards in this shared Workspace. Let's copy them to our Workspace now so we're ready to use them. They are as follows:

- **Vulnerability Publishing**

  - `https://trello.com/b/RF4Wrbi8/vulnerability-publishing`

- **Vulnerability Disclosure**

  - `https://trello.com/b/ANRLGfgO/vulnerability-disclosure`

- **CVE Publishing**

  - `https://trello.com/b/DbZgiL4T/cve-publishing`

Copy these templates the same way we did with our first board. We'll need each of these to cover different phases in our testing, disclosure, and publishing. Now, let's review the boards and how they'll be used.

Research to disclosure

Let's say we found vulnerabilities in the **Poodle Groomer 5000** application. If we did, we'd need to then disclose that information to the vendor. Since this itself is a whole process, we need to organize. We're going to move our research to a disclosure-specific board to track disclosures. The best way to do this is to copy the card to a new board, which you can do by clicking **Copy** in the properties of the card:

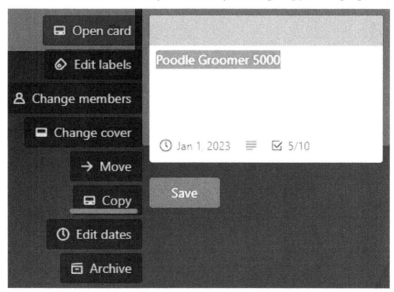

Figure 10.20 – Clicking Copy in the properties of the card

Clicking **Copy** will bring up the menu seen in the following screenshot. I like doing this without attaching the checklist since we'll need to create new checklists for our disclosure process:

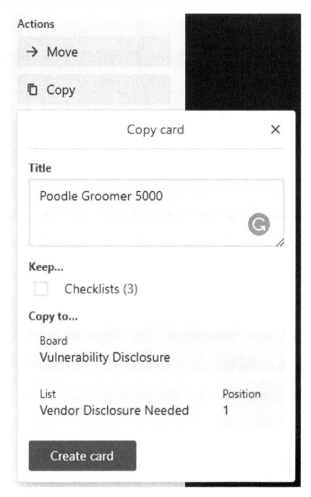

Figure 10.21 – Moving the card to another board

Click **Create card** to copy your new card on our other disclosure board. Once it's copied, you can navigate to the board and see that you have your new card:

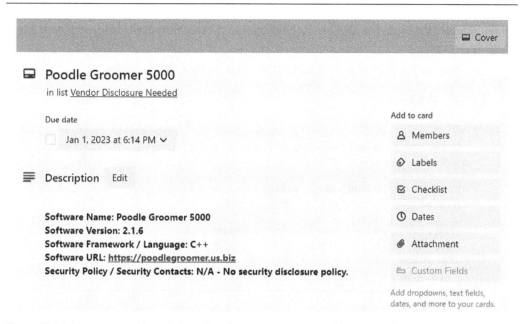

Figure 10.22 – Our new card has all the values from our previous card but none of the completed checklists

Now, we can add our disclosure-based checklists from the template on the vulnerability disclosure board.

Click **Checklist** and we'll add the checklists from the template on this board. You'll have a few to add, as shown in the following screenshot:

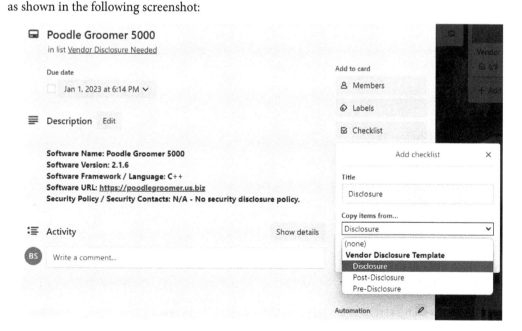

Figure 10.23 – Copy over the disclosure, post-disclosure, and pre-disclosure checklists

Once you've added the cards, you should now be able to see the checklists needed for completing this phase of the process:

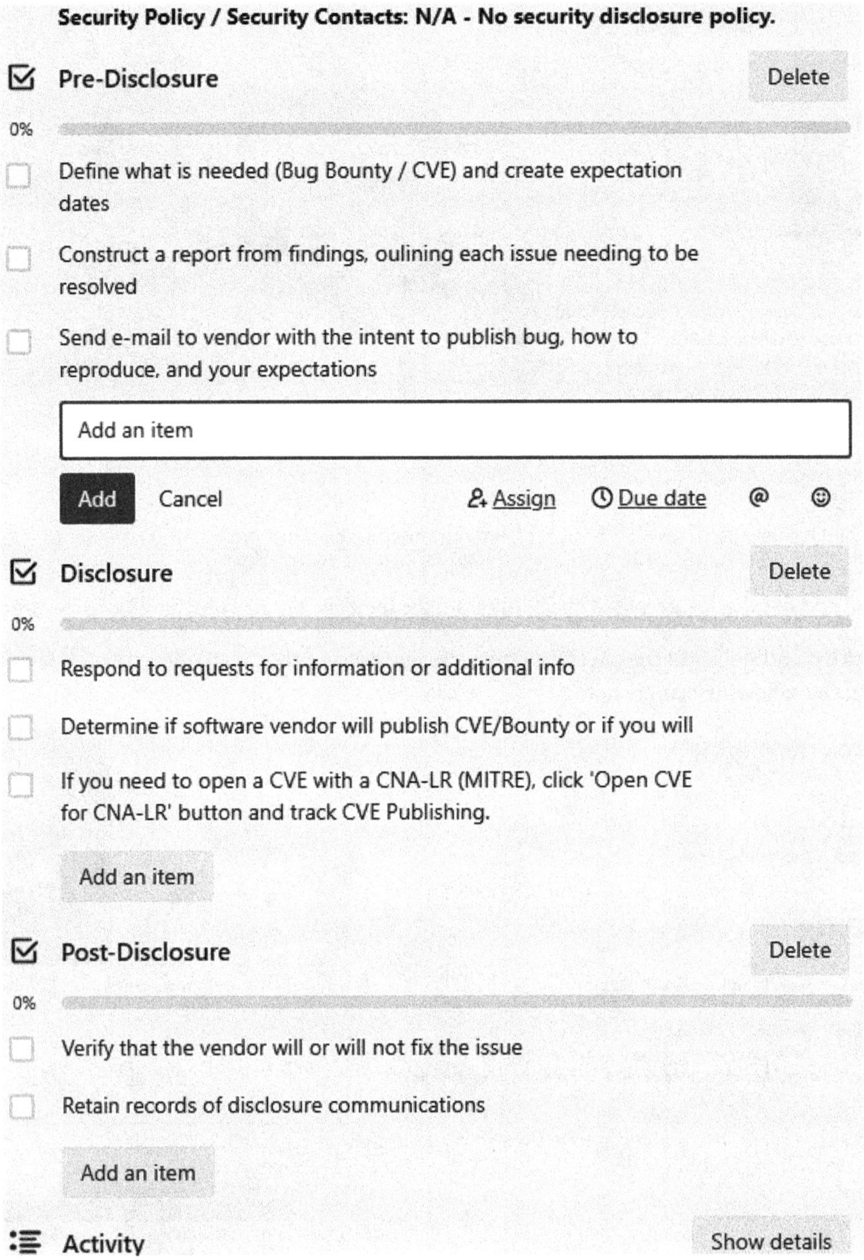

Security Policy / Security Contacts: N/A - No security disclosure policy.

☑ **Pre-Disclosure**   Delete

0% ▨▨▨

☐ Define what is needed (Bug Bounty / CVE) and create expectation dates

☐ Construct a report from findings, oulining each issue needing to be resolved

☐ Send e-mail to vendor with the intent to publish bug, how to reproduce, and your expectations

┌──┐
│ Add an item   │
└──┘

[Add]   Cancel   &+ Assign   ⏱ Due date   @   ☺

☑ **Disclosure**   Delete

0% ▨▨▨

☐ Respond to requests for information or additional info

☐ Determine if software vendor will publish CVE/Bounty or if you will

☐ If you need to open a CVE with a CNA-LR (MITRE), click 'Open CVE for CNA-LR' button and track CVE Publishing.

   Add an item

☑ **Post-Disclosure**   Delete

0% ▨▨▨

☐ Verify that the vendor will or will not fix the issue

☐ Retain records of disclosure communications

   Add an item

☷ **Activity**   Show details

Figure 10.24 – Our new checklists are now set up for the next set of tasks needed to disclose a vulnerability

This same process is used in the event of a CVE being opened, as seen in the second checklist. You'd simply copy the card to the **CVE Publishing** board. Similarly, you'd also follow the same procedure we used for the **Publishing** template. The **Publishing** checklist can be found here:

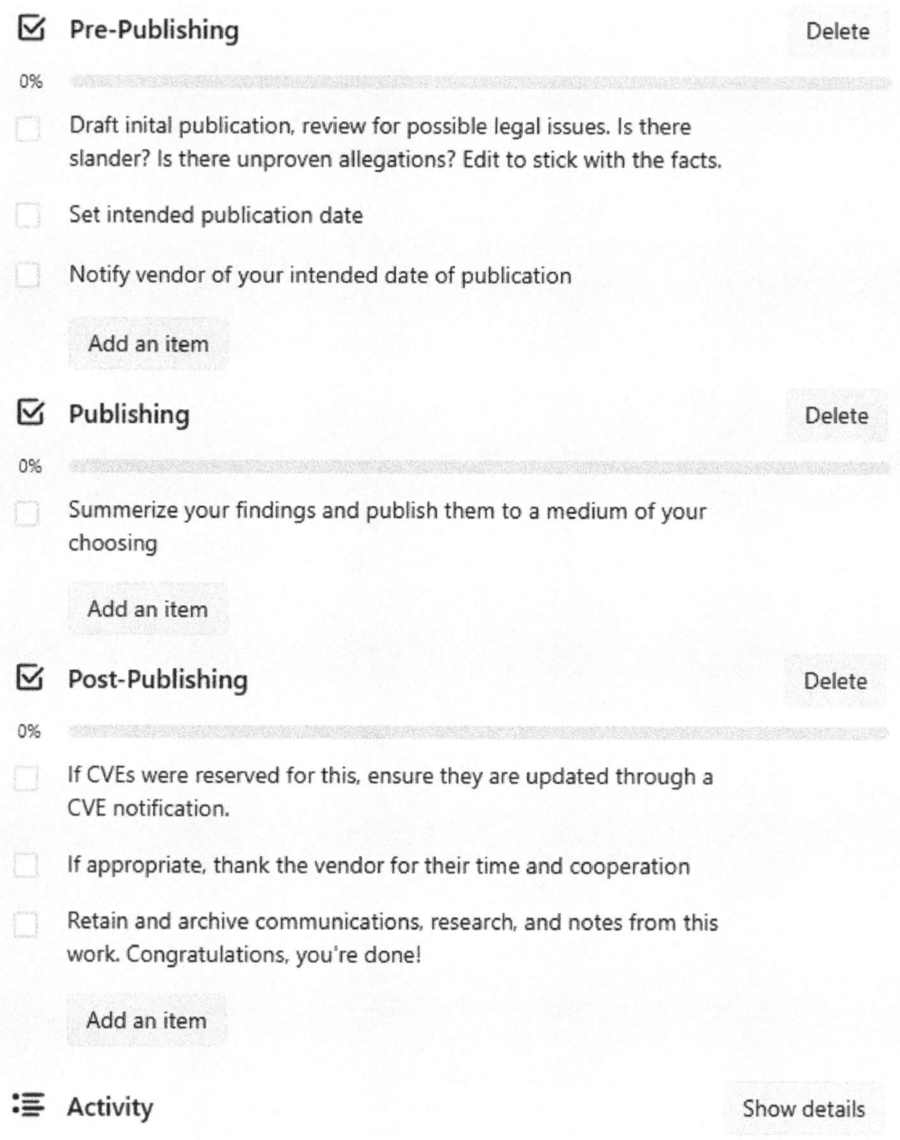

☑ **Pre-Publishing**   Delete

0%

☐   Draft inital publication, review for possible legal issues. Is there
       slander? Is there unproven allegations? Edit to stick with the facts.

☐   Set intended publication date

☐   Notify vendor of your intended date of publication

       Add an item

☑ **Publishing**   Delete

0%

☐   Summerize your findings and publish them to a medium of your
       choosing

       Add an item

☑ **Post-Publishing**   Delete

0%

☐   If CVEs were reserved for this, ensure they are updated through a
       CVE notification.

☐   If appropriate, thank the vendor for their time and cooperation

☐   Retain and archive communications, research, and notes from this
       work. Congratulations, you're done!

       Add an item

≔ **Activity**   Show details

Figure 10.25 – The Publishing checklist

The CVE checklist can be found in the following screenshot:

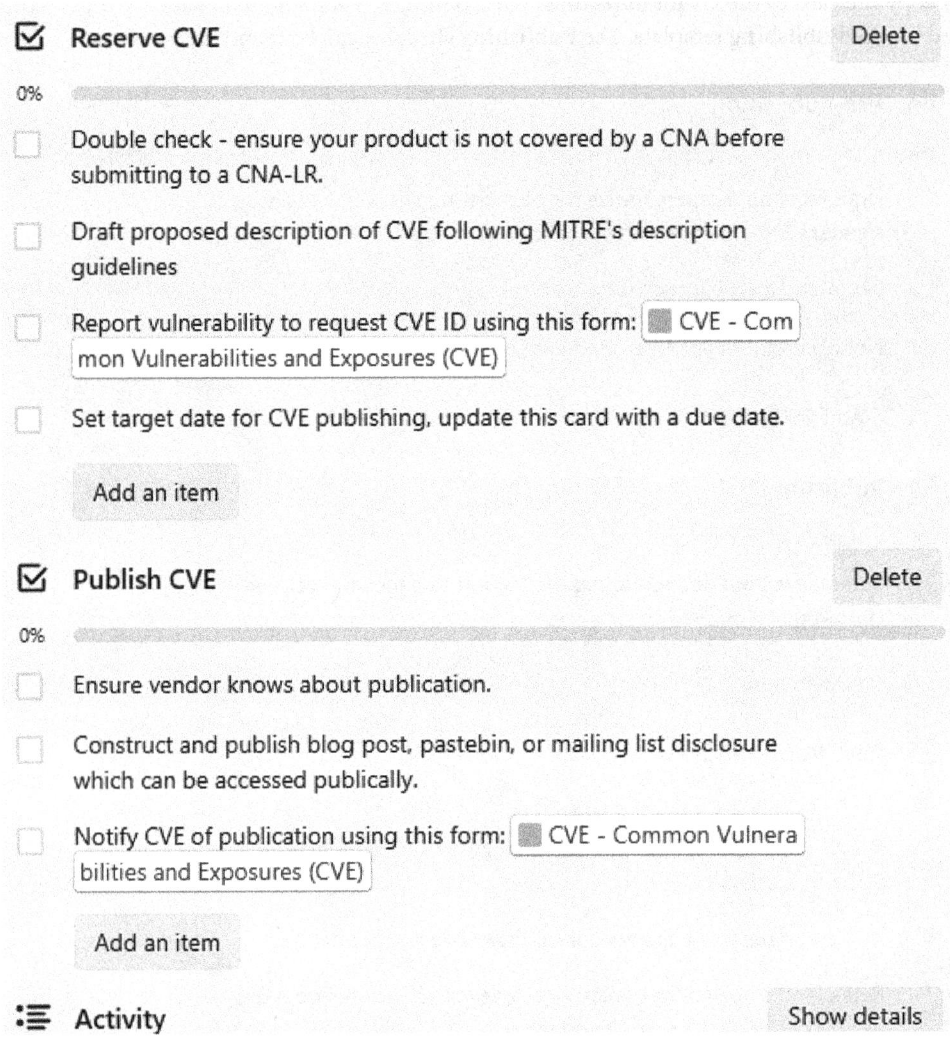

☑ **Reserve CVE**   Delete

0% ▭▭▭▭▭▭▭▭▭▭▭▭▭▭▭▭▭▭▭▭▭▭▭▭▭▭▭▭▭▭

☐ Double check - ensure your product is not covered by a CNA before
submitting to a CNA-LR.

☐ Draft proposed description of CVE following MITRE's description
guidelines

☐ Report vulnerability to request CVE ID using this form: ▦ CVE - Com
mon Vulnerabilities and Exposures (CVE)

☐ Set target date for CVE publishing, update this card with a due date.

Add an item

☑ **Publish CVE**   Delete

0% ▭▭▭▭▭▭▭▭▭▭▭▭▭▭▭▭▭▭▭▭▭▭▭▭▭▭▭▭▭▭

☐ Ensure vendor knows about publication.

☐ Construct and publish blog post, pastebin, or mailing list disclosure
which can be accessed publically.

☐ Notify CVE of publication using this form: ▦ CVE - Common Vulnera
bilities and Exposures (CVE)

Add an item

☰ **Activity**   Show details

Figure 10.26 – The CVE checklist

These templates can be made even more special using the automation capabilities that Trello allows. For example, you could automatically trigger the actions described previously if conditions are met. Feel free to use these as you look into organizing your research, or let these give you the inspiration to go and make your own organizational tools. For more information on getting started with Trello, see the *Further reading* section of this chapter.

With our resources now wrapped up, let's close this chapter with our final words of encouragement and a summary.

Summary and final words

Hello security researcher,

If you've arrived here, that means you've completed this book. While creating this book, it was my sincere wish to create something you could use to give you a thorough understanding of the vulnerability research and disclosure process. I also wanted to cover the various perils you can expect along your journey of becoming a researcher and sharing your work. This collected set of knowledge is precisely what I wish I had when I began my path of publishing research and working with vendors of all sorts. I hope I have answered your research questions and encouraged you to find your place in the research community. It takes people from diverse backgrounds to better the software and systems most of us use.

Security research is a significant use of time and I applaud you for even considering a contribution to it. You will undoubtedly face discouragement and disappointment throughout your path should you find vulnerabilities to publish. Many vendors will try to suppress your work and subvert your valuable contributions. They will discredit you, lie to you, and try every discouraging technique they can find in their toolbox to devalue your work and suppress the open exchange of ideas that helps the people they're meant to serve. Changing the order of anything in this world is challenging and changing how software is built and serviced by vendors is no different. Your disruptive work will inevitably go against the flow of corporate initiatives, personal ambitions, intercompany politics, new features, and potential revenue streams. Despite these factors ultimately challenging your work, I encourage you to press on.

The mechanisms that drive the modern software industry have so many areas to improve on and the products of the industry are so ubiquitous in the day-to-day life of many people. Nothing will ever get better without the oversight of people who can expose these problems and identify better ways to operate these systems, which are required to be used to participate in modern society. So, it's up to us.

Researchers are the ones who are responding to these problems and will need to continue to do so for the foreseeable future. There's no governmental oversight in our near future that could cause a significant shift in these systemic problems. There's no backup on its way and we should not expect organizations to correct course now. Their problems in operations are a symptom of their oversight and through the lens of corporate risk, their customers being harmed might be considered an acceptable risk. Despite this, I am hopeful. Research publication has grown year after year and there are signs that corporate organizations have been pulled, kicking and screaming, into patterns where they have accepted that researchers exist and will publicize their work. Some organizations have even accepted that working with researchers might benefit them. They have used their relationship with the information security community in a traditional vendor form: as a marketable asset. These are all good signs of better things to come but the pressure needs to continue and I encourage you to participate in this work so you can be an important part of this shifting tide.

To help support your journey, I encourage you to build connections with other researchers to share knowledge and perhaps commiserate on the latest woe some vendor has put you through. These relationships will help ease the burden of carrying this alone, help you further your own research through collaboration, and enrich your research in untold ways. In terms of what is available to you in the information security community, remember that many researchers (some no longer with us) have contributed to the body of knowledge that we benefit from, sometimes at significant risk to themselves. Ensure that you honor and respect these contributions wherever possible by building on them, contributing to them in good faith, and pledging to use them for good. People are counting on you.

Closing out this text, I wish you the best of luck in your research career. Thank you for taking the time to contribute to something important, and I look forward to reading your publications.

Further reading

- *Getting Started with Trello*: `https://trello.com/en/guide`

- *Using Trello for Project Management: An Easy, Step-by-Step Guide*: `https://blog.hubstaff.com/trello-project-management/`

- *How to use Trello* (video): `https://www.youtube.com/watch?v=geRKHFzTxNY`

- *Product Management Crash Course and Trello Fundamentals* (video): `https://www.packtpub.com/product/product-management-crash-course-and-trello-fundamentals-video/9781803235646`

Index

Symbols

packtpub.com

Subscribe to our online digital library for full access to over 7,000 books and videos, as well as industry leading tools to help you plan your personal development and advance your career. For more information, please visit our website.

Why subscribe?

- Spend less time learning and more time coding with practical eBooks and Videos from over 4,000 industry professionals

- Improve your learning with Skill Plans built especially for you

- Get a free eBook or video every month

- Fully searchable for easy access to vital information

- Copy and paste, print, and bookmark content

Did you know that Packt offers eBook versions of every book published, with PDF and ePub files available? You can upgrade to the eBook version at packtpub.com and as a print book customer, you are entitled to a discount on the eBook copy. Get in touch with us at customercare@packtpub.com for more details.

At www.packtpub.com, you can also read a collection of free technical articles, sign up for a range of free newsletters, and receive exclusive discounts and offers on Packt books and eBooks.

Other Books You May Enjoy

If you enjoyed this book, you may be interested in these other books by Packt:

Penetration Testing Azure for Ethical Hackers

David Okeyode, Karl Fosaaen

ISBN: 9781839212932

- Identify how administrators misconfigure Azure services, leaving them open to exploitation
- Understand how to detect cloud infrastructure, service, and application misconfigurations
- Explore processes and techniques for exploiting common Azure security issues
- Use on-premises networks to pivot and escalate access within Azure
- Diagnose gaps and weaknesses in Azure security implementations
- Understand how attackers can escalate privileges in Azure AD

Practical Threat Intelligence and Data-Driven Threat Hunting

Valentina Costa-Gazcón

ISBN: 9781838556372

- Understand what CTI is, its key concepts, and how it is useful for preventing threats and protecting your organization
- Explore the different stages of the TH process
- Model the data collected and understand how to document the findings
- Simulate threat actor activity in a lab environment
- Use the information collected to detect breaches and validate the results of your queries
- Use documentation and strategies to communicate processes to senior management and the wider business

Packt is searching for authors like you

If you're interested in becoming an author for Packt, please visit `authors.packtpub.com` and apply today. We have worked with thousands of developers and tech professionals, just like you, to help them share their insight with the global tech community. You can make a general application, apply for a specific hot topic that we are recruiting an author for, or submit your own idea.

Share Your Thoughts

Now you've finished *The Vulnerability Researcher's Handbook*, we'd love to hear your thoughts! Scan the QR code below to go straight to the Amazon review page for this book and share your feedback or leave a review on the site that you purchased it from.

`https://packt.link/r/1803238879`

Your review is important to us and the tech community and will help us make sure we're delivering excellent quality content.

Download a free PDF copy of this book

Thanks for purchasing this book!

Do you like to read on the go but are unable to carry your print books everywhere?

Is your eBook purchase not compatible with the device of your choice?

Don't worry, now with every Packt book you get a DRM-free PDF version of that book at no cost.

Read anywhere, any place, on any device. Search, copy, and paste code from your favorite technical books directly into your application.

The perks don't stop there, you can get exclusive access to discounts, newsletters, and great free content in your inbox daily

Follow these simple steps to get the benefits:

1. Scan the QR code or visit the link below

https://packt.link/free-ebook/9781803238876

2. Submit your proof of purchase

3. That's it! We'll send your free PDF and other benefits to your email directly

www.ingramcontent.com/pod-product-compliance
Lightning Source LLC
Chambersburg PA
CBHW060537060326
40690CB00017B/3522